# Empire, Celebrity and Excess

# Empire, Celebrity and Excess

*King Farouk of Egypt and British Culture, 1936–1965*

Martin Francis

BLOOMSBURY ACADEMIC
LONDON • NEW YORK • OXFORD • NEW DELHI • SYDNEY

BLOOMSBURY ACADEMIC
Bloomsbury Publishing Plc
50 Bedford Square, London, WC1B 3DP, UK
1385 Broadway, New York, NY 10018, USA
29 Earlsfort Terrace, Dublin 2, Ireland

BLOOMSBURY, BLOOMSBURY ACADEMIC and the Diana logo
are trademarks of Bloomsbury Publishing Plc

First published in Great Britain 2023
This paperback edition published 2024

Copyright © Martin Francis, 2023

Martin Francis has asserted his right under the Copyright, Designs and
Patents Act, 1988, to be identified as Author of this work.

For legal purposes the Acknowledgements on pp. ix–x constitute
an extension of this copyright page.

Cover image: A portrait of King Farouk broken during the Cairo riots of 1952.
Photo by Hulton Archive/Getty Images.

All rights reserved. No part of this publication may be reproduced or transmitted
in any form or by any means, electronic or mechanical, including photocopying,
recording, or any information storage or retrieval system, without prior
permission in writing from the publishers.

Bloomsbury Publishing Plc does not have any control over, or responsibility for,
any third-party websites referred to or in this book. All internet addresses given
in this book were correct at the time of going to press. The author and publisher
regret any inconvenience caused if addresses have changed or sites have
ceased to exist, but can accept no responsibility for any such changes.

A catalogue record for this book is available from the British Library.

A catalog record for this book is available from the Library of Congress.

ISBN:  HB:    978-1-3501-2459-2
       PB:    978-1-3503-4533-1
       ePDF:  978-1-3501-2460-8
       eBook: 978-1-3501-2461-5

Typeset by Integra Software Services Pvt. Ltd.

To find out more about our authors and books visit www.bloomsbury.com
and sign up for our newsletters.

*For Sammy and Brenda*

# Contents

| | |
|---|---|
| List of Figures | viii |
| Acknowledgements | ix |
| List of Abbreviations | xi |
| | |
| Introduction | 1 |
| 1  Faruq, King of Egypt | 15 |
| 2  Indeterminacy: Farouk and the Official Imperial Mind | 23 |
| 3  Music Hall and Merry Monarchs | 43 |
| 4  Exile or Tourist? | 73 |
| 5  Excess | 99 |
| 6  American Farouk, Fictional Farouk | 125 |
| Conclusion: Two Funerals, 1965 | 149 |
| | |
| Notes | 160 |
| Bibliography | 199 |
| Index | 220 |

# Figures

| | | |
|---|---|---|
| 1 | Prince Farouk and Sir Miles Lampson at a RAF air display at Heliopolis, 1935 | 28 |
| 2 | Farouk, Queen Farida and their daughter Princess Ferial, 1939 | 37 |
| 3 | Carl Giles, 'Mother's Day', *Sunday Express*, 15 March 1953 | 59 |
| 4 | Farouk with Philip, Duke of Edinburgh (left) and Foreign Secretary Ernest Bevin (right), Koubbeh Palace, 31 January 1950 | 65 |
| 5 | Farouk with his mistress, Irma Minutolo, at a Monte Carlo casino, 16 February 1954 | 84 |
| 6 | Farouk shields himself from a paparazzi photographer at a Rome restaurant | 87 |
| 7 | Farouk and Narriman on Capri, August 1952 | 95 |
| 8 | Farouk's 'Secret Museum' | 115 |
| 9 | Farouk and playmates on the beach at Anzio, 4 August 1956 | 121 |
| 10 | *Abdullah the Great*: Abdullah (Gregory Ratoff) and Aziz (Martina Berti) | 145 |

# Acknowledgements

My first debt of gratitude is to my commissioning editor Maddie Holder, who has been such an enthusiastic and solicitous supporter of *Empire, Celebrity and Excess* from its formative days. The professionalism, efficiency and forbearance of all the team at Bloomsbury, most especially Abigail Lane, have made the progress from proposal to publication a genuine pleasure. I would like to thank the three anonymous readers of my manuscript for their constructive and astute suggestions, the incorporation of which has unquestionably improved the final version of this book.

Conducting research for this book was facilitated by the assistance of librarians and archivists at the following institutions: Langsam Library, University of Cincinnati; Sussex University Library; The British Library; National Archives, Kew; Middle Eastern Centre, St. Antony's College, University of Oxford; British Film Institute Archive; Mass-Observation Archive, University of Sussex; and British Cartoon Archive, University of Kent.

Even in a period marked by disruption and lockdown, no writer ever works entirely alone, and I hope my endnotes and bibliography do justice to my indebtedness to countless other scholars. More directly, I have benefited immeasurably from the advice and encouragement of Alex Windscheffel, Deborah Cohen, Geoff Eley, Max Jones, Vanessa Schwartz, Philippa Levine, Antoinette Burton and Laura Mayhall. Like so many others in our profession, I sadly miss the generosity and scholarly insight of Sonya Rose (1935–2020). At Sussex, Martin Evans and Hester Barron have (with varying degrees of success) valiantly striven to keep me out of trouble. Darrow Schecter has been a heartening companion through the valley of tears that constitutes being a fan of the New York Mets. Claire Langhamer's singular wisdom, keen critical eye and multiple acts of personal kindness, all had a role to play in helping me see this project through to completion.

For almost four decades, Stephen Brooke has been an inspiration (as both scholar and writer) and a cherished friend. The ways in which I continue to benefit from his altruism, erudition and emotional intelligence remain too myriad to detail, so I will content myself with thanking him for being such a steadfast ally of *Empire, Celebrity and Excess* on those occasions when I might otherwise have become seriously discouraged. Lewis Hayward always found time to talk about Farouk, even when attending to more pressing matters, not least steering his school through a pandemic.

I salute the memory of my parents, Barbara Francis (1933–2012) and Brian Francis (1928–2002), whose love and selfless dedication formed the bedrock of all my subsequent happiness and good fortune. I thank my in-laws, Alyce Friedman Assael and Henry Assael, for their unstinting support and liberal hospitality. It was entirely appropriate that it was under their roof, in the summer of 2021, that this manuscript was finally completed.

The joy that my wife, Brenda Assael, and son, Sammy, have brought to my life is simply too abundant and profound to be registered in words. Brenda has been an untiring source of encouragement and inspiration, even in the midst of completing her own book on the London restaurant and embarking on a challenging new scholarly enterprise, which (like Christopher Robin) has been taking her 'to Africa and back' on a daily basis. I'm truly fortunate to share married life with a formidable historian, indefatigable co-parent and matchless combination of hardboiled New York tenacity and sophisticated continental chic.

I cannot even begin to express the feelings of love and pride I have for our son, Sammy. Celebrating his achievements (as budding scholar and dedicated musician) and sharing in his passions (as voracious reader, nascent military historian and baseball aficionado) have provided a daily reminder of what really matters in life. I know that *Empire, Celebrity and Excess* isn't that book on the Second World War that Sammy wanted Daddy to write (I promise him, though, that this will be coming in due course), but it's dedicated – with all my love and devotion – to him, all the same.

# Abbreviations

BFI British Film Institute
CIA Central Intelligence Agency
FO Foreign Office
GFM German Foreign Ministry
LD Sir Miles Lampson Diaries
MOA Mass-Observation Archive
OSS Office of Strategic Services
RAF Royal Air Force
TNA The National Archive, Kew

# Introduction

'Who do you think you are? King Farouk?'. This verbal admonishment, directed by 1950s British parents towards their children when they made demands that appeared either unreasonable or unfeasible, is a striking testimony to the ubiquity of, and universal familiarity with, the figure who ruled Egypt between 1936 and 1952, and remained in the public spotlight throughout his reign and during the exile years which culminated with his death in Rome in 1965. Despite the fact that he never returned to Britain after a brief sojourn immediately subsequent to his accession, and that Egypt was never a formal British imperial possession, narratives about, images of and references to 'Farouk' – the Anglicized and popularized appellation of Faruq-al-Awwal, the tenth member of the Mehmet Ali dynasty to rule Egypt and the Sudan – insinuated themselves into every corner of British culture.[1] Critically, Farouk was not merely an instantly recognizable public figure. He also served as a widely accepted synonym in metropolitan Britain (and beyond, not least in the United States) for personal excess and the unapologetic pursuit of pleasure.

As an important figure in British imperial policy making and diplomacy, Farouk inevitably became a preoccupation of the British Foreign Office, but key figures such as Foreign Secretary Anthony Eden and Britain's Ambassador to Egypt, Sir Miles Lampson, seemed no less preoccupied with Farouk's colourful private life, justifying their voyeurism by their insistence on the geopolitical implications of matters of intimacy. Lampson, in particular, became almost pathologically fixated on Farouk's personal behaviour and picaresque adventures. In addition to his manifestation in newspaper coverage of the official worlds of British foreign policy and international affairs, Farouk was a constant presence in those same papers' gossip columns and celebrity features, even if the largely sympathetic reporting of his first marriage and accession in the mid-1930s had given way to less deferential (and certainly more salacious) treatment by the late 1940s. Farouk's distinctive appearance – notably his corpulent body, tarbush and dark sunglasses – made him a popular subject for newspaper cartoonists, notably Carl Giles of the *Daily Express*. Farouk featured prominently in cinema newsreels and was even referenced in feature films. When Jack Lemmon's C.C. Baxter is mistaken for a unscrupulous philanderer in the 1960 film *The Apartment*, he is explicitly likened to Egypt's (by then) ex-ruler.

Lewd banter about Farouk featured in the stage act which contributed to the notoriously bawdy Lancashire character comic Frank Randle falling foul of Blackpool council's by-laws on obscenity. At a more refined (if hardly less suggestive) level of comedic improvisation, in his Las Vegas cabaret show, Noel Coward reworked the lyrics of Cole Porter's well-known song *Let's Do It* to include a reference to Farouk's amorous propensities. The memoirs of women who worked in Allied headquarters in wartime Cairo frequently incorporated stories about the stratagems required to evade the amorous advances of Egypt's libidinous monarch, while British soldiers brought home with them ribald songs about Farouk they had lustily sung on active service in the Western Desert. Popular interest in Farouk's excesses was not confined to sex. No magazine feature on the casinos of the Riviera was complete without an anecdote about Farouk's legendary wins and losses at their tables. The publications of British philatelists, numismatists and philumenists expressed their admiration, and envy, for Farouk's gargantuan collections of stamps, coins and matchboxes. The more prurient were intrigued by extraordinary collections of clothing, perfumes, furniture, motor cars and (allegedly) pornography which were recovered from the king's palaces and auctioned off by Egypt's nationalist rulers after Farouk fell from power. If the scale of such wealth and flamboyance made Farouk seem like a fantasized figure from the overblown orientalist imaginary, he could sometimes progress from the domain of representation to that of the immediate and (near-) tangible. A guidebook for British travellers to the Bay of Naples, published in 1955, itemized the specific restaurants and nightclubs on the island of Capri where a fortunate tourist might be likely to encounter the exiled monarch at play.

The fact that Farouk was present everywhere – from the domains of imperial officials and policy makers to the populist discourses of celebrity, sensationalism or tourism and the idioms of vernacular speech – signified a wider disruption to the co-ordinates of British culture between the 1930s and 1950s. The presence of Farouk in such a variety of texts and contexts was not just testimony to the performative potential of a single, albeit, larger-than-life historical actor. It also exposes the way that, as Britain's formal imperium came to an end, the discursive components of British imperialism, never particularly secure in the first place, began to attach themselves to, and incorporate themselves within, cultural formations whose derivation and constitution appeared to have limited connection to the British Empire, real or imagined. Official and popular narratives of Farouk reveal that those varied cultural and social features of postwar Britain that have been seen as part of the reconstitution of Britain's discursive terrain in the aftermath of empire – liberalization in the spheres of sexuality and personal conduct, 'Americanization', consumer affluence, increased interaction with the European continent, new forms of mass leisure, the emergence of celebrity culture – did not, as most historical accounts imply, take place independently of the dismantling of empire. Stories about Farouk show how discourses of empire merged into an evolving, but no less globalized, domain of cultural knowledge.

Critically, such discursive dispersal ensured, if not erasure of the trauma of decolonization, at least a restorative measure of distance and disassociation. If, as Todd Shepard argues, the French came to terms with the end of their empire by effectively denying that Algeria had ever been French, the British seemed to have effected a similarly brazen stratagem, in which a major protagonist in the narratives of late British imperialism was reimagined and recontextualized to such an extent that he appeared to lack any substantial identification with empire whatsoever.[2] Stories about Farouk therefore dramatized the shift from a colonial to an emerging postcolonial culture.

This book provides the first account (scholarly or popular) of the place of King Farouk in British culture between the late 1930s and early 1960s. It is not a biography of Farouk but rather a reflection on how narratives and representations of Egypt's last king illuminate, but also problematize, our understanding of the contours of British history in the middle decades of the twentieth century.[3]

Representations of Farouk within the mindset of British imperial policy making see-sawed from ill-disciplined child and oriental despot to Westernized modernizer and genuine partner in a more egalitarian conception of empire. Furthermore, after the Second World War, Farouk's status as both an international playboy and (for the last thirteen years of his life) high-profile exile meant he could no longer be confined within the recognized spaces of empire. The geographical co-ordinates of his story were not just the lavish palaces of Cairo and Alexandria but also the European playgrounds of the *beau monde*: the Riviera, Capri and Rome's Via Veneto. The – already contradictory – discourses of the so-called third British empire now competed for the privilege of defining Farouk with a variety of associations derived from popular culture and the mass media, ranging from the robust traditions of English music hall to the more self-consciously modern (and often trans-national) sites of mediatized celebrity, mass leisure and consumption. Farouk's increasing autonomy from the discourses of imperialism also encouraged an alignment between the Egyptian monarch's private appetites and public anxieties surrounding, initially, the corrosive effects of the Second World War on sexual standards in the 1940s, and, subsequently, increased affluence in the 1950s. However, while Farouk dramatized issues that clearly had a broad contemporary resonance, he was regularly comprehended through affinities to people and places that were as temporally and geographically dispersed as the Egyptian Pharaohs, the Roman emperors, Henry VIII of England, *belle epoque* Paris and Monte Carlo in the 'Naughty Nineties'. Narratives about Farouk's already outlandish lifestyle were inevitably often embellished, and the king had an impressive fictional life, not merely in films and novels but in the apocryphal concoctions of fantasists and charlatans.

Farouk was therefore a transversal figure, able to confound the prescriptions of spatial, temporal and conceptual confinement. Politics and celebrity, empire and Europe, imperial and postcolonial: when considering British perceptions of Egypt's notorious monarch, it becomes abundantly clear that pairings such as these should be regarded not as oppositional but, rather, as startlingly interdependent. More critically, Farouk's ability to disrupt categorical boundaries should not be comprehended as an idiosyncratic corollary of the singular privileges accorded by his extraordinary wealth, royal status and fame. Rather, the failure to 'fix' Farouk was emblematic of the much wider precariousness and indeterminacy that characterized British culture during the eras of late imperialism and decolonization.

Chapter 1, 'Faruq, King of Egypt', provides a brief outline of Farouk's life, locating him in the context of Egyptian politics between the 1930s and 1950s.

Chapter 2, 'Indeterminacy: Farouk and the Official Imperial Mind', focuses on how Egypt's ruler was presented and comprehended by British diplomats and policy makers. Understandings of Farouk in the Cairo Residency and Whitehall disclosed a wider confusion about the nature of Egyptian identity, a disorientation rooted in its apparent incompatibility with many of the conventional hierarchies and arrangements on which imperial rule were predicated, notably in regard to issues of sovereignty, race and the geographical ordering of empire. Far from offering a means of clarification, Farouk's complex ancestry, and his apparent ability to move from exemplifying the cosmopolitan culture of Egypt's multinational elite one minute to fashioning himself as a tribune of Arab nationalism in the next, only aggravated British mystification about Egypt. Those British officials who emphasized the king's capriciousness, cruelty and sensuality reanimated the hackneyed repertoire of orientalism, but they were soon required to acknowledge the distinctly modern aspects of Farouk, not least the fact that coverage of the king in the British press became increasingly characterized by popularization, personalization and the publicization of stories about his intimate life. Moreover, his (well-reported) hedonistic excursions to the pleasure resorts of the Riviera and Italy ensured that Farouk seemed able to disregard the designated spaces of the imperial mindset, exploiting new structures of globalization which confounded the ostensible binaries between 'Orient' and 'Europe'. Obliged to come to terms with Farouk's status as not merely a monarch with critical significance in British imperial policy making but as a highly mediatized celebrity, diplomats and policy makers accommodated themselves to, and even reiterated, the conventions of celebrity culture.

Chapter 3, 'Music Hall and Merry Monarchs', considers the place of Farouk in British popular culture and entertainment. For all his significance as an exemplar of modern conceptions of celebrity, the appearance of Farouk in the routines of music hall performers such as Frank Randle or Max Bacon suggested the resilience of older, more vernacular and more visceral forms of popular culture in 1940s and 1950s Britain. Celebrity culture has often been associated with a media focus on the personal lives of public figures as a means to create affinities between female audiences (and consumers) and the famous. By contrast, Farouk's gambling and womanizing were aligned in British popular culture with a robust pursuit of masculine pleasures and privileges, and a rejection of puritanism, middle-class moralizing and the obligations of home and family. In this sense, Farouk's popularity calls into question one-dimensional models of male domestication and working-class embourgeoisement in the middle decades of the twentieth century. This not to say that Farouk did not also have a presence in the more sedate and respectable world of working-class associational culture, given his legendary status among those engaged in the hobbies of matchbox, stamp and coin collecting.

The British public were also fascinated by the fact that Farouk was a king, but one whose allure was not predicated on the blend of political passivity and domestic virtue which has been a dominant motif in explanations of royal adaptation and survival in the modern era. As profiles of the Egyptian king regularly acknowledged, both Farouk's solicitous guarding of his royal prerogative and his full-blooded pursuit of personal pleasures meant he had greater affinity with some of Britain's historical rulers, notably Henry VIII, Charles II and George IV, than with his contemporary, the decidedly bloodless George VI. Public interest in Farouk suggested that the House of Windsor's concoction of public spectacle and private probity was not the only script about monarchy available to Britons in the twentieth century, and that we could do more to acknowledge that there might also have existed a measure of regret among the British public for the passing of a time when kings still knew how to live like kings.

Of course, the House of Windsor survived, but the House of Fuad did not. Chapter 4, 'Exile or Tourist?', begins by addressing Farouk's status, after 1952, as an ex-king. Farouk was merely one of a number of deposed monarchs (other notable examples being the former rulers of Romania, Bulgaria, Italy, Albania and Yugoslavia) whose aimless, tawdry (and often tragic) lives in exile received considerable attention in the British press. These deracinated and displaced ex-royals found their loss of formal status was countered by their growing value as celebrities, but their fates also served as a proxy for broader uncertainties about dramatic social and geopolitical change. Indeed, exiled monarchs might be usefully placed alongside postwar Displaced Persons and Commonwealth immigrants settling in metropolitan Britain as totemic symbols of the estrangement and dislocation that characterized the decades immediately after 1945. In fact, it is not altogether outlandish to argue popular interest in the exiled Farouk was an exercise in psychological displacement, an unconscious disclosure of the melancholy, loss and dispossession that might have been expected to have accompanied the end of Britain's empire, but which was peculiarly absent from the dominant public narratives surrounding decolonization in the 1940s and 1950s.

The second half of this chapter discusses the cultural geographies of Farouk's exile, more specifically the popular understandings of the pleasure zones of Deauville, the Cote d'Azur, the Amalfi coast and Rome's Via Veneto, where he spent a large part of the final thirteen years of his life. These were places that, in the 1950s, became associated with an internationalized celebrity culture, contemporary style and affluent modernity. Farouk was to be found eyeing aspiring starlets on the beach during the Cannes film festival and was one of the earliest victims of the paparazzi photographers who created the cultures of excess and exposure that constituted *dolce vita* Italy. However, in British culture, Farouk's affiliation with these rich men's resorts also drew on older, even archaic, associations, ranging from a folk memory of the pre-1914 aristocratic gilded age to long-standing notions of the intrinsic debauchery of the 'sinful' Mediterranean. Indeed Farouk's perambulations underlined the resilience of the Mediterranean as a discrete, albeit fantasized, unit in the British imaginary, even in an age in which one might have expected it to have been superseded by new, politically derived zones of demarcation. Farouk's years of exile coincided with the expansion of mass tourism, and the ostentatious vulgarity of the ex-king at play ensured that even his wealth and fame failed to impede his alignment with the less prepossessing aspects of modern, democratic, conceptions of leisure and travel. Indeed, regularly spotted at casinos, hotels, nightclubs and beaches, Farouk himself actually came to feature in the informal and formal itineraries of Mediterranean tourists in the 1950s.

Chapter 5, 'Excess', considers how stories about Farouk dramatized contemporary concerns about both new sexual standards and the impact of increased affluence in metropolitan Britain. Farouk had a walk on part in narratives about wartime Cairo which emphasized its reputation for sexual licence and easy virtue. In these, it was not always possible to identify the king's philandering with the uncontrolled passions of the colonial other, since their plots were just as likely to incorporate notions of female agency and mutual sexual pleasure. After the war, coverage of Farouk's sexual escapades reflected more relaxed attitudes to sex in the popular press, and changing attitudes to adultery and divorce. However, both his prematurely ageing body and royal status excluded him from the growing correspondence between sexual allure and a commercially driven emphasis on youthful modernity and meritocracy. Farouk was all too obviously a playboy rather than a Playboy. Here, Farouk serves as testament to the possibility that older understandings of sexuality might have still had a role to play in British culture, even at the dawn of the so-called 'sexual revolution'.

Farouk's apparently irrepressible pursuit of pleasure was not confined to sex. He also had a proclivity for the accumulation of treasure, high-stakes gambling and gargantuan meals. In the late 1940s, press coverage of Farouk's life of flamboyant self-gratification offered a vicarious release for Britons from the austerity and officially endorsed strictures of self-abnegation that characterized the years of the Attlee government. In the 1950s, by contrast, Farouk seemed to offer an extravagantly exaggerated version of the corrupting powers of conspicuous consumption that accompanied dramatically rising living standards. Farouk's penchant for outlandishly expensive kitsch (fully revealed in the auction of the royal collections after his fall in 1952) seemed indicative of a more general coarsening of society and culture promoted by the 'age of affluence'. Both his unsightly corpulent body and his unapologetic kleptomania offered cautionary tales of the moral and social costs of an excessive concentration on personal prosperity and material accumulation.

Chapter 6, 'American Farouk, Fictional Farouk', considers two of the most dramatic instances of the British failure to 'fix' Farouk: his prominence in

American culture and his presence in stories that were entirely fabricated or fictionalized. Since the United States played such a critical role in the emergence of new globalized identities (notably of celebrity and conspicuous consumption), it was probably inevitable that Farouk would feature in American popular culture, whether it be the serialization of his ex-wife's memoirs in the *Ladies Home Journal*, the titles of jazz recordings or the machinations of American publicists. Farouk was also of interest to the African-American press, who sequestered his racial indeterminacy to the requisites of racial pride. The shared familiarity with Farouk in the popular imaginaries of both Britain and the United States challenges simplistic notions that the 'Americanization' of British culture after the Second World War inevitably entailed a turning away from imperially derived cultural associations. Rather, it underlines how 'Americanization' was the product of complex patterns of global interaction and integration, which included the incorporation of referents which had first emerged in the contexts of British imperialism. America was the co-author of these transnational scripts about Farouk, and while he never actually crossed the Atlantic, this did not prevent the widespread dissemination of apocryphal stories about his relationship with Florida madams and New York call girls.

The fictional Farouk was not confined to the world of tabloid sensationalism. His larger-than-life personality attracted novelists as diverse as Gore Vidal, Lawrence Durrell and Barbara Skelton, who included him (sometimes, but not always, under an assumed name) in their fiction. The imperatives of Americanization and fictionalization converged in a 1955 feature film *Abdullah the Great*, where a thinly disguised portrayal of Farouk exposed the paradoxical and contradictory discourses which surrounded the recently deposed king.

Finally, a short concluding chapter, 'Two Funerals, 1965', uses the fact that Farouk and Winston Churchill died in the same year as an entry point into a discussion about how Farouk's posthumous path to near-obscurity reflects a narrowing of how we understand the operation (and discursive possibilities) of empire.

In what particular ways might a study of King Farouk in mid-century British official and popular culture contribute to a refashioning of the historiography of modern Britain? In the introduction to his *Capital Affairs*, first published in 2010, Frank Mort appealed for a 'breaking out of the discrete and compartmentalized way that post-war English history has traditionally been told'. In fact Mort himself then went some considerable way to rectify this situation, his cultural history of London between 1945 and 1964 deploying new and imaginative approaches to the connections between government and society, or between public and private identities.⁴ This study of Farouk likewise encompasses a variety of empirical contexts which are rarely juxtaposed in the historiography of modern Britain: official records produced by the imperial British state, published memoirs, tourist guides and travelogues, mass-circulation newspapers, illustrated magazines, novels and feature films. However, while Mort brings together what historians have previously endeavoured to keep apart, he does so on a single site, the 'urban prism' of postwar London. By contrast, any appraisal of Farouk has to be much more de-centred and dispersed. This is not merely because geographical mobility (as a prerogative of elite cosmopolitanism and, later, as a requirement of exile) was an important feature of Farouk's personal history. Rather, it is an acknowledgement of the multi-sited nature of the creation of late-imperial and post-imperial British culture.

It is also important that we are much more expansive and imaginative when we determine precisely what those multiple sites might be. At the most immediate level, Farouk requires us to restore Egypt to a more significant place in the British cultural imaginary. While the 'new imperial history' has made it almost impossible to ignore the mutually constitutive relationship between metropolitan Britain and its imperial possessions between the eighteenth and twentieth centuries, some aspects of this story have remained relatively neglected. In particular, the study of Britain's presence in North Africa and the Middle East has largely remained the preserve of diplomatic historians, and there has (ironically given the region's centrality to the arguments of Edward Said's seminal study *Orientalism*) been a notable lack of scholarship dedicated to the cultural interaction between metropolitan Britain on the one hand and Egypt, Palestine and Arabia on the other.⁵ In fact the lack of formalized colonialism in Egypt actually encouraged colonial discourse, albeit based, not on territorial authority but on 'mythological authority over the collective imagination'.⁶ Farouk's pervasive presence in British popular culture suggests that Egypt and the Arab world need to be inserted into our understanding of how empire was imagined in the metropole, and how the colonial imperative was domesticated.

However, Farouk's particular itineraries and their intersections with a range of globalized, trans-national phenomena (notably monarchy, celebrity culture, exile and tourism) also demonstrate that the ending of the British empire cannot be mapped by focusing exclusively on the axes between metropole and colony. Other parts of the world, notably continental Europe and the United States, were deeply imbricated in the way the British understood their empire, and certainly in the way they negotiated its demise.⁷ Antoinette Burton's pioneering study of South Asian public intellectual Santha Rama Rau's life and career in both India and the United States offers a model of how to address issues of cosmopolitanism, transnationalism, race, globalization and the reach of colonial and postcolonial cultures beyond the boundaries of formal empire. While concerned with a figure who (while renowned) lacked Farouk's international celebrity status, Burton's study has had a critical influence on how this study of Farouk emphasizes the multi-sited nature of identity formation and the value of seeking out connections between individual lives and geopolitical change.[8]

Ann Laura Stoler has long argued for the necessity of moving beyond constricted models of empire, insisting that imperial formations were never 'clearly bordered or bounded polities'. This book shares Stoler's desire to seek out the 'indeterminate spaces and ambiguous places' that, while they might nominally seem to have little connection to empire, were not 'beyond the reach of imperial will'. If the designated borders of empires were 'not necessarily the force fields in which they operated or the limits of them' during the heyday of the European empires, then this contention is surely even more pertinent during the era of their dissolution.[9] More specifically, it is vital to move beyond the peculiarly irrepressible myth that, it was only after its overseas empire was dismantled that Britain accommodated itself to closer engagement with its European neighbours. At the very least, the situating of Farouk's high-living in popular imaginings of the two-shored Mediterranean adds further freight to the surely not unreasonable demand that the long-established dichotomy between empire and continental Europe in the writing of British history be finally discarded.[10]

If Farouk calls into question existing spatial understanding of both empire and decolonization, he also can help us clarify issues of temporality and periodization; expressly when, if at all, did British empire end? Despite the critical role accorded to empire in narratives of modern British history, the ending of imperial dominion was, until relatively recently, accorded only peripheral significance in the voluminous historiography of post-1945 Britain. However, in the last decade historians have looked beyond the apparent lack of unrest or controversy in debates over decolonization within British domestic politics in this period to acknowledge that disengagement from empire (especially in Kenya, Malaya and Cyprus) was often accompanied by protracted counterinsurgency campaigns, and resort to violence and brutal coercion.[11] At the same time, studies of various aspects of British mass media have seriously questioned the notion that decolonization was something that only happened 'overseas'.[12] In a highly significant intervention, Jordanna Bailkin has recovered the extensive links between the afterlives of empire and the creation of the postwar British welfare state.¹³ Nevertheless, in contrast to scholarship on France, there has been little effort to bring the end of empire into dialogue with other critical cultural forces operating in postwar Britain, notably the impact of consumer affluence and Americanized mass culture.¹⁴ Even mass immigration from its former colonies, one of the most visible aspects of social change in post-1945 Britain, has, until very recently, remained oddly disconnected from its imperial associations, despite the pleas of Bill Schwarz and others to recognize how the settlement of migrants from the Caribbean and South Asia caused the colonial frontier (and its associated racial discourses) to be 'brought home' to Britain in the late 1950s and 1960s.¹⁵

However, while Bailkin laments that the history of postwar Britain has remained 'a pristinely metropolitan story', she is not content to merely criticize. She also offers a plausible explanation for this deficiency, namely that it is because 'the timeline of the empire's death is so hazy, and geographically uneven' that 'its intersection with other themes of postwar history has been so difficult to discern'.¹⁶ This study of Farouk shares this insistence on the indeterminacy of empire's end, but extends that characterization beyond time and space, to encompass the unstable and porous nature of the demarcations between discursive categories and designations.¹⁷ While its agenda is broader, this book fully shares Bailkin's determination that we should do much more to isolate the precise ways in which the histories of the postwar and the post-imperial might have interacted.

At a more general level, Farouk disrupts the rarely established, but too often simply assumed, linear narratives of modern British history. The fact that Farouk was comprehended through associations as varied as the Riviera of the Naughty Nineties, the robust plebeian culture of the British music hall and the orientalist fantasies of the harem suggest that we should be careful not to overestimate the reach of self-consciously modern nostrums such as 'the domesticated male', the 'affluent worker', a 'democratized monarchy' and the 'mediatized celebrity'. Farouk's perambulations also demonstrated the resilience of older geographical imaginaries – notably the 'Mediterranean' pleasure zone – which confounded the nominal geopolitical reordering of the globe (not least the creation of 'the Middle East' as a distinct entity) during the Cold War. In short, Farouk calls into question the status of the late 1940s and 1950s as a critical 'moment of modernity' in British history.¹⁸ Moreover, popular interest in Farouk's lifestyle and adventures requires us to confront an affective domain of longing, fancy and fantasy (combined with a sense of ill-defined restlessness), which existed among the British public, but has rarely been acknowledged in the dominant, materialist-based, historical narratives of postwar Britain.[19] At the very least – as the complex and multiple representations of Farouk make manifest – the fact that Britain lost control of its empire, not merely literally and materially but discursively, underlines the benefits of incorporating into British history that recognition of the 'tenuousness of the postwar world' that, in recent years, has inspired so much innovative scholarship on continental European history in the decades immediately after 1945.[20]

This book also offers methodological claims which are not confined to the field of British history (even in its globalized incarnations). Foremost among these is an insistence that case studies constructed around narratives, and representations, of individual lives can contribute to an understanding of the broader patterns of political, social and cultural change. Contradicting the baleful censure of one widely publicized historiographical intervention, this study of Farouk reminds us that generalized and abstract forces in history certainly *can* be recovered from attention to the personal and the particular.[21] At a most immediate level, Farouk confirms that matters of state and matters of intimacy were intrinsically tied, and this book contributes to a growing body of scholarship examining the shared terrain between international history and the history of the emotions.[22] More generally, historians need to be able to successfully oscillate between the very small and the very large, to seamlessly move between the domain of the individual life (and even body) or anecdote, on the one hand, and the grand narratives of diplomacy and geopolitics, on the other. They also need to be more willing and eager to abandon the compartmentalization that continues to beset historical research and writing.[23] International relations were not confined to the world of formal politics but were constantly shaped and comprehended through myriad other formations, encompassing, in the specific case of Farouk, sexuality, celebrity, monarchy, orientalism, modernity, affluence, popular entertainment, fiction, geographical imaginaries, popularized history and nostalgia, Americanization and cinema.[24] Only by understanding that all these elements were not distinct and discrete, but were entangled, and often mutually constitutive, can one begin to make sense of the multidirectional forces that characterized the late imperial world.

While this book is not intended as a biography of Egypt's last king, it does possess a distinct affinity with new forms of historical writing which focus on individual lives. The historical biographer David Nasaw has argued that, 'in the process of researching and writing about individual lives embedded in particular times and places, biographers discover and reveal the ways in which their subjects assume, discard, reconfigure, merge and disassociate multiple identities and rules'.²⁵ Indeed Jo Burr Margadant has gone so far as to assert that the subject of biography is no longer 'the coherent self' but rather 'an individual with multiple selves whose different manifestations reflect… the demands and options of different settings, or the varieties of ways that others seek to represent that person'.²⁶ Such sentiments obviously accord with an investigation of the multiple narrative representations of Farouk, although this book ultimately resists the more extreme poststructuralist contention that the notion of a unified and continuous unified subject is a chimera, and that lives and experiences are little more than texts.²⁷ That said, there is definitely a marked correspondence between this study of Farouk and Matt Houlbrook's self-consciously postmodern biography of 1920s British confidence trickster Netley Lucas. Houlbrook demonstrates how, like Farouk, Lucas could move between ostensibly discrete worlds, producing narratives which confounded national borders and cut across different genres and media.²⁸ Moreover, just as Lucas' chameleon chicanery is deployed by Houlbrook to dramatize the social and cultural changes of post–First World Britain, the lack of fixity surrounding Farouk should be taken as both symptomatic and representative of the instability and fluidity which characterized the world he inhabited in the 1940s and 1950s.

Reiterating that what follows is not a biography (in either its conventional or poststructuralist variety) does not imply that this book is not replete with stories and anecdotes about one of the twentieth century's larger-than-life historical figures. While they are capable of bearing considerable interpretational weight, and lend themselves to various forms of deconstruction, it cannot be denied that these stories are arresting, and frequently entertaining, in their own right. Britain's ambassador in Cairo will be found encouraging Egyptian female socialites to become Farouk's lover in order to gain surreptitious pro-Allied influence over the king during the Second World War. Farouk takes a blow torch to the chest hairs of his barber, and pockets a watch that had been given to Randolph Churchill by his father, Winston. In a Cairo jewellers, Farouk approaches a young woman choosing an engagement ring, dismisses her fiancé and announces his intention to marry her. On his honeymoon, the king smashes the camera of a hapless British tourist who tried to photograph him in the lobby of a Deauville hotel. Farouk threatens to sue a Florida brothel keeper who had named him as one of her clients, despite the fact the king had never even visited the United States. Both Orson Welles and Errol Flynn turn down the chance to play Farouk in a feature film about his life. Even as such stories are scrutinized for their value to the historian committed to recovering broader historical identifies and patterns, it should not be forgotten that it was predominantly through such tales (in their unproblematized and un-deconstructed forms) that the British public came to know, and to make sense of, Egypt's celebrated monarch.

By the time he died in 1965, Farouk of Egypt was a very fat man who had become the subject of some very tall stories. Most of these stories were outlandish and many were undoubtedly apocryphal. Farouk's effortless crossover from fact to fiction may not be sufficient to designate him as a harbinger of the postmodern condition. However, it offers striking verification of how it proved impossible to confine Egypt's last king within the approved demarcations of imperial jurisdiction during his lifetime, and why, long after his death, we should seek to understand him, and his world, by forcefully repudiating the established conventions and partitions of British history.[29]

1

# Faruq, King of Egypt

Faruq al-Awwal was born on 11 February 1920 at the Abdin Palace in Cairo. His official title at birth was His Sultanic Highness Faruq bin Fuad, Hereditary Prince of Egypt and the Sudan.[1] His father was Ahmad Fuad I (1868–1936), Sultan of Egypt since 1917. Fuad belonged to the dynasty founded in 1811 by Mehmet Ali, an Albanian volunteer in the Ottoman army, and was the last surviving son of the Khedive Ismail, who had presided over Egypt's economic modernization and cultural reorientation towards Europe in the 1860s and 1870s. At the outbreak of the First World War, Britain (which had occupied Egypt since 1882) took the opportunity to end Ottoman suzerainty over Egypt. The existing Khedive was deposed and replaced by his uncle, Hussein Kamil, who took the title Sultan of Egypt. Kamil died in 1917 and was succeeded by Fuad. The protectorate did not long outlast the First World War. In 1922 Egypt was declared independent, although British troops remained in Cairo, and the High Commissioner retained the power to veto or suggest ministers. Under this new arrangement, the Sultanate was abandoned, and Fuad was declared king of Egypt on 15 March 1922.

Fuad's inclinations were inherently autocratic, and he succeeded in modifying the constitution in 1923 to extend his powers. He personally selected his own ministers and regularly flouted the constitution. Despite being in debt when he ascended the throne, Fuad managed to become very rich during his reign, acquiring a personal fortune reported to be in the region of 100 million dollars and some of the most valuable land in Egypt. Fuad was a cultivated and cosmopolitan king, a patron of the arts and scholarship, who genuinely sought to raise the educational standards of his subjects. However, like many products of the Ottoman world, he held ordinary Egyptians largely in contempt and made little attempt to master Arabic. His peremptory manner and barking voice (the product of a bullet which lodged in his throat after he had been shot by his own brother-in-law) did little to endear him to courtiers, politicians and the few members of the ordinary Egyptian public he was exposed to. Fuad's legacies to Faruq were a gilded-cage upbringing and a commitment to asserting royal prerogative, even when it contradicted the insistence in Egypt's constitution that 'the nation is the source of all power'.

Most of Faruq's formative years were spent in the pampered splendour of the 400 rooms and ornamental gardens of Cairo's Koubbeh Palace, in the company of his mother, his four sisters, multiple ladies-in-waiting and an English nanny, Ina Naylor (who later became a vexation for the Foreign Office after she threatened to write her memoirs).[2] Faruq was educated by private tutors until he was sixteen. Fuad's cosmopolitan inclinations encouraged the king to accede to British pressure to provide his son with the educational experience of an English gentleman. Faruq's failure to satisfy the school's Latin entry requirement quashed an attempt to enrol him at Eton. However, Fuad was persuaded to send Faruq to the Royal Military Academy in Woolwich (much to the relief of the British, who feared if the impressionable young prince attended his father's alma mater, the Turin Military Academy, he might come under the sway of Italy's fascist regime). While Woolwich lacked the cache of Sandhurst, it had important connections with the British imperial presence in Egypt, its old boys including General Gordon and Evelyn Baring, Consul-General of Egypt from 1883 to 1907. Faruq arrived in Britain in October 1935, but, failing the entrance exam for the Academy, was obliged to register as an extramural student. 'Prince Freddy', as he was known to the residents of Kingston-upon-Thames (where the prince and his entourage occupied a mansion overlooking the Surrey Downs), spent most of his time playing squash or shopping in the West End.

When King Fuad died on 29 April 1936, Faruq was obliged to return to Egypt. Faruq did not formally ascend the throne until he reached his majority in July 1937. In the meantime, his powers were transferred to a Regency Council, presided over by his uncle, Prince Mohamed Ali. It was during the Regency that the Anglo-Egyptian Defence Treaty of August 1936, a response to nationalist pressure, placed continued British military occupation on a more internationally acceptable legal footing. The Treaty also eradicated the position of High Commissioner, its incumbent, Sir Miles Lampson becoming ambassador instead. Lampson was initially well disposed towards Faruq, but the young king found the ambassador increasingly overbearing, and by 1937, their relationship was characterized by barely concealed mutual contempt. To the alarm of the Foreign Office, Faruq seemed to be more attracted to his Italian, rather than his British, connections. Even while residing in Surrey, Faruq had been under the sway of anti-British courtiers such as General el-Masri, who was later to pass

British secrets to the Axis and who attempted to escape Egypt in order to join Rommel's forces.

Faruq faced several challenges on his accession. At the most immediate level, his own family provided a series of unwelcome distractions. His uncle, Mohamed Ali, clearly believed his age and self-consciously projected sophistication made him more qualified to be monarch than his inexperienced and immature nephew. Faruq had to remain alert to his uncle's frequent attempts to exploit Lampson's frustrations with the king as a means to advance his own claims on the throne. Faruq's mother was another source of familial vexation. Nazli Sabri had been Fuad's substantially younger second wife. For all his public commitment to modernizing Egypt, ostensibly symbolized by his decision to abolish the veil in 1927, Fuad had decidedly traditional Ottoman views about his own family, and Nazli was sequestered in the king's harem. When Fuad died, Nazli was only forty-one and was determined to catch up on the emancipation that she believed other women of her class and generation had enjoyed. Nazli became a devotee of the nightlife of both Cairo and several European capitals, and embarked on a series of romantic adventures, including what may have entailed a secret marriage to Hassanein Pasha, Faruq's Oxford-educated First Chamberlain.

In the spring of 1937, Faruq and Nazli embarked on an unofficial tour of Europe, during which the former frittered away his time in various Swiss resorts and alienated his British hosts by turning up late for dinner with Foreign Secretary Anthony Eden (his excuse being that he had decided to go swimming) and for a ceremony with the vice-chancellor of Cambridge University (this time, Faruq had been buying puppies). The Foreign Office was much more concerned about Nazli, especially the fact that she had been photographed in London without a veil, and her indiscreet assignations in her suite at Claridges with Hassanein. Egypt's Queen Mother, averred one anxious official, 'may be going too fast for a Muslim country'.[3] Given Faruq's later scandalous reputation, there was inadvertent irony in British efforts to keep Nazli and Faruq apart in the early years of his reign, lest the young king be tainted by his mother's disreputable private life. By the final years of his reign, Nazli and Faruq were estranged. When Fazli allowed Faruq's sister, Fathia, to marry a Christian in San Francisco in 1950, the king's response was to expel them both from the royal family. Nazli outlived Faruq and died in California in 1978, two years after Fathia was shot dead by her then ex-husband.

Faruq's wayward relatives were ultimately less challenging than the three-way power struggle between the monarchy, the Cairo Residency and the Egyptian parliament, which remained the dominant political configuration in Egypt throughout his reign. Parliament was dominated by the Wafd, a pro-independence movement which took its name from the Arabic word for 'delegation', and was headed after 1927 by Mostafa el- Nahas. Nahas' distracting outward squint and lack of social refinement led him to be initially underestimated by both the court and the British, and his career was constantly beset by allegations of corruption. However, his populist demeanour gave him a credibility on the Arab street that few elite politicians could match, and he became a mainstay of Egyptian politics until the very end of Faruq's reign. The British wanted to use the monarchy to contain the Wafd's nationalist ambitions, but it was no less committed to ensuring Farouk's authority – vis-à-vis both parliament and the Cairo Residency – was not unduly extended. Egypt's prime ministers in the early years of his reign were members of the Wafd, but, outside parliament, Faruq's prerogatives were jealously guarded by the director of his royal cabinet, Ali Maher. Even when the Wafd were in government, Faruq retained the power to appoint prime ministers, dismiss administrations and dissolve or prorogue parliament. His assent was also required for all government bills.

The opening years of Faruq's reign seemed decidedly propitious. Having an Egyptian mother and a fluency in Arabic that his father conspicuously lacked, the young king appeared genuinely popular with his people. Repudiating the Ottoman sensibilities of his forbears, Faruq benefited from an alignment with a dynamic culture of national pride (and cultural effervescence) that had accompanied Egypt's ostensible progress to independence. His youth and handsome appearance appealed to the self-conscious modernity of the middle-class effendi, while the peasant *fellahin* were attracted by his apparent combination of traditional religious piety and a commitment to improving the social welfare of his citizens. Ali Maher attempted to build on the goodwill towards Faruq exhibited by the devout and the traditionalist elements of Egyptian society by promoting the king's candidacy for the Caliphate, a position of spiritual-temporal leadership in the Islamic world that had remained dormant since 1924. While this effort came to nothing, it demonstrated a serious attempt to project Egypt as a regional power and added further to Faruq's positive public image.

Faruq's popularity was further enhanced by his marriage in January 1938 to Safinaz Zulficar, who immediately took the name Farida (meaning, ironically in the light of Faruq's subsequent infidelities, in Arabic 'the only one'). As the daughter of a high court judge and a lady-in-waiting to Queen Nazli, Farida satisfied the social expectations of the pasha classes, but she also possessed a glamorous modernity that harmonized with the aspirations of a young nation, especially the bourgeois effendi. Faruq and Farida had three daughters: Ferial (born 1938), Fawzia (born 1940) and Fadia (born 1943).

It was during the Second World War that Faruq's reign (and reputation) took a turn for the worse, establishing a trajectory that would culminate in the demise of Egypt as both a monarchy and a part of the British Empire. Egypt proclaimed its neutrality in 1939 but still complied with its obligations under the 1936 Treaty, placing its resources and communications at Britain's disposal and accepting the imposition of martial law. Moreover, the Wafd declared that its nationalist aspirations did not preclude unequivocal support for the Allied cause for the duration of the war. However, once Italy entered the war in June 1940, the Foreign Office became rattled and sought to tighten control over Egypt's internal politics. Ali Maher, who had been appointed prime minister in 1939, had extensive Italian connections, and Faruq himself was suspected of harbouring pro-Axis sympathies. When Ali Maher refused to declare war on Italy, Lampson demanded Faruq dismiss his government. After stalling for a week, Faruq complied. However, the military successes of Axis forces in North Africa in 1941 and 1942 aggravated lingering suspicions in the Residency about the loyalty of the court to the Allied cause. When Faruq contemplated restoring Maher to the premiership, Lampson decided dramatic action was required. On 4 February 1942, 600 British troops, tanks and armoured cars surrounded the Abdin Palace. Lampson sent an ultimatum to the king, instructing him to appoint Nahas as prime minister, or abdicate. When Faruq failed to respond by the designated deadline, the ambassador went in person to the palace, bearing a letter of abdication drafted by Walter Monckton, the author of Edward VIII's abdication letter, who happened to be resident in Cairo in his capacity as director of Britain's Middle East propaganda operations. Faruq was visibly shaken by Lampson's ruthlessness and meekly capitulated to the ambassador's instruction to summon Nahas.

Faruq's submission to Lampson was comprehended by many Egyptians as a national humiliation. Nationalism now aligned itself with anti-monarchism, and the Wafd's apparent collusion in the humbling of Faruq ensured that the ultimate beneficiaries of what became known as the 'Abdin incident' were the more radical elements in Egyptian politics. These included not merely the Muslim Brotherhood (which equated both British imperialism and the monarchy with a Western decadence that was corroding traditional Islamic values) but also several junior officers in the Egyptian army (notably Gamal Nasser and Anwar Sadat) who responded to Faruq's abasement by embracing republicanism. Faruq himself never recovered from the Abdin incident, taking solace in the increasingly reckless and unconcealed pursuit of private pleasure, for which he was to become legendary. In 1943, a serious car accident required surgery, the details of which are obscure, but which many Egyptians speculated had led to both the king's dramatic weight gain and a shift in his personality towards increased narcissism and self-absorption.

In the last months of the war, Faruq tried to restore his standing within Egypt, and beyond, by taking a lead in the creation of the Arab League, a regional organization of states (initially composing Egypt, Iraq, Transjordan, Lebanon, Saudi Arabia and Syria) to foster economic development and secure common political objectives. If this appeared to signify a desire to free himself from imperial superintendence, Faruq nevertheless could not escape the dilemma that any British military evacuation would leave his throne exposed to potential revolution. Lampson's replacement at the Cairo Residency by the less imperious figure of Sir Ronald Campbell in early 1946 eased tensions with the British, but Foreign Office frustrations with the king continued, centred on the failure to resolve the future status of British troops in Egypt and Faruq's dynastic claims to be recognized as king of Sudan.

In 1948 Faruq joined the other Arab states in a war against the newly created state of Israel. Faruq may have been manipulated into this decision by rogue members of the British intelligence services operating in Cairo, but his primary motivation was to prevent King Abdullah of Transjordan seizing the mantle of defender of the Palestine Arabs. A series of Egyptian military defeats were aggravated by a scandal which implicated the palace in the purchase of defective weapons, and Faruq's reputation took a further dive. The king's decision to employ former Wehrmacht officers as military advisors also created unwelcome publicity overseas. At home, the disasters of the Arab-Israeli war coincided with Faruq's announcement of his divorce from Farida in November 1948. The king's shameless parading of his mistresses in public and Farida's failure to produce a male heir ensured the news hardly came as a shock among the Cairo elites. However, the unceremonious casting aside of a well-liked consort all but obliterated any remaining affection for Faruq among the Egyptian public.

Facing growing hostility at home, Faruq decided to spend more time in Europe, or, more accurately, the hotels and casinos of the Cote d'Azur, Deauville and the Bay of Naples. High-stakes gambling was accompanied by the voracious consumption of food and the relentless pursuit of various inamorata, his paramours ranging from princesses (foreign and domestic) to belly-dancers and aspiring movie starlets. In May 1951, Faruq attempted to restore his popularity by marrying Narriman Sadek, a seventeen-year-old daughter of a middle-ranking civil servant. Narriman was in fact already engaged, to a Harvard doctoral student, Zaki Hashem. She was reputedly shopping with her fiancé for an engagement ring in the royal jewellers on Abdel Khalik Sarwat Street in Cairo, when her blonde hair and voluptuous figure were clocked by its owner, Ahmed Naguib. Naguib persuaded Narriman to return in two days to view a ring he would arrange to be transferred from his Alexandria branch. After they left, Naguib called Faruq's valet, to recommend the king take the opportunity to meet Narriman. Two days later, Narriman was trying on rings in Naguib's shop, when Faruq entered. The king quizzed the overawed teenager about her life and interests.[4] The fact that Narriman was already engaged only encouraged Faruq in his pursuit of a new bride. Narriman's father was instructed to tell Hashem that his forthcoming marriage had been quashed by royal decree. The jilted fiancé's only consolation was that Faruq had promised to secure the return of any presents Hashem had sent to Narriman. Faruq's reign may have been entering its twilight years, but his sense of majestic entitlement was in no way yet diminished.

Faruq's decision to marry a young woman whose lack of aristocratic refinement required her to be secretly sent to the Egyptian embassy in Rome to study history, etiquette and four languages clearly had an element of cynical populism about it. However, if marrying this 'Cinderella of the Nile', as Narriman was soon dubbed, was intended to endear the king to the masses, it failed in its objective. The four-month long European honeymoon spree which followed the lavish wedding festivities alienated the Egyptian public, not least because it coincided with Ramadan. Nevertheless, Faruq could console himself with the arrival of a male heir, when Narriman gave birth to Ahmad Fuad in January 1952.

In that same month, an escalating standoff between nationalist Egyptians and the British military exploded into violence after British troops, pursuing nationalists who had attacked British ships and installations at Ismailia, killed fifty Egyptian auxiliary police officers. On 26 January – 'Black Saturday' – an incensed mob, encouraged by nationalist agitators, burned and ransacked the centre of Cairo, destroying many of the hotels, clubs, restaurants, cinemas and department stores that were the social and cultural infrastructure of the British community in the city. The riots suggested that the Egyptian government had lost the ability to maintain order and the British contemplated restoring a full military occupation. Faruq eased tensions with the British by dismissing the Wafd government, but political instability continued. When Faruq decided to arrest the leaders of the Free Officers Movement, a cell of republican nationalists within the army, he prompted a mutiny of junior officers on 23 July 1952. Faruq panicked and put out feelers for the British to intervene, but his secret messages were intercepted. Some of the Free Officers felt Faruq was guilty of treason and should be killed, but, after an intervention from the leader of the revolutionary command council, Gamal Nasser, it was decided to force Faruq to abdicate, in favour of his son. On 26 July, Faruq, Narriman and their children left Egypt on the royal yacht.

King Ahmad Fuad's regency ended in June 1953. Faruq played no further role in either Egyptian or British imperial politics. While he did send a communication to the British government during the Suez crisis, offering to mediate, it was ignored: the Eden administration had no intention of restoring the Egyptian monarchy, even if they had succeeding in overthrowing Nasser.[5] Faruq settled into a life of exile in Italy, first on Capri and then in a villa outside Rome. His second marriage ended in 1953, when, tiring of his philandering, Narriman and her mother returned to Cairo. In 1959 Faruq was granted Monegasque citizenship by Prince Rainier of Monaco, producing the unintended consequence of barring him from the casino at Monte Carlo, which had become something of a home away from home. Fortunately, there were still the casino at Cannes and the gaming rooms of Rome's Circolo Degli Scacchi to satisfy Faruq's predilection for high-stakes gambling. He remained a subject of celebrity gossip and popular interest throughout the 1950s, but became an increasingly pathetic figure in the last years of his life, which was spent, in deteriorating health, amidst the dubious and seedy pleasures of Rome's notorious Via Veneto.

Faruq, once King of Egypt and the Sudan, Sovereign of Nubia, Kordofan and Darfur, died in Rome on 18 March 1965. A post-mortem was never completed, but it is most likely he died of a cerebral haemorrhage. The ex-king was only forty-five years of age. His life, and indeed his reign, had been short and tragic. However, while the story of *King Faruq* as a political figure was confined to Egypt in the final decades of British imperial supervision, the story of *King Farouk* not king of Egypt but 'king of the night' was to extend much further, and much deeper, into the weft and weave of British national culture.

2

# Indeterminacy: Farouk and the Official Imperial Mind

On the evening of 17 August 1951 a modest awards ceremony in the English coastal town of Folkestone honoured the contestants in that year's *Daily Mail* International Cross-Channel Swimming Race. Swimmer after swimmer came to the podium to emphasize the fellowship and concord between nations that had been fostered during the competition. However, when Mareen Hassan Hamad, the Egyptian who had made the fastest crossing of the twenty miles from the Kent coast to the Pas-de-Calais, was invited to say a few words, his team manager, Brigadier-General Mohammed Sabri Bey, rose in his stead. To the consternation of those present, he declared that his swimmers had chosen to decline their prize money, in protest at what they regarded as the relentless and unwarranted slandering in the British press of their monarch, King Farouk. While the *Daily Mail* indignantly responded by accusing Sabri Bey of politicizing a sporting event, it was hard not to accept that the Egyptian swimmers had a legitimate grievance.[1] Britain's mass-circulation newspapers – not merely the *Daily Mail* but also the *Daily Express* and the *Daily Mirror* – at the time of Farouk's accession in 1936, had presented him as a glamorous and handsome modernizing prince. However, by the late 1940s, the popular press had come to portray the Egyptian king as a grotesquely bloated and garishly debauched potentate, a simultaneously ludicrous and sinister figure, possessed of apparently insatiable appetites for food, gambling, sex and intrigue.

The Egyptian swimmers' indignation elicited a degree of sympathy from within the British diplomatic elite. The Foreign Office was already troubled that excessive press attention to Farouk's picaresque adventures, often coloured by a peculiar concoction of censure, titillation and ridicule, might jeopardize Britain's relationship with Egypt, which, while never formally a British possession, had, for seventy years, been critical to Britain's imperial authority in the Mediterranean, Africa and the Middle East, not least in its responsibility for the Suez Canal, Britain's vital lifeline from Europe to its Indian empire. By 1951, the combination of Indian independence and the strains of imperial overstretch might have suggested Egypt was now much less pivotal to British interests, and the British military presence in Egypt had already been substantially whittled down in the years immediately after 1945. However, as the shattering events of the 1956 Suez crisis were to reveal, not merely was Britain far from wholehearted in its resort to imperial decommission after the Second World War but Egypt remained important in Britain's imperial story, almost to the very – bitter – end.[2] Discussions over press coverage of Farouk in Whitehall and the Cairo embassy in 1950 and 1951 ranged from overwrought panic (one – unrealized – suggestion was that King George VI himself should be asked to make a plea to the press to display greater responsibility) to a resigned acknowledgement that a combination of media trivialization of current affairs and Farouk's undoubted personal failings made a satisfactory outcome unlikely. As one Foreign Office official put it, 'King Farouk, by his way of life, invites ribald comment, and nothing is likely to curb the essential vulgarity of our popular press'.[3]

Ultimately, the Foreign Office determined that attempts to curtail press coverage of Farouk's scandalous private life were either undesirable or unfeasible. When Foreign Secretary Herbert Morrison personally approached his former wartime cabinet colleague and proprietor of the *Daily Express*, Lord Beaverbrook, he was robustly rebuffed.[4] At one level the tension between the Foreign Office and the mass-circulation daily newspapers was a story of how the ordered progress of British politics and diplomacy had become a collateral victim of the rise of what was later to be termed 'celebrity journalism'. In the first half of the twentieth century the British popular press had increasingly prioritized entertainment over information about public events. The necessity of offering a steady supply of 'human interest' stories created a focus on a select cast of notable public figures – aristocrats and plutocrats, socialites, actors, entertainers and sports personalities – whose lives could be chronicled over months and years. These lists of noteworthy figures also increasingly extended to politicians and royal personages. Moreover, as sexuality was granted increased significance in conceptions of personal identity, information about the private and intimate lives of celebrities was seen as critical to their representation in the mass media. Farouk's often outlandish private life inevitably drew him into this new conception of the public sphere as articulated by the British press. He was rendered even more vulnerable by being foreign, and by a new climate after 1945, in which discretion and deference had been dealt a massive blow by a desire among journalists not to repeat the acquiescence shown towards the social and political establishment that had characterized the British press during the 1936 Abdication crisis.[5]

The inability of the British diplomatic elite to prevent Farouk being framed not by the protocols of imperial officials and policy makers but by populist discourses of celebrity, gossip or sensationalism reflected a broader failure to fix Farouk securely in the rubrics of imperial rule, which had been evident from the beginning of his reign. Understandings of Farouk in the Cairo Residency and Whitehall disclosed a wider confusion about the nature of Egyptian identity, a disorientation rooted in its apparent incompatibility with many of the conventional hierarchies and arrangements on which imperial rule were predicated, notably in regard to issues of sovereignty, race and the geographical ordering of empire. Farouk's complex lineage, and his apparent ability to move from exemplifying the cosmopolitan culture of Egypt's multinational elite one minute to presenting himself as a tribune of Arab nationalism in the next, only aggravated British mystification. Those British officials who emphasized the king's capriciousness, cruelty and sensuality reanimated the hackneyed repertoire of orientalism, but they were soon required to acknowledge the distinctly modern aspects of Farouk, not least the fact that coverage of the king in the British press became increasingly characterized by popularization, personalization and the publicization of stories about his private life. Moreover, his highly publicized junketing in the pleasure resorts of the Riviera and Italy allowed Farouk to disregard the assigned spatial arrangements of empire, exploiting new dynamics of globalization which confounded the ostensible binaries between 'Europe' and 'Orient'. Obliged to come to terms with Farouk's status as a highly mediatized celebrity, diplomats and policy makers accommodated themselves to, and to a surprising degree, internalized, the precepts of celebrity culture.

I

Defining 'celebrity culture' is far from straightforward. Historians have come to celebrity relatively late in the day, the topic previously being the preserve of scholars in the fields of sociology, media studies and cultural theory. This is ironic, given that one of the pioneers in the study of celebrity was the historian of modern America, Daniel Boorstin. Boorstin was responsible for the much-quoted definition of a celebrity as 'a person well-known for his well knownness', a depressing example of the trivialization of Western culture at the hands of an irresponsible mass media. For Boorstin, modern celebrity culture was distinct from earlier forms of fame, which rested on achievement rather than mere visibility.[6] Subsequent commentators have been more positive about celebrity, identifying it as a function of modern democracy, permitting ordinary people to enjoy the benefits of fame, which had previously been confined to a narrow elite.[7] Historians have tended to eschew the taxonomies of celebrity, which often do little more than reiterate value judgments, and which tend to break down when subjected to sustained scrutiny. For example, while it might be a stretch to identify Farouk as an 'achieved celebrity' (whose fame is based on merit), he would nevertheless satisfy the criteria of both of the two remaining categories of celebrity adopted by Chris Rojek, being not merely an 'ascribed celebrity' (dependent on birth and rank) but also an 'attributed celebrity' (a media creation, whose celebrity is regardless of any intrinsic merit or achievement).[8] Historians have been equally sceptical that celebrities did not exist before the twentieth century, although they have also conceded that celebrity culture undoubtedly intensified in the era of the Hollywood film and the glossy magazine.[9] Farouk's celebrity did not entail the commercialization of an individual which the Hollywood system promoted, but it was no less dependent than that of movie stars on a mass media that constructed and disseminated his fame.

In the person of Farouk, modern celebrity culture was to confront what has been termed the 'official mind'. While Gallagher and Robinson, in their classic exploration of Britain's fashioning of its emerging African empire in the nineteenth century, applied this notion to almost everyone (from the prime minister to the lowliest consular official) undertaking imperial responsibilities in the Victorian era, Thomas G. Otte focused his dissection of the official mind between 1865 and 1914 on diplomats who represented Britain abroad and senior officials in the Foreign Office.[10] It is the late-imperial successors to the categories of official Otte is concerned with – especially the British Ambassador and his advisors in the Cairo Residency, the Foreign Secretary himself and senior civil servants in Whitehall – that feature prominently in this chapter. While Egypt was part of Britain's imperial system; the fact that it was neither a Dominion nor a colony meant that it was to be the Foreign Office, and not the Colonial or India Offices, that was to play the critical role in shaping British understandings of both Farouk and his kingdom.[11]

The accepted understandings and unspoken assumptions of the Foreign Office 'official mind' reflected the social exclusivity of the section of society from which the diplomatic elite were recruited. Their values and beliefs were inculcated at the public schools and ancient universities they had attended, in which intellectual attainment was seconded to notions of gentlemanly conduct and the lionization of service, as opposed to self-advancement.[12] Senior officials literally 'spoke the same language', in terms of both social class and a patriotic pride that made them jealous guardians of British prerogatives and imperial security. Sir Miles Lampson, ambassador to Egypt from 1936 to 1946, had attended Eton, as had both his immediate successor (between 1946 and 1950) Ronald Campbell and the long-serving foreign secretary Anthony Eden (1935–1938, 1940–1945, 1952–1955). Campbell and Eden also went to Oxford, as did the final ambassador to Egypt during Farouk's reign, Ralph Stevenson (1950–1952). Given the formative cultures from which they emerged, such men were inevitably attracted to paternalistic genres of public service, of which imperial diplomacy sat at the apex.[13] In the middle decades of the twentieth century, Britain clung to imperial rule, less from economic priorities than because it was embedded in the self-imagery of its leading political class.[14] It is hard not to be struck by the ostensibly irreconcilable imperatives of celebrity culture and the official mind: self-publicity versus public service, personality versus character, democracy versus elitism. In fact, as we shall see, the two formations proved impossible to disentangle, and the official mind found itself unable to repudiate the prerogatives of celebrity culture, even if it had wanted to.

Farouk became king in 1936, the year in which the Anglo-Egyptian Treaty confirmed that Egypt was a sovereign state. However, it also made Egypt's nominal independence conditional on the continued safety of imperial communications and the maintenance of British troops in the Suez Canal zone. This arrangement was yet another stage in British imperialism's idiosyncratic relationship with Egypt, a country which it had occupied since 1882, but which had officially remained a province of the Ottoman Empire until 1914, before briefly becoming a British Protectorate for the eight years prior to independence in 1922. British power in Egypt was far from overwhelming, and its continued presence was in fact only made possible by the promotion of policies that met the interests of a significant portion of the Egyptian elite. However, Britain retained a virtual monopoly in terms of foreign influence over independent Egypt, and the retention of Britain's imperial prerogatives was made abundantly clear in the decision to appoint the existing High Commissioner, Sir Miles Lampson, as Britain's first ambassador to Egypt.[15]

British policies towards Egypt in the 1920s and early 1930s have been characterized as a 'neo-colonial settlement' which essentially invented the Egyptian monarchy so as to create the conditions for collaboration with the nation's elites while weakening revolutionary fervour. Many conservative and aristocratic Egyptians also saw the value of a monarchy, in their case as a means to ensure that while Egypt emerged as a modern, developmental, nation-state, it would also be an authoritarian one. Egypt therefore was a place where colonial ideology worked in a complex conjunction with indigenous cultural values, especially the aristocratic codes of the pasha class. Supported by the aristocracy, state bureaucrats, the landowning elite and much of the religious establishment, the monarchy simultaneously appeared to combine the birth of a modern Egyptian nation and the paternalistic ideology of British colonialism.[16] In the interwar years British travellers, artists, businesspeople, teachers, nurses and engineers resident in Egypt exemplified an understanding of empire which permitted them to have close social relations with the corresponding Egyptian elites, and, as James Whidden has expertly demonstrated, the worlds of the colonizer and the colonized frequently overlapped.[17] However, little of this liberal vision of the social relations of empire found its way in the official mind of the Residency. More specifically, Lampson seemed to have absorbed little of the nuanced political approach to Egypt adopted (albeit unevenly) by the British since 1919. In many senses, he was a throwback to the high-handed style of Lord Cromer, consul general in Egypt from 1883 to 1907, who had famously belittled the Khedive Abbas Hilmi. Lampson's barely concealed contempt for both Egyptian politicians and the young monarch was to set

**Figure 1** Prince Farouk and Sir Miles Lampson at a RAF air display at Heliopolis, 1935 (Keystone-France via Getty Images).

the tone for relations between Residency and Palace in the first ten years of Farouk's reign.

Attempts by British policy makers to control and contain the young Egyptian monarch were often as much literal as they were discursive. Immediately after Farouk's accession, both Lampson and foreign secretary Anthony Eden were eager to prevent the sixteen-year-old king from falling under the sway of anti-British factions in the Egyptian court.[18] Lampson's initial option was to keep Farouk in England until he was twenty-one, but, appreciating this might suggest to the Egyptian people a Machiavellian plot to maintain control over their young, and at this point popular, monarch, he suggested the alternative option of bringing a British tutor to Egypt.[19] The unfortunate recipient of this assignment was a young master at Eton, Edward Ford. While the Foreign Office went to great lengths to ensure Ford was not seen as a British spy, he did regularly report back to the ambassador, in lengthy handwritten reports which recorded – in meticulous detail – Farouk's narcissism and selfishness, aggravated by being surrounded by the obsequious flattery of his entourage.[20] Lampson, concerned about pro-Italian sentiments among Farouk's inner circle, used palace servants to report on court intrigue, and, during the Second World War, supposedly encouraged noted Jewish beauty Irene Guinle to become the king's mistress, in order to sway him against the Axis.[21] When Farouk travelled outside Egypt in 1936 and 1937, the Foreign Office intervened to prevent the king making official stops in Italy and (less successfully) tried to steer him away from the distractions of European night life.[22]

Back in Egypt, Lampson sought to curtail Farouk's 'nocturnal excursions' to night clubs and casinos, fearful of the negative impact on respectable Muslim opinion.[23] The ambassador was no less committed to the, ultimately thankless, task of 'keeping him [Farouk] away from women'.[24] An early marriage only temporarily halted Farouk's waywardness, and Lampson expended no less effort during the war years on keeping tabs on Farouk's extra-marital affairs than he did on keeping up with the tortured trajectories of Egyptian high politics. Farouk inevitably resented these exercises in surveillance, scrutiny and control. Lampson's notorious insensitivity and high-handedness towards the king betrayed proconsular proclivities that stood in stark contrast to wartime conceptions of empire that emphasized not exploitation and domination but trusteeship and partnership.[25] The fact that Lampson was almost three times as old as Farouk probably made it inevitable that the ambassador would regularly – in both official correspondence and his private diary – disparage the young monarch as 'the boy'.[26] However, Lampson's self-adopted role as a stern father admonishing his prodigal charge also suggested that the ambassador continued to subscribe to long-established notions of colonized subjects as intrinsically childlike and insufficiently mature for self-government.[27]

During the war years, British military commanders, convinced that the strategic necessity of keeping Egypt out of Axis hands was more important than the ambassador's personal dignity, were vociferous critics of Lampson's lack of respect for Farouk.[28] Air Marshal Sholto Douglas contrasted Lampson's treatment of the king as 'nothing but a naughty and rather silly boy' with the overtures to Farouk from the Italians and Germans, who 'treated him as an adult'.[29] To Lampson's fury, Douglas attempted to befriend Farouk, becoming part of his social circle and accompanying him to Cairo night-spots.[30] However, the disagreement between Lampson and Douglas over how to handle Farouk may be seen less as a conflict over means and ends in diplomacy, and more as emblematic of the unresolved tension between two visions of how Britain's interests could best be promoted in the era of the so-called 'Third British Empire'. The level of scrutiny exercised over Farouk by the Residency initially abated after 1945, when the Foreign Office curbed the practice of interfering in Egypt's internal affairs, deciding that entanglement in court and party political conflicts made it more difficult to resolve the contentious issue of retention of British forces around the Suez Canal. However, it was reversed at the end of the decade as Egypt's ill-advised war against the nascent Israeli state left the nation's politics on point of collapse.[31]

Parallel with Britain's shifting strategies over how best to manage imperial tutelage in a nominally independent nation was Britain's ongoing inability to properly situate Egypt in the geographical arranging of empire, a problem which Farouk's complex ancestry and public personality confounded, rather than clarified. Egypt was comprehended through the overlapping, contradictory and ill-defined appellations of the Arab world, the North African littoral, the Levant, the Islamic world, the eastern Mediterranean and the Near East. While the term 'Middle East' increasingly became the default description for the cluster of nations that emerged from the collapsing Ottoman Empire after 1918, this did not preclude continued recourse in understandings of Egypt to pre-1914 romantic and escapist conceptions of 'the Orient'.[32] This notable indeterminacy in imperial discourses surrounding Egypt was even more evident when it came to its monarch. As nationalist critics pointed out, both Farouk's Circassian and Albanian ancestry and his Ottoman cultural heritage meant he had shallow roots in Egypt. Naquib, the man who overthrew Farouk in 1952, declared that the Mehmet Ali dynasty had 'always been a stranger' to the Egyptian people.[33]

In fact, Farouk was less alien to Egyptians than his father (who, unlike his son and heir, spoke no Arabic), his mother was an Egyptian commoner, and he succeeded in his early years in embodying the youthful spirit of national regeneration which characterized Egypt in the late 1930s.[34] However, the British seemed preoccupied with Farouk's non-Egyptian bloodline. During the Second World War, repeated references were made to Farouk's Albanian patrilineal great-great grandfather. This not merely associated the king with the lionization of the Albanian brigands-turned-partisans who featured in the picaresque narratives authored by British Special Forces operatives serving in the Balkans.[35] It also offered reassurance that the fact that Farouk's father had been educated in Italy and served in the Italian military was unlikely to secure an alliance between Egypt and Britain's fascist enemy, on the (somewhat flimsy) basis that Mussolini had invaded Albania in 1939 and deposed Europe's only Muslim ruler.[36]

Other intimations of Europe in Farouk's heritage and personality reinforced the difficulty of containing the king, not merely geographically but temporally. Farouk spoke English with a slight French accent, and boasted matrilineal descent from one of Napoleon's officers, inheriting from his ancestor his hefty 'heavy dragoon' physique.[37] The physical environment of royal Cairo under Farouk remained the ersatz version of Second Empire Paris created by his grandfather, the Khedive Ismail.[38] One British travel writer saw in Farouk's rococo opulence the elusive echo of the court of Napoleon III, now 'dim and gay and very far away'.[39] Those fortunate (or unfortunate) enough to visit the king's private apartments would have found there an extraordinary seven-piece bedroom suite made by the Second Empire French cabinet-maker Antoine Krieger, inspired by the furnishings of Napoleon and Josephine's palace at Malmaison. Others felt that Farouk had greater affinities with the unapologetic splendour and autocracy of the Bourbons, and his execrable taste in ornate furniture was disdainfully labelled 'Louis Farouk'.[40]

Farouk was at the apex of a rarefied social elite in Egypt that was unequivocally cosmopolitan, incorporating Turks, Germans, French, Greeks, Lebanese and Copts.[41] It was these aristocratic circles with which British diplomats and administrators were most familiar, their interaction with middle-class Egyptian effendi (let alone the *fellahin* masses) proving negligible. In particular, Farouk had close personal relations with Egypt's Jewish community, Helene Mosseri serving as his social organizer, and renowned beauties Irene Guinle and Lilianne Cohen were to be found among his romantic entanglements.[42] The king's Jewish circle offered a model of cultural cosmopolitanism that was not bounded by the formal arrangements of empire.[43] Farouk's highly personal ties to Egypt's Jews undoubtedly meant that the British were perplexed, not to say flabbergasted, when, at the end of the Second World War, the king refashioned himself as head of the Arab League and granted asylum to the notorious pro-Axis anti-Semite and Palestinian Arab nationalist Amin Al-Husseini, the Mufti of Jerusalem.[44] By 1949 Farouk was becoming framed within the uncompromising binaries of the postwar Middle East. Israel and its supporters within the international community were eager to publicize evidence of Farouk's wartime flirtation with the Axis, and the subsequent employment of former Wehrmacht general Wilhelm Schmitt by the Egyptian military.[45]

However, if Farouk was now an Arab, he was set apart from an Arab world that was identified in the British imperial imaginary with the romance of the desert Bedouin. Farouk seemed to embody the European vices of materialism and superficiality, rather than the chivalry and asceticism regularly attributed by British travel-writers to the nomadic desert Arab.[46] The fact that Farouk's wealth and mobility were concretized not by the lavish reception tent of his contemporary, the Saudi monarch Ibn Saud but by the Egyptian king's extravagant private yacht underlines his association with the maritime Levant, or even with the boundless ocean beyond, as opposed to the arid desert that featured so disproportionately in British preconceptions of Arab culture and identity.[47]

One strategy of distancing Farouk from the Arab world might have been to emphasize Egypt's Pharaonic, as opposed to its Muslim, past, especially given the king's preference for the coastal cities over Egypt's rural and devoutly Islamic hinterland. When Farouk appeared on the cover of *Time* magazine (for the second time) in 1951, he was portrayed wearing the tarbush (soon to be repudiated by nationalists as a symbol of Egypt's discredited monarchic and Ottoman pasts, but, at this point explicitly associated with the cosmopolitan Mehmet Ali dynasty), but in the background loomed the ancient and familiar landmarks of the Pyramids and the Sphinx.[48] The Egyptian national revival of the 1930s and 1940s was accompanied by renewed interest in Egyptology, while the last years of Farouk's life and his early years in exile coincided with several opulent cinematic spectacles of ancient Egypt, which would have been viewed by British audiences.[49] However, much to the disgust of his tutor Ford, Farouk himself appeared to possess little interest in his Pharaonic predecessors, beyond the adoption of pseudo-Pharaonic décor for his private night club and rest house, built in the shadow of the Pyramids.[50]

Farouk's physiognomy exacerbated the inability to fix him in an imperial system predicated on distinct racial hierarchies. In 1938 one British newspaper remarked that the king possessed the 'blue eyes and fair hair of the Scandinavian'.[51] That Farouk's facial chromatics might place him both inside and outside the standard binaries of racial difference that empire regularly (although not universally) traded in was made obvious in British discussions about Egypt's relationship with the Sudan. Under the complex triangulated colonialism of the Condominium, Sudan was a colony of Egypt as well as of Britain, and Farouk was eager to draw clear demarcations between Egyptians and their black African neighbours to the south.[52] The British had no wish to contest such racially informed distinctions.[53] In a 1951 satirical cartoon in which Farouk is portrayed opening a casino in the Sudan, while he is presented as a humanized hippopotamus, his whiteness is starkly contrasted with the black bodies and grotesquely stereotyped faces of the black Africans surrounding him.[54] At one point, the Foreign Office and Colonial Office both became apprehensive about reports that Farouk was looking to buy a hunting lodge in Kenya. While such concern was largely about the threat to established structures of imperial demarcation between Britain's North African sphere of influence and its sub-Saharan colonies, it also suggested unease about the possibility of Farouk sharing in the dividends of whiteness enjoyed by Britain's settler elite in its East African possessions.[55] The inability to ascribe to Farouk the clear signifiers of racial difference may be usefully compared to his contemporary and fellow *bon vivant* Porfirio Rubirosa, whose black Hispanic identity was concealed through adopting the comportment and protocols of American and Parisian high society. Like Rubirosa (and another legendary playboy of non-European heritage, Aly Khan), Farouk exploited the Mediterranean as a playground for the super rich where race, at least among wealthy sybarites, was conveniently demoted.[56]

Of course a lack of chromatic distinction in British official (and popular) understandings of Farouk does not mean that we can afford to overlook the racial, and indeed racist, contexts here. The British undoubtedly regarded Egyptians as an inferior race, even if their conceptualization of racial difference was less about physiology or ethnographic categorization and more to do with issues of character, culture and morality. Works such as Edward William Lane's *Manners and Customs of Modern Egyptians*, first published in the 1830s, articulated a vision of Egyptians as savage, debased and parasitic that cast a long shadow into the next century.[57] The quintessential cruelty, backwardness and indolence of Egyptians, it was suggested, were both compounded by and attributed to their Muslim faith. Such sentiments of racial essentialism and deprecation endured into the era of Farouk, and indeed his nationalist successor, Nasser. A disturbingly large number of British novelists writing between the 1930s and

1950s testified to what they saw as the degeneracy, superstition and ill-discipline of the Egyptian *fellahin*, exemplified by Lawrence Durrell's disparagement of the Cairo masses as 'apes in nightgowns'.[58]

Nor can we disregard the fact that, in the immediate postwar decades, decolonization and mass immigration from the former colonies contributed to a dramatic reiteration of the demarcations of racial difference in metropolitan Britain.[59] While the primary indicators of racial difference in 1950s Britain were predominantly focused on skin colour (largely because West Indian immigrants, who could not – unlike South Asians – be differentiated by religion or language, were the predominant focus of official and media scrutiny in this decade) cultural values and practices were no less significant in fashioning postwar conceptions of race and nation. The anti-Commonwealth immigrant backlash which tried to reestablish Britain as an exclusively white nation was intrinsically linked to metropolitan responses to anti-colonial insurgency in black Africa.[60] However, racial politics in Britain in the 1950s were undoubtedly also entwined with dramatic events taking place in Malaya, Cyprus and in Egypt, especially the 1952 Cairo riots and the 1956 Suez crisis. During Suez, the British media regularly identified Nasser with interwar European dictators, but some observers noted the Egyptian leader's 'hooked nose and fuzzy hair', while British newspapers felt little queasiness in publishing letters from readers declaiming the Egyptians as a 'dirty race'.[61]

Priya Satia has asserted that orientalist conceptualizations of the desert Arab in the period during, and immediately after, the First World War were rarely grounded in empirically justified racial categorizations, as opposed to cultural understandings derived from myth, landscape and even notions of mystical enchantment.[62] Similarly, the absence of the more obvious physiological signifiers of racial difference did not preclude Farouk from being interpreted by British imperial policy makers within the rubrics of orientalism.[63] However, the fact that official British understandings of Farouk were frequently mediated through letters and memoranda produced by Lampson ensured that the attribution of the qualities of 'orientalism' to the king could not fail to disclose the intrinsic ambiguity of the term. Lampson's despatches frequently described Farouk as 'oriental', an appellation that has added significance in the light of his previous posting as ambassador in Peking.[64] Indeed Lampson insisted that 'Egypt, like China, is a land of paradox'.[65] A *Picture Post* article in 1942 asserted that 'Egypt is in Africa and not very far from Europe, but the habits of mind of its people are what we know as "oriental"'. As a consequence, Lampson's experience of the Far East made him 'admirably equipped' to deal with Egypt's ruler.[66]

Other diplomats, while they lacked Lampson's apparent belief in potential commonalities between the rulers of China and Egypt, were no less comfortable with applying the label 'oriental' to Farouk and his circle. David Kelly, bemoaning the erosion of British control over Farouk after he returned to Egypt on his father's death, explicitly referenced the sinister influence of his 'oriental court'.[67] Journalists were quick to appropriate notions of the capricious oriental potentate in their characterizations of Farouk, presenting him as equally capable of kindly attentiveness and a ruthless disregard for the lives and feelings of others.[68] Farouk's maliciously warped sense of humour (claims were made that he shaved off the chest hairs of his barber with a blowtorch or that he installed a horn on his car that imitated the screams of a dog run over) was cited as evidence of the continuities in the king's bloodline from the 'remorseless tyrants', Mehmet Ali and his immediate successors in the early nineteenth century.[69] One of Lampson's senior assistants, Laurence Grafftey-Smith, referencing Farouk's 'dark heredity', relayed a (unverified) story about Farouk laughing, as some of his servants, believing they were fishing out gold pieces from a bucket, discovered that the vessel was filled, not with water, but with acid.[70]

Orientalist visions of non-European rulers traded not merely in notions of cruelty, atrocity and depravity. They also emphasized sensual, especially sexual, indulgence.[71] When Narriman Zadek, who became Farouk's second wife, was poached from her fiancé by the king, gossip columnist William Hickey maintained that, while it might offend Europeans, such behaviour was entirely compatible with Muslim convention.[72] However, the most important substantiation of the ongoing pertinence of orientalist conceptions of sexuality in popular understandings of Farouk was repeated press reports of the king's predilection for the belly-dancer Samia Gamal. The fact that the legendary abdominal gyrations of Egypt's 'national dancer' owed more to a fantasized Orient created in North American cabaret culture in the 1920s than it did to North African or Ottoman traditions should have been self-evident.[73] The combination of ballet skirt and silver brassiere Gamal wore while dancing for Farouk at Deauville in 1950 (and the accompanying jazz soundtrack) was hardly authentic.[74] However, salacious British journalists seemed unable to believe that Gamal's writhing and beckoning body was not part of a 'centuries-old rite of seduction', or an attempt to dramatize an ancient tale of 'virgins sacrificed and drowned in the Nile'.[75]

We now know much more about how colonial subjects were not simply the passive victims of orientalist essentialism but rather developed sophisticated forms of response and resistance.[76] In the case of Farouk, what seems particularly germane is the notion of 'code switching' between 'oriental' and 'modern' aspects of identity and performativity.[77] If the king seemed eager to preserve the prerogatives of his dynastic predecessors, he also embraced the prospects (and especially the pleasures) of the modern world.[78] Indeed, in the period around his succession and subsequent marriage to his first wife, Farida, both imperial officials and the British press were captivated by the apparent intimations of self-conscious modernity in the public and private lives of this 'new kind of king in an ancient land'.[79] In a clear alignment with Farouk's own publicity machine, the young couple were presented as relaxed, informal and democratic.[80] The king's enthusiasm for motor cars and aircraft matched a 1930s preoccupation with the romance of glamourized technology.[81] While Farida may have observed tradition by being absent from the wedding ceremony, she still wore a dress from a Parisian fashion house, while her trousseau contained lingerie from an American designer, who commented on the young Queen's 'beautifully proportioned' and slim figure.[82] The British press was particularly taken by Farida's breaking convention, when she appeared in public with her husband, her yashmak little more than 'a strip of white tulle'.[83] Not merely did Farouk not sequester his new bride in the harem. His devotion to his first-born child, a daughter, appeared to belie stereotypes of orientalist misogyny.[84]

Indeed, when by late 1940s, it became obvious that Farouk had become tired of Farida, the king's failure to continue to satisfy the requirements of a modern companionate marriage became an important component in the increasingly negative coverage of Egypt's ruler in the British press.[85] Significantly, Farouk's later defence of his conduct attempted to resurrect his modern credentials by insisting that, rather than adopt the 'traditional Muslim privilege' of simply taking additional wives, he had pursued the 'Western' convention of divorcing his wife, before taking up with another woman.[86] However, Farouk's preference for serial monogamy over polygamy did little to convince his critics that he had not abandoned the progressive and modernizing imperatives of his early reign. Eileen Bigland, who visited Egypt in the mid-1940s, credited Farouk with an ongoing commitment to economic development and improving the conditions of the rural poor.[87] In 1949 Lord Strang visited welfare centres and agricultural institutes in the Delta in the company of Farouk, and claimed to have detected 'stirrings of social conscience in what one might have thought to be unlikely places'.[88] However, by this time, the dominant view in Britain was that all of Farouk's energy went into his private pleasures, and his self-declared interest in social reform had become intermittent and incoherent.[89]

**Figure 2** Farouk, Queen Farida and their daughter Princess Ferial, 1939 (Keystone/Getty Images).

## II

What further encouraged a marked polyvalence in the way Farouk was comprehended within the official imperial mind was that he became an increasingly peripatetic figure, whose personal itineraries were no longer confined to the kingdom he ruled. Lampson's efforts to contain and control Farouk had culminated in the 1942 'Abdin incident'.⁹⁰ However, by 1946, a more realistic appreciation of Britain's waning power led to Lampson's successor,

Ronald Campbell, recommending to the Foreign Office that it would be profitable to get Farouk and Farida out of Egypt, after seven years of confinement: 'They all need some fresh air and wider horizons.'[91] While political concerns made formal state visits abroad inadvisable, Farouk welcomed the opportunity (especially after the failed war against Israel) to set out on a series of hedonistic excursions to the pleasure resorts of Europe. No longer obliged to remain in the designated spaces of the imperial remit, Farouk exploited the emergence of new structures of globalization which were driven by commercial and cultural imperatives which confounded the conventions of geopolitics. Specifically, he thereby transgressed the ostensible binaries between 'Orient' and 'Europe'. As one 1950 profile observed, Farouk and his royal sisters chose 'their clothes and their atmosphere and their acquaintances impartially from anything that takes their fancy in either East or the West'.[92] French writer and filmmaker Jean Cocteau, after regularly spying the (by now exiled) Egyptian monarch in the lobby of a Cannes hotel in 1953, averred that Farouk exhibited a penchant for revolving doors, foyers and vestibules, emblematizing the restless impermanency of modern life.[93] However, Farouk was not merely geographically unmoored. He had also become discursively 'translated person' who was placed beyond simple and straightforward cultural allegiances and reclamations.[94]

Farouk's abandonment of his palaces and the world of court intrigue for the casinos and grand hotels of southern Europe reiterated the increasing impossibility of framing him predominantly, let alone exclusively, within the discourses and practices of imperial governance. This development was strikingly encapsulated in a feature on the exiled Farouk's arrival on Capri in 1952, in which the former sovereign was described as being at equal risk from the 'assassin's bullet' and from 'the telephoto lens' of the press.[95] By the late 1940s, Farouk had become a prominent figure in the world of celebrity culture. This should not imply that he satisfied every criteria of the modern celebrity. A noteworthy component of celebrity culture is the affective affinity between the public and the celebrity, the creation of a persona with which mass audiences can identify.[96] This was not entirely true of Farouk, public interest in whom lacked the extensive emotional investment that typified people's relationships to entertainers or film stars. However, representations of Farouk in the late 1940s increasingly displayed the priorities of popularization and personalization (and the publicization of intimate lives) that were the hallmark of celebrity culture.[97] Critically, he became a highly mediatized personality, a regular presence in English-language popular newspapers and magazines, and in newsreels, at a time when figures for both middle-market newspaper circulation and cinema attendance remained at record levels.⁹⁸ In the press, Farouk's ubiquity was so established that it was sometimes not even necessary to refer to him by name. The *Daily Express* flagged up articles on the king with a crudely rendered image of dark glasses placed under a tarbush. Even a caricature of the face these accessories framed was deemed surplus to requirements.⁹⁹

While celebrity journalism might have been predicated on a 'depoliticized view of the world as a site of melodrama', the geopolitical significance of Egypt meant that Farouk's significance as a political figure obviously could not be simply demoted or disregarded by Britain's imperial rulers.¹⁰⁰ However, in attempting to comprehend, and manage, Egypt's wayward monarch, diplomats and policy makers were obliged to accommodate themselves to the precepts of celebrity culture. Foreign Office officials conceded that it was necessary to report on Farouk's private proclivities, as these often had political implications. In the process, they compounded the capital of intimate lives and 'human interest' stories well beyond the gossip columns of popular newspapers. British officials were certainly alert to the diplomatic consequences of Farouk's gallivanting. Sometimes these concerns might appear local or relatively contained, for instance the need to ensure that Queen Frederica of Greece's claims of improper advances from Farouk did not jeopardize the position of Egypt's Greek community.¹⁰¹ However, on other occasions the king's peccadillos had more serious import for British interests. During the war Lampson had been anxious that the women who shared Farouk's bed might steer him towards the Axis cause. After the war, Farouk's gambling and womanizing risked providing succour for the republican and nationalist movements in Egypt that Britain was desperate to keep in check.

Farouk himself was not entirely oblivious to such worries. In 1950, he took care to ensure that photographs of himself in bathing trunks on the beach at Deauville would not appear in the Egyptian press.¹⁰² However, it seems unlikely that observant Muslims were reassured when the king attempted to mitigate his regular presence at the resort's casino table, by making it abundantly clear that the bottle at his side contained only lemonade or Coca Cola. Farouk's sybaritic tastes did not necessarily shock his subjects, but his lack of discretion in such matters generated criticism at home that was brought to the attention of Residency officials. In the summer of 1951, Farouk's lavish thirteen-week honeymoon with his second wife, Narriman Sadek, in which they booked all 150 rooms at the Caesar Augustus Hotel in Capri and 32 rooms at the Carlton in Cannes, coincided with the holy month of Ramadan. The ambassador, Ralph Stevenson, minuted, 'The king in him is fighting a losing battle with the man.'¹⁰³ When it had became apparent, by 1949, that Farouk intended to divorce his first wife, Farida, and marry Narriman, the British Embassy in Cairo legitimized its interest in terms of the impact of the king's decision on court politics (notably which political faction had influence over Farouk) and regional geopolitics. The *Daily Express* diplomatic correspondent Sefton Delmer claimed that Farouk's divorce and remarriage had compromised his prestige among Arabs at home and abroad to such an extent that he had been obliged to make concessions to Egypt's Wafd Party and was powerless to prevent Iraq and Syria from merging under a single Hashemite ruler. However, Delmer concluded his commentary in the melodramatic refrain of the gossip column: 'It is amazing what a pair of beautiful eyes can do in the world even today.'[104]

Indeed, official discussions of Farouk's remarriage required taking seriously the same innuendo and gossip that dominated coverage of Farouk in the popular press. Diplomats, no less than celebrity journalists, privileged exposure and revelation. Lampson had already established a precedent in this regard in the immediate aftermath of the Abdin incident. The ambassador had both his wife, Lady Lampson, and the wife of the minister-resident in Cairo, Lady Lyttelton, write up their individual accounts of a private audience with Farida, in which the then Queen shared candid details of her marital difficulties. The resulting reports may have seemed closer to an exclusive 'confessional' interview with a Hollywood celebrity than a Foreign Office communique, but they were nevertheless typed up and sent on to Eden at the Foreign Office.[105] In the postwar period, Stevenson regularly passed on gossip about the king to his peers in Whitehall, including descriptions of the physical attributes of his intended new bride (not necessarily in altogether favourable terms, Narriman being dismissed on one occasion as a 'dumpy girl').[106]

Foreign Office surveillance of Farouk and Narriman's honeymoon stay in Italy matched the modus operandi of celebrity reporting, trailing Cadillacs with Egyptian license plates with 'glamour girls inside' and appropriating private conversations between the wife of the British ambassador in Rome and her Egyptian equivalent to confirm a reported spending spree by the royal couple in the salons and jewellers of the Eternal City.[107] The usually bloodless disposition of official memoranda was eschewed in favour of an animated and sprightly mode that often appeared indistinguishable from the lexicon of media sensationalism.[108] One memorandum, replete with references to 'the most beautiful women' who featured in Farouk's circle, offered a breathlessly tabloid approach to the question of 'Who Will Be the New Queen of Egypt?'[109] Foreign Office claims that their interest in Farouk's private pleasures was merely a corollary of political prerequisites became increasingly questionable, especially once Farouk went into exile. In December 1952, a report from the British Embassy in Rome on Farouk's activities in Italy unapologetically conceded that such a document had little political value, but 'As we used to take an interest in the junketings of the royal playboy when he still wore a crown, it would seem churlish in us to ignore him now'.[110] The author of the report clearly seemed oblivious to the implication of his statement, namely that the purpose of a diplomatic memorandum was little more than to relay gossip.[111] Farouk's status as a mediatized celebrity not merely permitted him to operate outside the discursive domain of the official imperial mind. More significantly, it revealed that this imperial mindset itself was having to engage with a rapidly changing world, and in so doing, was undergoing a process of significant, if possibly inadvertent, reconfiguration.

# 3

# Music Hall and Merry Monarchs

'There won't be a fuss, will there?' This was the rather disingenuous response from character actor, musician and comedian Max Bacon to a *Daily Express* reporter on 30 October 1951.[1] The correspondent had approached Bacon to secure the latter's perspective on events that had taken place the previous evening at the Victoria Palace Theatre. The theatre and its legendary impresario Jack Hylton were playing host to the Royal Variety Performance, the annual revue of music, comedy, dance and magic by leading popular entertainers that was broadcast live on the BBC, attended by senior members of the royal family. In 1951 the royal party was composed of Queen Elizabeth and Princess Margaret. The king was unable to attend, still incapacitated after an operation to remove his left lung in the previous month. Awareness of the rapidly deteriorating status of George VI's health was still confined to a narrow tight-lipped circle. Prior to the show, the queen replied to a solicitation about the king's recovery from comedian Bud Flanagan with a reassuring insistence that 'He is going on nicely, thank you'.[2]

However, if *the* king was absent, it was not to be the case that the evening was to proceed without *a* king. The cast list for the show was over 300 strong, with appearances by the Tiller Girls, Richard Murdoch and Kenneth Horne, Jimmy Edwards and Florence Desmond. Max Bacon was not officially on the programme. The warm-up act was assigned to the Crazy Gang, a comedy sextet famed for combining groaningly corny slapstick with startlingly clever wordplay. All six performers were dressed in scarlet and black royal livery, exploiting the comic potential of the preposterously archaic costumes still worn by royal attendants at formal occasions.[3] If the king had been present, it is unlikely (despite his notorious sartorial punctiliousness, constantly alert to even the most minor and esoteric infringements of official dress codes) that he would have been offended by this skit on royal ceremonial, since he was an unapologetic admirer of the knock-about antics of the Crazy Gang, whom he regularly invited to perform private shows at Windsor. However, one component of the Crazy Gang's routine was to cause a minor commotion in official circles, requiring the attention of senior figures in both the royal household and the Foreign Office. While the six comedians were clowning around in front of the footlights, they were interrupted by a (clearly staged) altercation taking place in the stalls. An usher was confronting a man bearing a strong resemblance to King Farouk of Egypt. In fact this 'Farouk' was Max Bacon, sporting round dark glasses, tarbush, waxed moustache, a tightly fitting white uniform jacket with suspect decorations across the chest and a flamboyant cape. The usher insisted that 'Farouk' was sitting in somebody else's seat and demanded to see his ticket. Bacon fumbled in his pocket and produced a receipt for a French casino, before being unceremoniously ejected from the auditorium.

On the following day, Bacon made light of his impersonation of Egypt's monarch. However, twelve days later the British ambassador in Cairo, Ralph Stevenson, wrote to the Foreign Office to inform them that Farouk himself had found out about the skit, and was 'much hurt', especially since this insult to his dignity had taken place during an event attended by members of the British royal family. The Foreign Office made clear to Farouk that they fully shared his indignation at the 'deplorable taste' of the sketch by a man they disdained as 'an alleged comedian', and offered heartfelt apologies. They also sought to reassure the Egyptian monarch that the British royal party had not yet arrived at the theatre at the time when the warm-up routine was in progress. A personal intervention from Foreign Secretary Anthony Eden ensured a letter of apology to the Egyptian ambassador in London was sent by the Lord Chamberlain, who, while usually associated in the public mind with his responsibility for maintaining public decency on the London stage, was also one of the most senior members of the British royal household.[4] The 1951 Royal Variety Performance was apparently not the only occasion on which irreverent depictions of Egypt's king had come to the attention of Britain's most prominent theatrical censor. A Foreign Office memorandum in February 1952 claimed that it had been made aware of a number of variety acts which contained unflattering and scurrilous references to Farouk. However, Eden himself annotated the memorandum to record that it was his understanding that 'These [sketches] have been stopped by [the] Lord Chamberlain'.[5] Even if the notorious prohibition on stage acts or plays featuring living British royal personages could not necessarily be extended to foreign monarchs, the Sixth Earl of Clarendon, whose term of office as Lord Chamberlain (1936–1952) almost exactly coincided with Farouk's reign in Egypt, clearly took seriously his powers to withhold a licence from any stage routine which represented a living person 'in an invidious manner' or might 'be calculated to impair friendly relations with any Foreign Power'.[6]

The incident at the 1951 Royal Variety Performance was clearly another example of how Farouk's fame and ubiquity exposed a growing inability in the postwar era to segregate the world of imperial statecraft from the world of celebrity culture, a premise that has already been advanced in the previous chapter. However, it also offers an entry point into two additional themes, which will be the concern of the remainder of this chapter. First, since Farouk was regularly referenced in the world of popular entertainment (and popular leisure more generally), how might these references further our understanding of the sensibilities and values of those who consumed these popular diversions? Does Farouk's representation as a debauched, profligate and self-indulgent pleasure seeker require us to revise models of mid-twentieth-century British popular culture that emphasize modernity, commercialization, Americanization, feminization, embourgeoisement and domestication? In particular, did popular knowledge of what were presented as Farouk's distinctly masculine distractions reveal the resilience of older, more visceral and vernacular forms of popular culture well into the 1950s? Second, the fact that much of Farouk's disquiet arose from the fact that he had been lampooned at an important event in the official British royal calendar was a reminder that, whatever his deficiencies as a man, Farouk was also a king, and one who demanded the respect and propriety appropriate to his royal status. While (to the continued vexation of the Foreign Office) the British public were unlikely to treat the king with the gravitas and deference he felt he was entitled to, part of their fascination with Farouk derived from the fact that he *was* a monarch, albeit one with a very different public personality to that of their own sovereign and his family. While this distinction could be deployed to reiterate the British monarchy's moral probity and selfless devotion to public duty, it also revealed that the British public may have possessed a secret yearning for a more robust vision of royalty (encapsulated not just by Farouk in the present but by the fantasized folk memory of a number of colourful monarchs from Britain's historical past). For those willing to make the connection, Max Bacon's rendering of Farouk as an exuberantly spirited larger-than-life potentate at the Variety Performance undoubtedly offered a stark contrast with the twitchy nervousness, faltering speech and distressingly cadaverous features of Britain's all-too-mortal monarch.

# I

The 1951 Royal Variety Performance had been unusual in being held at the Victoria Theatre. Its usual venue was the London Palladium, whose managing director since the war had been the dynamic, if controversial, Val Parnell. Parnell demoted established domestic variety acts in favour of high-profile (and equally high-priced) big name acts from the United States. In the late 1940s and early 1950s the top of the bill at the Palladium featured Judy Garland, Bing Crosby, Peggy Lee, Frank Sinatra, the Andrews Sisters and, by 1953, even the precursor to rock and roll, Johnnie Ray. In 1948, the debut at the Palladium of Danny Kaye proved to be a sensation: queues stretched around the building, tickets were exchanged on the black market at exorbitant rates, and cabinet ministers and royalty flocked to the actor-singer-dancer-comedian's dressing room. The apparently endless succession of breezily self-possessed and American stars of theatre, screen and radio across the stages of the West End seemed to epitomize an invigorating and sophisticated freshness that contrasted dramatically with the shoddy obsolescence of the old-style music hall.[7]

Even within British variety, a new generation of entertainers (drawing albeit, less from their American competitors, and more from an appreciation of the absurd and the irreverent, forged by the experience of wartime national service) turned their backs on the hoary traditions of Dan Leno or George Robey. In particular, comedians such as Harry Secombe or Jimmy Edwards rejected the conventional music hall monologue or sketch, preferring a new style of fast-paced, and frequently absurdist, humour.[8] In this new environment, the traditional music halls played to dramatically shrinking audiences, who endured increasingly moribund acts in increasingly dilapidated buildings: the world so ferociously disparaged in John Osborne's *The Entertainer*.[9] Some venues, lacking the capital and entrepreneurial nous of Parnell's Moss Empires circuit, were forced to resort to the tawdry voyeurism of the 'girlie show'. Such desperate measures might have temporarily postponed the demise of individual establishments, but they failed to arrest the decline of the sector as a whole: in the thirteen years after the end of the war, over a hundred halls permanently closed their doors.[10]

By the late 1950s both the audiences and the talent (including, significantly, Val Parnell) of British music hall had relocated to the increasingly dominant medium of television. For contemporary commentators, the changing nature of mass entertainment both contributed to and provided a potent symbol of a profound shift in British culture.[11] With popular performance now primarily consumed within the intimate domain of the family sitting room, the privatized family, rather than the broader community (defined by class, region or neighbourhood), became the critical arena in which identities were established. Television seemed to mark the triumph of a sanitized, domesticated and homogenized culture; in the eyes of its critics, moreover, it was also an overly commercialized, Americanized and inauthentic one. The most notable contribution to this critique was, of course, Richard Hoggart's *The Uses of Literacy*, an unequivocal indictment of modern mass media for its role in denuding popular culture of its integrity and veracity.[12] The extent to which these claims can be borne out by the historical record (and their relationship to broader questions about 1950s affluence and the possible embourgeoisement – and, indeed, feminization – of the British working class) remains a matter of serious contention among historians.[13]

It is at this juncture that Farouk returns to our narrative. As a figure with such prominence in British popular culture, representations of Egypt's monarch offer a useful index of what may, and what may not, have changed in the decade and a half after 1945. References to Farouk in popular culture disclose the unevenness of change across this period, highlighting the resilience of older, more localized, forms of popular pleasure-seeking. The cultural changes which came to characterize the very late 1950s were not necessarily as prevalent in the earlier part of the decade, and Farouk's deployment in popular entertainment is a reminder of the continued purchase of more venerable cultural forms and styles in the immediate postwar years. In this, as in so many other aspects of his public image, Farouk's status as a modern celebrity should not be allowed to obscure the longer-established connotations through which he was also comprehended.

As will be seen, popular referencing of Farouk proved to be particularly apposite in a number of highly specific social and cultural milieu, ranging from the working-class seaside holiday to the associational world of male hobbyists. It is therefore worth repeating that Farouk's appropriation by comic writers, illustrators and performers, and his presence in more private and colloquial forms of humour, can be found across the social spectrum. Indeed it would hardly be an exaggeration to assert that making fun of Farouk was something of a national pastime in late 1940s and early 1950s Britain. The Foreign Office would undoubtedly been appalled to discover that, even among the well-bred and the well-educated, there was little inhibition in pursuing the humorous possibilities offered by Farouk's sexual peccadilloes, even at the cost of a marked insensitivity to their political ramifications. Undergraduates celebrating the University of Cambridge's Poppy Day Rag in November 1951 had hoped to include a tableau of 'Farouk and His Harem' in the Rag cabaret, but were forced to abandon their plans after Egyptian students protested.[14]

Such lighthearted lampooning of Farouk was fully compatible with middle-class and middlebrow tastes. Studies of the nineteenth-century middle classes have revealed that the prescriptive power of the imperatives of moralization and respectability did not foreclose increasing middle-class forbearance towards (at least certain forms of) less virtuous forms of amusement. This indulgent acceptance of occasional hedonism clearly intensified in the interwar period, a corollary of the self-conscious 'modernity' which accompanied the expansion of the so-called 'new' (i.e. salaried, technical and commercial, as opposed to employer- and professional-dominated) middle class. By mid-century, the lower middle class, in particular, had found it relatively straightforward to combine, in Peter Bailey's playful configuration, 'prudery and rudery'.[15]

Farouk's buffoonish sexual escapades aligned him with popular middlebrow entertainment genres such as the Whitehall farces, the series of long-running comic plays which first debuted in the West End in September 1950. The Whitehall faces, like their precursors authored by Ben Travers at the Aldwych theatre in the 1920s and 1930s, offered absurd and preposterous scenarios involving innocent misunderstandings, infidelity, cuckolding, borrowed clothes and misplaced trousers. While their plots nominally varied, the farces always contained stock characters such as the hen-pecked husband, the lecherous man about town, the repressed official and the nymphomaniac. Popularized stories of Farouk's unprepossessing flight from a lover's bedroom, when their husband unexpectedly returned home, clearly echoed the plots of British stage farces (and, for more highbrow audiences, those of French *belle epoque* playwright Georges Feydeau), and it is surely not inappropriate to surmise that Farouk was comprehended through popular performative forms such as these.[16] This, in turn, illustrates that Farouk's status in British popular culture was frequently grounded in his affinity with indigenous, if clearly not exactly autonomous, cultural formations.

Farouk's immediately recognizable appearance ensured that he was enlisted in the peculiarly twentieth-century British propensity for 'fancy dress', the more democratized successor to the masquerades and costume balls of earlier epochs.[17] Max Bacon was by no means the only person who saw the comedic potential of donning dark glasses and tarbush. In 1952 a Pathe newsreel recorded a man dressed as Farouk at the opening of a charity football match.[18] At an annual Christmas party at the Hastings Sun Lounge in the early 1950s, a children's fancy dress competition featured the expected generic national costumes and renderings of nursery rhyme figures. However, first prize was awarded to four-year-old Adrian Wilms, who turned up as Farouk, his home-constructed costume consisting of fez, sunglasses, cigarette holder and precariously attached moustache fashioned from what appears (from a photograph) to be carpet material. Around his neck hung a crudely made cardboard placard on which, in clearly an adult hand, was inscribed 'No Bathing in My Canal'.[19] One will undoubtedly be relieved to hear that this topical reference to the tussle between the Egyptian king and the British government over who exercised sovereignty in the Suez Canal zone failed to attract the attention of nervous Foreign Office officials, who continued to be exercised by aspects of British popular culture that might create offence in Egypt, or with Farouk personally.

Farouk's distinctive physical and sartorial attributes were no less attractive to cartoonists. Initially, his appearance was in cartoons which offered pictorial comment on specific events or developments in international affairs. For example, David Low, in the *Daily Herald*, placed Farouk in cartoons illustrating the latest machinations of the British government, the Egyptian court, the Wafd and the Muslim Brotherhood over control of the Canal Zone, or represented him as an Olympic athlete to make a caustic observation about the shared problems of the Egyptian and Iranian monarchies.[20] However, such representations of Farouk's role in politics and diplomacy, increasingly referenced his well-publicized private indulgences. Low's cartoon 'The Gambler's Grab' embodied Egypt's attempt to wrest control of the Suez Canal from the British in the form of Farouk eagerly seizing his winnings (namely the title deeds to the Canal) from Foreign Secretary Herbert Morrison, portrayed as a casino croupier.[21] It was this conflation between political satire and an explicit citation of Farouk's personal vices that most vexed the Foreign Office. In September 1951 the *Sunday Express* published a cartoon by Carl Giles which addressed efforts by the Soviet Union to offer support to Farouk's ailing regime. In the cartoon, a court lackey, facing a bloated Farouk, reclining in luxury while a young woman caresses his toes, suggests 'As a gesture to our glorious allies would your Majesty like to inspect the valiant workers in the factories instead of the casinos?'[22] The Foreign Office was sufficiently concerned about the cartoon's content to have it expurgated from copies of the newspaper that were distributed among British troops in the Canal Zone. This blatant censorship succeeded in rousing the righteous indignation not merely of the Express newspaper group but also from a very different point on the political spectrum, the Communist *Daily Worker*.[23]

After Farouk's fall from power, his presence in exclusively political cartoon satire inevitably diminished (although his ghostly presence did occasionally skulk in the margins of commentary on the struggles of Egypt under the nationalist rule of Colonel Nasser).[24] However, Farouk continued to appeal to cartoonists, who now used him as a more abstracted symbol of uncontrolled appetites, high-living and the pursuit of private pleasure, usually in a relatively non-judgemental, often indulgent and rarely moralizing, mode. In 1945 Carl

Giles introduced his single-panel cartoon 'The Giles Family', which was to feature regularly in the *Daily Express* and *Sunday Express* for the next forty-five years.[25] The Giles family, and their popularity in a mass-market family newspaper, were emblematic of the contradictory forces at work in postwar Britain. This fictional family, which seemed to embody long-established working-class attitudes and conventions, while living in a suburban home that became increasingly filled with modern consumer goods and appliances, was an unfeasible fantasy, but one which spoke to both a newly aspirational disposition after the war and to a culture that, while less deferential, still exhibited a robust Tory patriotism and distrust of postwar collectivism. Farouk frequently appeared in the more outlandish and fanciful adventures of the Giles family. On one occasion, he is there to greet the Giles family, as they disembark on a holiday in Monte Carlo. On another, transported to the surface of the Moon, which bears an uncanny resemblance to the beach at Blackpool, the family encounter a lunar inhabitant who bears a remarkable similitude to Egypt's ex-king, who is selling carpets and souvenir postcards. At a wedding service attended by the Giles family, the recognizable tarbush and dark glasses of Farouk can be spotted among the congregation, seated in proximity to Grandma, the cartoon family's legendary working-class matriarch.[26]

## II

By inserting Farouk into the world of a recognizably familiar (if not necessarily typical) English family, Giles reflected a broader trend in which the Egyptian king appeared in cartoon scenarios which drew on the everyday situations and environments of British life. This was particularly true of cartoons composed by Joseph Lee for the *Evening News*. In Lee's work, Farouk makes his presence felt in recognizably British interiors, streets and vistas. An aged spinster, holding a large heart-shaped Valentines' card in a faded Edwardian drawing room, suggests to her female companion that Farouk, as a now divorced ex-king, might be 'feeling lonely' and available 'on the rebound'.[27] In a recognizably suburban setting, a father who had ventured that, since the government had now increased the allowance available for Britons to travel abroad, he had determined 'to go abroad this summer to see Farouk's girl friends' is being chased by his outraged wife onto their rooftop.[28] Among a group of shabbily dressed working men playing cards in their local pub, one man berates his fellow player: 'You raised us to tuppence on a hand like yours? Who d'y' think you are… King Farouk?'[29]

In a cartoon published soon after he went into exile, Lee imagines Farouk as a recognizable, and not entirely incongruous, figure seated in the distinctive, and unequivocally plebeian, setting of the garden of an English village inn.[30]

The Foreign Office memorandum of February 1952, drafted (as discussed previously) in response to mounting concerns about unfavourable references to Farouk in metropolitan Britain, noted that 'hostile articles and unfriendly cartoons' in some newspapers 'in turn have inspired a number of sketches in the music halls'.[31] Unfortunately, unlike the newspaper cartoons, the specific content of these routines is now lost. There are tantalizing, if rare, references in the review pages of the theatrical press, although these focus on the more imaginative (and most likely, atypical) comic deployment of Farouk on the music hall stage. For example, one of the turns in a variety show at the Glasgow Empire in October 1953 was the comic duo Medlock and Marlow, who performed wearing 'lifelike masks of famous personalities' which included Bette Davis, Groucho Marx and Winston Churchill, in addition to Farouk.[32] However, it is most likely that Farouk featured in the acts of the comedians who, together with singers, acrobats, magicians and jugglers, were the main attraction in variety shows. Individual comic gags or sketches incorporating Farouk have not survived, even in the forensically detailed reports on various music hall acts assembled by Mass-Observers in the mid-1940s. However, it doesn't require too much imagination to envisage the uses to which Farouk's grotesquely bloated body and his reputation as a ludicrous and lecherous buffoon were put by music hall funnymen. For, as Mass-Observation's various surveys of British humour all concluded, the most popular jokes at mid-century were those that foregrounded 'extreme sexual vulgarity, and intimate discussion of physical functions'.[33] The less prepossessing aspects of Farouk's life neatly aligned themselves with music hall jokes of, what one Mass-Observer scornfully dismissed as, 'the double bed and lavatory type'.[34] One can certainly imagine the possibility of blending racist caricature with Farouk's sexual escapades provided handy material for the risqué (albeit always restrained through recourse to innuendo and euphemism) routines of the legendary 'cheeky chappie' Max Miller, music hall's last truly legendary figure.[35]

Moreover, Farouk's incorporation into the traditions and conventions of music hall were encouraged by his association with the indomitable Gracie Fields. By the late 1940s, while Fields no longer enjoyed the extraordinary popularity and affection she enjoyed during the Depression, she remained Britain's pre-eminent female variety artiste, even if her chosen media had become film and vinyl, rather than the provincial halls in which she had crafted her reputation as an unpretentiously gifted musical comedienne.[36] By this point, she had made her home in Capri, which is where she regularly encountered Farouk. Indeed in the early days of his exile in 1952, Fields entertained Farouk and his family at La Canzone del Mare, her restaurant and swimming pool complex on the island. (The press reported that Fields had given the ex-king's children a dog, and received a recipe for scrambled egg in return.)[37] While this personal interaction took place at a geographical and temporal distance from Fields' years on the revue circuit, cartoonists immediately framed the relationship between ex-king and 'Lancashire Lass' in the context of music hall. Low predicted that the new star attraction at the 'London Collodium' would be Farouk and Fields performing her hit song 'The Biggest Aspidistra in the World'.[38] Giles created an imaginary billboard for the 'Palaseum Theatre', which included 'our Gracie' and Farouk reworking several of the former's most popular songs to create new numbers such as 'Don't Turn Farouk's Face to the Wall, Mother'.[39] Farouk also demonstrated a personal interest in some less-renowned variety performers. In 1954, he attended a stage show at a casino in Rome which featured the 'Mighty Mannequin', glamorous British strongwoman Joan Rhodes who had toured provincial music halls alongside Mushie the Lion and Elro the Armless Wonder. The ex-king was so taken with Rhodes' combination of a chorus girl figure with the ability to break ten-inch nails that he requested a private meeting to find out more about how she achieved her feats of strength.[40] Such lowbrow diversions of a high-born royal underlined Farouk's association with, and comprehension through, the forms and connotations of well-established modes of British popular culture.

The comic universe of variety and music hall was certainly not innocuous, and early twenty-first century commentators have often felt understandably queasy when they are obliged to confront the unedifying xenophobia, sexism, homophobia and body-shaming which these routines regularly traded in. We might also speculate on how far routines featuring Farouk incorporated some form of racial caricature, given the way race had been regularly intertwined with other issues in music hall songs and entertainment in the past.[41] What might seem particularly disconcerting to us today is that, while such humour was rarely granted the designation of 'wholesome', it was accepted as 'family entertainment'. However, on one notable occasion, Farouk was to be a presence in the routines of one of the most notoriously reprobate exponents of music hall stand-up comedy. Historians, taking their cue from the over-determined models of cultural theorists, have regularly identified the British seaside holiday, not as a mere routine annual treat for the urban working class, but as an opportunity to live out (albeit in a manner that was geographically and temporally compressed) the transgressive possibilities of liminality and the carnivalesque. Seaside resorts have been presented as places in which the usual constraints on personal conduct are suspended, so as to create increased leniency towards exposed bodies, sexual promiscuity, drunkenness, raucous ribaldry and temptations to extravagance.[42]

Many of these claims for the liberating and transgressive potential of the seaside are seriously overblown, and we would be well advised to heed George Orwell's typically shrewd caution, in his commentary on the grotesquely prurient comic postcards of Donald McGill, not to confuse 'a harmless rebellion against virtue' with 'a serious attack upon morality'.[43] However, it would be churlish not to concede that seaside holidays permitted a temporary triumph of frivolous pleasure-seeking and the casting aside of inhibitions. The unapologetically vulgar pursuit of private – often illicit – pleasures in the seaside resort provided yet another readily available framework through which Farouk might have been made familiar and intelligible to the British public. One might, for example, consider the correspondence of Farouk's roguish sexual escapades with the lecherous men leering at women with grossly over-emphasized breasts and buttocks who feature in McGill's saucy postcards. Or how Farouk's notorious plumpness may have recalled the abnormally sized bodies which constituted an important element in the freakshow displays which (in contrast to urban areas, where they were in declining genre of public amusement) retained their popularity in seaside resorts, especially Blackpool's notorious 'Golden Mile', into the 1940s.[44]

Indeed mid-century Blackpool was credited (although not universally) for its singular raunchiness, and it is not surprising that in the early 1950s, the resort's Central Pier hosted the twice-nightly Summer Scandals, performed by music hall's most outrageous comic, Frank Randle.[45] Randle was a notoriously irresponsible purveyor of lewd and low humour, in which he unashamedly acknowledged, and indeed celebrated, the baser needs of the human body. His stage persona was a gurning, leeringly lascivious, not to say priapic, reprobate, but he was also the last survivor of a strongly localized (i.e. Lancashire) working-class culture.[46] However, even here, in this decidedly delimited and vernacular comic universe, Farouk could find a place. Randle received regular summonses to Blackpool magistrates court, on charges of obscenity and performing unlicensed sketches. In September 1952, he was prosecuted for a variety of offensive items, which included Randle asking the audience, as what the press identified as 'a silent Chinaman' shuffled across the stage, 'Is that King Farouk?'[47]

Notwithstanding the reference to Farouk in the routine of a man regularly identified as Britain's most disreputable comic, it would be unwise to associate Egypt's ruler exclusively with forms of popular leisure which appeared to promote, albeit momentarily, the triumph of misrule and the violation of taboos. Farouk was just as likely to have been comprehended through varieties of working-class pleasure seeking which traded in much more conservative, albeit populist, idioms. Farouk's fondness for the casino table made him a potential confederate for the large number (possibly as high as 75 per cent) of Britons who participated in organized mass betting. True, the sums bet on horses, dogs and football, which were usually small, and easily accommodated within working-class domestic budgets, bore little comparison to the staggering wins (and losses) Farouk achieved in the high-stakes card games he played with his wealthy peers. However, Britons who gambled undoubtedly felt an affinity with Farouk's apparent disavowal of puritanical moralizing, not least because, while betting had become increasingly accepted among the British public, important agents of disapproval (notably the churches and the Home Office) remained, ensuring that paternalistic, restrictive legislation on bookmaking continued to be enforced.[48]

Such attitudes can be situated in well-established traditions of plebeian indulgence of elite hedonism. In the nineteenth century such dispensation took the form of the vicarious pleasures offered by music hall *lions comiques*, with their riotously exaggerated caricatures of aristocratic womanizing, gambling and drinking.[49] In the interwar years, working-class racegoers shared in the delight of high-status owners such as Lord Derby or the Aga Khan, when their horses won the day. Unlike a figure such as the wealthy Maharajah of Rajpipla, popular with racecourse crowds in the 1930s because of his playboy lifestyle, Farouk never put in a personal appearance in the VIP enclosure at Ascot or Epsom. However, the fact that the king was both a racehorse owner (with a fine complement of Arab horses in his private stables in Egypt) and an inveterate high roller may well have granted him admission to the confraternity of those working-class male (and, to a lesser extent, female) punters who optimistically pressed a modest handful of coins into the hands of the street bookies and runners that, on Friday afternoons, plied their trade in back yards and the corners of public bars in Britain's towns and cities.[50]

Commentators on modern celebrity culture have sought to explain how ordinary people living nondescript lives have developed such high levels of presumptive familiarity, not to say identification, with people whose extraordinary and rarefied lives are so radically and profoundly different to their own.⁵¹ Farouk's presence in British culture, by contrast, accords with older traditions of assumed affinity which were rooted in the belief that both aristocratic and working-class pleasure-seekers shared a common antagonism towards the moralizing prescriptions of middle-class reformers. Such notions, which appalled twentieth-century socialists as much as they had nineteenth-century Nonconformist liberals, had very little to do with the supposedly 'democratic' imperatives intrinsic in the rise of modern celebrity culture. Rather, they were the reflection of a society in which acquiescent and deferential responses to social hierarchy retained considerable purchase. The pursuit of working-class pleasures might be more credibly identified as a form of robust popular Toryism, rather than as an exercise in 'cultural resistance'.⁵²

## III

If analogies, and explicit references, to Farouk in the provinces of the music hall, the seaside resort and the bookie's lair suggest the resilience of cultural formations which would have been recognizable to the late Victorians and Edwardians, the gender politics of Farouk's significance in British popular culture were equally backward-looking. Historians have, with justification, highlighted the way that the emergence of modern celebrity culture from the 1920s onwards was closely linked to an appreciation of the significance of women as the pre-eminent consumers of the 'human interest' stories which became an increasingly important feature in the content of national newspapers.⁵³ In tandem, historians of gender have detailed how, in this same period, rising levels of female employment, increased opportunities for heterosocial engagement, the cults of both romantic love and domesticity and the emergence of the 'companionate marriage', all served to erode the stark gender segregation that had purportedly characterized earlier periods of British history. On whose terms this new disposition in gender relations was settled and how novel or profound it was have inevitably been the subject of considerable scholarly debate.⁵⁴ It is not the purpose here to attempt to conclusively resolve the question of how far mid-century Britain experienced the 'domestication of the male'.⁵⁵ Rather it offers a more modest assertion, namely that the incorporation of Farouk into British popular culture discloses the continued claims, made in the immediate postwar era, on behalf of the pursuit of specifically *masculine* pleasures and diversions.

Moreover, it should not be forgotten that, for many men, enforced (if not necessarily absolute) homosociability was a critical aspect of their early adult lives. This was obviously true of the several million men who spent the Second World War in uniform. Moreover, the decision to retain conscription into the postwar period resulted in around two and a half million young men being called up between 1948 and 1960. The social and cultural significance of postwar national service, long neglected by scholars, has recently received its due attention, and there is now much greater awareness that conscription, rather than state welfare, may have been the critical site of interaction between many young British men and the state during the 1950s. While some men served in various wars of colonial counterinsurgency (most notably in Malaya, Kenya and Cyprus), the vast majority were confined to the mundane world of army bases on British soil.[56] For national servicemen, of both the 1939–1945 and 1948–1960 cohorts, military discipline, monotony, privation and irksome regulations (and, for those who faced combat, acknowledging the possibility of death or wounding) required the fostering of both individual and collective strategies of survival. Denied the ability to freely express discontent, soldiers' disaffection and disrespect sought outlet through comedy and song. As has been the case throughout history, soldiers' songs offered what one folklorist has neatly summarized as 'an informal channel of protest against circumstance and against oppressive, incompetent, unpopular or overbearing military authority'.

Many of the songs sung by postwar national servicemen were drawn from the repertoire of their predecessors in the Second World War (and, in many cases, the First World War and even the conflicts of the nineteenth century). In the North African campaign, one of the most popular songs among the troops of the Eighth Army was entitled 'King Farouk'. Various versions of the song were in existence, although they were all sung to the tune of 'Saleem el Malik', the Egyptian national anthem:

Old King Farouk
Put Farida up the chute
Then went for a week
To Skanderia, on the scoot

Now the poor little Queen's
Got another pup to wean
Kwise kateer, mungariya
Shufti kush, bardin

Then sing Sieg Heil for Egypt's King
And to his feet your tributes bring

> Kwise kateer, King Farouk
> Kwise kateer, King Farouk
> Oh you can't fuck Farida
> If you don't pay Farouk

The song registered both Farouk's pleasure-seeking ('Skanderia' is a corruption of Iskanderiya, the Arabic form of Alexandria and 'on the scoot' is slang for drinking and philandering) and his supposed pro-Axis sympathies ('Then sing Sieg Heil'). It also commingled sexual ribaldry with orientalist and sexist stereotypes. Farouk gets Farida pregnant ('up the chute') and the element of male sexual fantasy is extended into speculation that Egypt's Queen is so subservient to her husband that she is willing to prostitute herself on his command. The assembling of random Arabic words and phrase is largely meaningless, but does contain at least one example of sexual obscenity ('Shufti kush, bardin' appears to be a rendering of an uncouth request for a woman to expose her genitalia). It is hard not to conclude that the song's male fantasies about both Farouk and his queen were a projection of the soldiers' own sexual frustration. Indeed an alternative version of the song avowed:

> Queen Farida, Queen Farida
> All the boys want to ride her
> But they never had a chance
> Their ambition to enhance
> Stanna shwya, pull your wire
> King Farouk, bardin

'Pull your wire', it probably goes without saying, was soldiers' slang for male masturbation.[57] Significantly, despite its apparent topical and contingent elements, this song retained its place in the repertoire of soldiers' songs throughout the period of postwar conscription, and at least one former national serviceman recalls it being sung by British troops deployed in the Middle East during the Suez crisis of 1956.[58] As with his appearance in the comic routines of Frank Randle, the Farouk who featured in the uncouth songs of working-class soldiers was a reflection of the survival of decidedly visceral and vernacular idioms within mid-century popular culture.

The violence, discomfort, lack of privacy and petty restrictions which characterized service life undoubtedly contributed to an increasing positive valuation of men in this period of the attractions of romantic heterosexual love, marital companionship and domestic intimacy. However, while Geoffrey Gorer's oft-cited survey of popular attitudes towards love, sex and marriage (conducted in early 1951) recorded extensive enthusiasm for the pleasures of hearth and home, a significant number (14 per cent) of male respondents, when given a completely free choice, preferred the company of their own sex.[59] There were still plentiful venues for the practice of homosocial forms of leisure and recreation, ranging from working-men's clubs to the locker rooms and terraces of football and rugby teams. In the spring of 1953, two journalists accompanied an English rugby club on their 'big spree' to Dieppe, where the all-male unit interspersed an occasional competitive match with a full-blooded commitment to overeating, heavy drinking and rowdy behaviour in the hotel bar. The most frenetic partier was identified as Tim, 'who laughs so much and re-orders so often'. Significantly such unrestrained pleasure-seeking gained him the soubriquet of 'the Farouk of the club'. Many of the club members were married men, suggesting homosocial gratifications and domestic obligations were not mutually exclusive.[60]

Nor should it be forgotten that many men found a wholehearted commitment to domesticity was compromised by the strain of having to continue to live with their wives' parents, a not uncommon situation in the immediate postwar years in which affordable housing remained in short supply. Gorer found that having to share a house, and interference from in-laws, was cited by his respondents as a critical cause (and was certainly a more significant factor than infidelity) in creating unhappiness in marriage.[61] The disruptive presence of the mother-in-law served as a crystallization of male ambivalence about married life, which explains its established standing in the repertoire of music hall comedy.[62] When the exiled Farouk's marriage collapsed in March 1953, popular press coverage assumed recognition of, and affinity with, hoary depictions of the long-suffering bogeywoman of male humour. When the mother of his second wife, Narriman, tried to entice her daughter back to Egypt, Farouk was alleged to have claimed that Naguib's nationalist regime had attempted to break up his marriage 'by using the most powerful of weapons – the mother-in-law'.[63] Displaced male resentment, not to say barely suppressed aggression, directed at their wives' mothers was articulated in a Giles cartoon in which Farouk launches, grenade-style, a pot plant at the head of Narriman and her fearsome-looking mother, as they head, suitcases in hand, to the airport.[64]

It would be unfair to present Farouk's ability to illuminate the form and function of distinctly masculine cultures solely in terms of unrepentant misbehaviour or vicious misogyny. Farouk also appears as a thread within the fabric of more sedate and innocuous male pleasures, ones that belonged to an associational culture which could comfortably coexist with domesticity.[65]

**Figure 3** Carl Giles, 'Mother's Day', *Sunday Express*, 15 March 1953 (British Cartoon Archive, University of Kent GAO840).

Egypt's ruler had acknowledged affinities with the subcultures of male hobbyists and enthusiasts. When, after the 1952 revolution, Farouk's possessions were auctioned off, Britain's amateur philatelists and numismatists were captivated by the detailed inventories which listed the king's unparalleled collections of postage stamps, coins and banknotes. There was particular excitement when some of the unique items from Farouk's stamp collection came up for sale in both Bristol and Birmingham in the early summer of 1954, although an auctioneer bemoaned the fact that most of the Farouk lots were 'rather too costly for the average British collector' and that they had been bought instead by bidders in 'the dollar countries'.[66]

Farouk was also a notable cartophilist, which may explain why a certain A. J. Cause, the author of a book popularizing cigarette card collecting published in 1951, was eager to record that a copy of his book had been sent to, and accepted by, the Egyptian monarch. Farouk would probably have been nonplussed by the author's emphasis on the autodidactic possibilities offered by the tightly compressed description on the reverse sides of the cigarette card illustration. (Information covering 'every known field of human knowledge and interest' was made available 'which could otherwise only be obtained from the public libraries'.)[67] However, if the desire for self-instruction and self-improvement was an aspect of cigarette card collecting that had more appeal, and pertinence, to working-class British males than it did to the privileged and carefree monarch, it was not presumptuous or unreasonable for the amateur cartophilist to take pride that their low-profile, often disdained, pastime was shared by one of the world's richest sovereigns. However, that did not mean that the disparity in wealth and status between the two types of collector could always be disregarded. In 1954 the head of the London Cigarette Card Company wrote to his local MP to enquire how he might go about collecting an outstanding debt of £89 4s. from Farouk.[68]

Farouk also appeared to be taxing the patience of the officials of the British Matchbox Label and Booklet Society, an esoteric body of which the king was an official patron. At their annual exhibition in London in October 1952, the Society still lionized Farouk as 'the world's most distinguished philumenist' (matching the breathless admiration for Farouk's reputed collection of 150,000 matchbox covers expressed by attendees of the previous year's annual Collectors and Hobbyists Rally at Caxton Hall), but expressed some concern that the recently deposed king had failed to pay his annual 12s. 6d. subscription. Charles Crampton, designated as the Society's Foreign Relations Officer, disclosed that 'I sent him a reminder… to the palace in Cairo three days before the abdication, but I expect it was overlooked'.[69]

As with his attraction to music hall comics or newspaper cartoonists, Farouk's presence in the milieu of amateur hobbyists and collectors had occasion to attract the fretful attentions of Foreign Office officials. Yet again, Whitehall mandarins found themselves burdened with the ultimately doomed assignment of ensuring that the imperatives of statecraft and the dispositions of popular culture remained appropriately and securely segregated. In late 1949, the Egyptian charge d'affaires in London contacted the Foreign Office 'in a state of some agitation'. He had received a letter from Joseph Ciemniewski, a former Polish soldier now settled in Maida Vale. Ciemniewski, an avid philatelist, claimed to have been in possession of a rare Czechoslovakian stamp which, knowing that Farouk was an ardent stamp collector, the Pole decided to send to the king. While the stamp was mailed by registered post, Ciemniewski failed to take any additional methods to secure or insure his package. This was in spite of the fact that he enclosed an accompanying letter which indicated that he believed the value of the stamp was at least £5,000. Ciemniewski had established that his letter had been received, but not the stamp, and, as a consequence, he was insisting that Farouk was liable for either payment for the stamp or the return of his property.

What was more ominous for the Foreign Office was that Ciemniewski had threatened that, unless he received satisfaction from Farouk, he would go on hunger strike to publicize his claim in the popular press. The Foreign Office passed the matter over to the police, who, after interviewing both Ciemniewski and a number of stamp dealers, determined that, while the Polish philatelist had, at some point, genuinely been in possession of the rare stamp (and had most likely been telling the truth when he claimed to have mailed it to Egypt), its actual value was closer to £2 than it was to £5,000. The chief inspector who interviewed Ciemniewski indicated that the Pole remained resentful about the loss of the stamp, but had promised not to take any steps to seek publicity. This response was hardly surprising, since the police officer had informed him that sending the stamp out of the country was actually a criminal offence, although, since the Pole was being co-operative, the inspector was confident that Customs and Excise could be persuaded not to pursue the matter further.[70]

While few ordinary Britons went so far as to attempt extortion of Farouk, Ciemniewski's story illustrates, albeit in extreme form, the level of presumed familiarity between ordinary Britons with otherwise unremarkable lives and the rarefied world of Egypt's opulent monarch. Farouk was comprehended not solely through the tropes of exoticism (in both its orientalist and celebrity guises) but also through understandings that were grounded in distinctly specialized, parochial and vernacular elements of British popular culture.[71] However, it is important to recognize that Farouk was a monarch, and not merely a man, and here the motifs of familiarity and affinity operated slightly differently, refracted through both responses to the contemporary British monarchy and the folk memory of the nation's flamboyant royal past.

## IV

In the past four decades historical scholarship has become increasingly sophisticated in its efforts to explain one of the paradoxes of twentieth-century Britain, namely how an all-too-evident decline in the formal political power of the monarchy was accompanied by a no less startling increase in its public significance. David Cannadine's argument, first articulated in the early 1980s, that the House of Windsor's success lay in its ability to project an image of monarchy that was simultaneously homely and stately, has retained its status as a fundamental premise in historical elucidations of royal survival.[72] However, it has been supplemented and enriched by a range of studies, many of which have highlighted the highly contingent and conditional dimension to public support for a hereditary monarch in an age of mass democracy.[73] The universal effectiveness of royal ceremonial has been questioned, as has the extent to which royal interventions in national politics can be considered negligible after 1918.[74]

Historians have demonstrated how the monarchy became associated with philanthropic causes, and was popularized through new media technologies, visual images and material culture.[75] More critically, they have also revealed how the monarchy became a critical constituent of wider cultural configurations, notably national integration, imperial identities, celebrity culture, popular religion, affective life and public morality (and how changes in all these areas across the century can account for changing royal fortunes).[76] While most scholarship has focused on the production and projection of popular monarchy, there has also been increased attention to the reception and internalization of the discourses of royalty among the British public, with the first attempts to more systematically isolate the precise reasons why the monarchy resonated with ordinary Britons.[77]

What is missing from this scholarship is any sustained recognition that the projection and reception of the British monarchy did not exist in a vacuum. Those concerned with royal fortunes in the 1930s, encouraged by the priorities of contemporary observers such as Kingsley Martin and the founders of Mass-Observation, have noted that understandings of the British crown in the Depression years drew (overtly and covertly) on a vocabulary of constitutionalism and social cohesion that was violently juxtaposed with the pretensions and personality cults of continental dictators.[78] However, there has been less attention to considering how attitudes to the British monarchy might have been shaped by comparison with *other monarchs*, both contemporary and historical.[79] An analysis of the wedding of the Duke of Kent (George V's youngest surviving son) to Marina, Princess of Greece and Denmark, in 1934, includes an intriguing comment that, while the House of Windsor's survival instinct caused it to become a more exclusively 'British' institution after 1917, it is important not to exaggerate the monarchy's insularity in this period.[80] Royal cosmopolitanism on its pre-1914 scale may be beyond recovery, but it is clearly the case that the British public, at the very time they were forming an estimation of their own royal family, had (not least through newspapers and newsreels) other crowned heads available for scrutiny and comparison. Between 1936 and 1952, one of these was King Farouk.

What were the modes through which Farouk's status as a monarch were articulated and comprehended, and what do they tell us about understandings of monarchy (including Britain's own) more generally? Since he was neither a constitutional monarch nor a despot, Farouk's royal status was potentially open to a range of interpretative possibilities. As has already been demonstrated, Farouk was clearly susceptible to a broader trend in which understandings of monarchy were determined less by conventions of statecraft and more by the idioms of popular culture. However, popularized images of Farouk also suggest that the appeal of monarchy in the middle decades of the century was not necessarily dependent on the blend of the mundane and the exalted that has been such a critical motif in narratives of royal adaptation and survival in Britain.

At the time of his accession, British diplomats were confident that the combination of Farouk's apparent youthful informality and the majestic splendour of the Egyptian court neatly accorded with the House of Windsor's successful fusion of personal ordinariness and public spectacle. The Cairo Residency looked favourably on the Egyptian court's efforts to appropriate elements of the popularization of British monarchy. When Farouk made the first radio broadcast by an Egyptian monarch to his people on the eve of his coronation in 1937, he was adopting a new mode of communication which had been taken up by Buckingham Palace five years earlier.[81] Like the Windsors, Farouk and his advisors seemed to have understood how the public image of monarchy could be burnished by a well-publicized royal romance. British press coverage of Farouk's wedding to the commoner Safinaz Zulficar (who adopted the royal name of Farida) emphasized that despite the traditional ceremony (in which the bride was absent) and the fact that the marriage was arranged (by Farouk's mother, Queen Nazli), the young couple were very much in love. As with the newspaper reporting of the 1934 British royal wedding, Farouk and Farida were comprehended through a new emotional culture centred on love and personal fulfilment.[82]

However, parallels between the Windsors and the Egyptian royal family could only be stretched so far before they frayed, and eventually snapped. Commonality between the British and Egyptian courts could not, British officials made only too clear, be allowed to be interpreted (by either Farouk or his subjects) as the same thing as parity. Lampson's diaries disclosed a strong measure of condescension towards the House of Fuad, an entry in October 1938 explicitly comparing the 'brash arrivistes' of the Egyptian royal house with the quiet dignity of George VI and his family, with whom the ambassador was on close personal terms.[83] Among the litany of unfavourable comments about Farouk, made by his private tutor Edward Ford, was the snotty observation that there was 'something rather nouveau riche' about the young monarch.[84] The Foreign Office was reluctant to encourage a state visit by George VI to Egypt, since Farouk was 'wholly unfit for such an honour'.[85] A similar outlook informed Lampson's insistence that the British did not attempt to compete with Belgium's decision, in 1937, to invest Farouk with one of its highest honours – the Order of Leopold – by making the Egyptian monarch a Knight of the Garter. 'We do not know', the ambassador brusquely averred, 'how he [Farouk] is going to turn out', while a Foreign Office official declared that 'we should be very chary of giving high decorations to orientals'.[86] In this particular instance, there seems scant evidence of David Cannadine's controversial contention that, when it came to the honours system, 'across the varied races of empire, there was convergence and equality' between overseas imperial notables and British proconsuls.[87]

Moreover, as Farouk's lifestyle became more outlandish and, in the eyes of British officials, reprehensible, the Egyptian monarch was transformed into a self-evident countertype to his British equivalent. In a postwar culture keen to stress the value of the conventional family (in order to reverse a declining birth rate and rising levels of divorce and illegitimacy), the House of Windsor became a critical symbol of domestic virtue.[88] Where George VI embodied modesty, duty and discipline, Farouk represented vulgarity, self-indulgence and extravagance. In 1952, this contrast seemed to have been encapsulated in the tributes to his selfless sacrifice paid to George VI in the immediate aftermath of his death in February of that year, and Farouk's unlamented flight into exile, just over six months later. A Mass-Observation investigator recorded a conversation he overheard in the waiting room on Haslemere railway station. One man declared that the 'whole world' saw the death of George VI as a personal loss: 'You can tell that by the way they're turning up at the funeral. Except the Belgians. Even the King of Egypt's coming.' His companion retorted that they could 'do without' the King of Belgium, since his father had betrayed Britain in 1940. At this point the Mass-Observer intervened to declare – to general approval – that 'We could probably do without the King of Egypt, too'.[89] Farouk's abdication in 1952 appeared as a dire warning of the cost of failing to temper personal whims or maintain the probity of high office. Farouk's vulgarity suggested he had more in common with continental dictators than with constitutional monarchs, while his penchant for unconventional (often unsanctioned) uniforms aligned his visual iconography with Balkan strongmen and Latin American dictators in the late 1930s and early 1940s.

However, the conceit that by discursively distancing Farouk from his fellow royals in Britain he could serve to clarify and confirm the superiority of the Windsor model of majesty was, in practice, far from straightforward or secure. The changing nature of press coverage of royalty in British newspapers, and the British monarchy's own attempts to refashion their image in the era of mass democracy, had significant implications for the House of Windsor's insistence on its singular blend of heritage and virtue. The incorporation of the monarchy

**Figure 4** Farouk with Philip, Duke of Edinburgh (left) and Foreign Secretary Ernest Bevin (right), Koubbeh Palace, 31 January 1950. (Keystone/Hulton Archive/Getty Images).

into a wider celebrity culture might have ensured its continued pertinence and popularity from the 1920s onwards. However, it came at the cost of the creation of an apparent equivalence between royals on the one hand and socialites, entertainers and screen actors on the other, which diminished the distinctiveness of monarchy. This collapsing of the demarcation between ascribed celebrity (dependent on birth and rank) and achieved or attributed celebrity (based on personal merit or media construction) was encapsulated in the public image of Edward, Prince of Wales, in the 1920s and early 1930s. Media coverage presented the prince as the embodiment of wealth, good looks, charm and style, the very same attributes that were regularly attached to Hollywood stars. In the short term this helped invest monarchy with a fashionably modern allure. In the long term, it exposed the Windsors to a more intrusive, and critically less deferential, popular press. Celebrity journalism was predicated on providing revelations about the real person behind the public figure, and royals were ultimately no more successful than other public figures in controlling what aspects of their private lives were regarded as suitable for public consumption.[90]

It is clear that the British media believed that it had a licence to report, comment and speculate on Farouk's private escapades to an extent that was, in this era, inconceivable in regard to coverage of the British royal family. Nevertheless, even during the infamous self-imposed silence observed by Fleet Street throughout much of the Abdication crisis in 1936, efforts by the press to obtain candid photographs of Edward and Wallis Simpson marked the emergence of a new level of invasiveness within the rules of press engagement.[91] Moreover, after 1945, the press was determined not to repeat the docility and reverence that had characterized responses to the Abdication, and there was a distinct shift away from deference in press coverage of the engagement of Princess Elizabeth to Prince Philip in 1947 and of the Townsend-Margaret affair in 1953–1955.[92] Increased availability of previously concealed knowledge about the Windsors' private lives (however tame by comparison with, say, the 1990s or 1820s) exposed the conditional nature of royal prestige, particularly if a monarch's personal behaviour failed to match acceptable moral conventions among the wider public.

Any attempt to see stories of Farouk's extravagance and depravity as merely serving to reinforce the House of Windsor's unqualified reputation for simplicity and probity needs to be alert to this broader context, one which recognizes the ambiguous and conditional nature of royal authority and popularity. In a flattering item (reflecting the largely favourable representations of Farouk that appeared in the British press in his coronation year) in the *Daily Express* in June 1937, the young monarch was lauded for an act of personal generosity towards a British woman seeking funds to visit the graves of her father and grandfather (who had both died on government service) in Egypt. This story was juxtaposed with a piece not about George VI (whose coronation had been the previous month) but about the hotel where his brother, the Duke of Windsor, would be spending his honeymoon with the twice-divorced American for whom he had given up the British throne.[93] Royal scandals, and the tortured relationship between crown and public values they divulged, could easily come very close to home, and there was definitely no guarantee that they would be seen as the exclusive preserve of dissolute sovereigns in distant lands.

V

If Egypt's ruler was neither analogous to nor the antithesis of the Windsor model of royal survival and adaptation, what other scripts were available which allowed Britons to make sense of Farouk's majestic status? Geopolitics might be thought to have encouraged identification of Farouk with other Middle Eastern monarchs. Farouk's father, King Fuad, was, after all, the first incumbent of one of four new dynasties that the British helped establish in the region, in the wake of the collapse of the Ottoman Empire. (The others were Faisal in Iraq, Abdulla in Jordan and Ibn Saud in Arabia.) However, as has already been noted, it proved difficult to align Farouk with these 'desert kings', whose artificially created kingdoms lacked the coherence and august venerability of Egypt. As a ruler of a relatively recently established dynasty ruling over an ancient land (and one with extensive purchase in the Western imaginary) Farouk had more in common with Iran's Pahlavi dynasty, created in 1925 when military strongman Reza Khan declared himself Shah. Mohammad Reza Pahlavi, Khan's son and Iran's crown prince (before succeeding his father in 1941), had personal connections to Farouk, marrying the Egyptian king's sister, Fawzia, in 1939. The British press covered the marriage of Mohammad Reza with frequent cross-referencing to Farouk's wedding in the previous year, the common motif being the collocation of the youthful modernity of the royal couples with the ancient and opulent splendour of their two courts.[94] Farouk and Mohammad Reza were paired once again in the late 1940s and early 1950s, largely because they divorced their first wives, and remarried, at around the same time. Moreover the Shah's barely concealed womanizing, pursuit of several well-known Hollywood actresses and a penchant for Italian and Parisian nightclubs seemed to indicate he was a kindred spirit of his former brother-in-law.[95]

Another scandalous royal whose representation in British culture may have provided a template for understandings of Farouk was the ill-fated Carol II of Romania. This Ruritanian romantic adventurer attracted considerable press attention in the late 1920s and 1930s with stories of his reckless love for women, champagne and fast cars, and his operetta-style uniforms and decorations. There was particular curiosity about his scandalous affair with Elena Lupuscu, the green-eyed and Titian-haired Jewish wife of an army officer, which led to his temporary exile.[96] Carol's romance with Elena inspired both a John Buchan adventure yarn and an Ivor Novello play, *Glamorous Night*.[97] While it is true that such Ruritanian fantasies became less appealing to the British public in the late 1930s, as Romania swerved towards fascism, after the war, Novello returned to the world of fantasized operetta princes, ballrooms, royal yachts and opulent coronations in his penultimate play, *King's Rhapsody*.[98] No less enamoured by the overblown melodrama of Carol's live and loves was Terence Rattigan, whose 1953 play *The Sleeping Prince* featured a fictional Balkan Crown Prince who discards his wife when he falls in love with a chorus girl he encounters at the coronation of George V.[99] Of course, these Ruritanian princes – real and fantasized – usually possessed romantically congenial good looks and charm that Farouk (at least after the early 1940s) was unlikely to be credited with. However, the continued allure of the monarch as romantic adventurer once again suggests the inadvisability of consigning Farouk to the status of a discredited and disparaged paradigm of kingship. Furthermore, public interest in Carol II, as with its fascination with Farouk, demonstrates that popular expectations surrounding royal behaviour in mid-twentieth-century Britain were clearly not restricted to the rather insipid template offered by the House of Windsor.

Where Britons were most likely to find echoes and analogies of Farouk was in the cavalcade of monarchs from Britain's own historical past. A profile of Farouk in the *Observer* in 1952 insisted that understanding Egypt's ruler required abandoning present-day conceptions of monarchy as the 'epitome of domestic virtues and political neutrality'. Egypt, the article contended, could usefully be compared to Britain in the opening decades of the nineteenth century, a period of transition from aristocratic oligarchy to middle-class hegemony. In this context, with his combination of 'wit and intelligence' with 'disagreeable personal habits', Farouk recalled the gambling, gluttony and amorous debauchery of George IV.[100] Such comparisons concorded with popular interest in the aristocratic high-living and all-round naughtiness of the Regency period, which appeared a stark contrast with the stern moralizing of the Victorian era, and, more proximately, with the discipline and self-abnegation required by wartime and postwar austerity.[101]

The burdens of rationing and shortages, aggravated by high-minded official rhetoric (which seemed to make a virtue out of denying personal pleasure in favour of activities that were considered edifying and improving), may also explain the attraction of fantasized reconstructions of the Restoration. The folk memory of Charles II had long projected images of his reign as flamboyant and frolicsome, a period of exuberant self-indulgence and risqué glamour which stood in stark distinction to the grim-faced puritanism of the Interregnum which preceded it. In the late 1940s, the topicality of this contrast between Cromwellian puritanism and the sensuously colourful love life of the 'merry monarch' was not lost on contemporaries. The 1949 film *Cardboard Cavalier*, a vehicle for comedian Sid Field, used the setting of the Protectorate and Restoration as a pretext for a series of laboured gags about rationing, petty officialdom and puritanical prudishness.[102] Cinema audiences had already been exposed to fantasized renderings of Charles II and his court in films such as *Nell Gwynn* (1934), in which Anna Neagle's earthy and rumbustious portrayal of the most famous of Charles II's 'beauties' was matched by Cedric Hardwicke's presentation of a good-natured monarch who, for all his urbanity, liked to heartily sing along with the audience at the theatre and pursue both married duchesses and plebeian doxies.[103]

Charles (this time played by George Sanders) had a prominent role in the Hollywood costume melodrama *Forever Amber*, released in 1947. The film was based on the 1944 book of the same name by American author Kathleen Winsor. This sprawling, racy bodice-ripper, which attained immediate notoriety for its blatant sexual references and courtesan protagonist (but also received praise for its painstaking attention to historical detail), was a best-seller and was serialized over a total of thirty-seven weeks in the *Sunday Dispatch* during 1946–1947.[104] While instances of overt correspondence between the only well-regarded Stuart king and Farouk are not forthcoming, their shared reputation as sexually hyperactive pleasure seekers (and the prevalence of voluptuous eating scenes in these films) means that we should not discount the possibility that the mythologized Merry Monarch provided another reference point in public perceptions of Egypt's king.

Much more explicit was the association between Farouk and England's bluebeard king, Henry VIII. The legendary Tudor monarch had been memorialized as laying the foundations, not least in breaking with Rome, for the creation of national eminence under his daughter, Elizabeth. However, while the Virgin Queen appeared to have forsaken personal happiness in favour of the needs of her nation, Henry VIII let nothing impede his quest for power and pleasure. Henry's fame across the centuries rested on an indulgent response to his excesses, including his apparently insatiable appetites for wives, mistresses, majestic splendour and gargantuan feasts. The frequently reproduced image of an overweight, yet lavishly clothed monarch, belching and guzzling his food and throwing discarded chicken bones to his dogs, had long been familiar, but was further replenished in the mid-twentieth century by Alexander Korda's 1933 film *The Private Life of Henry VIII*. Charles Laughton's affectionate portrayal of Henry's pursuit of bawdy pleasures contributed to the film's extraordinary popularity, and he reprised the role twenty years later in *Young Bess*. Similar screen depictions of a heartily lascivious Henry in this period were supplied by (in the 1953 film *The Sword and the Rose*) James Robertson Justice and (on television in 1947 and 1952, respectively) Arthur Young and Basil Sydney.[105] The Tudor king was also referenced in the low humour and innuendo of the music hall, notably in Bert Lee's 1934 number (popularized by Stanley Holloway) 'With Her Head Tucked Underneath Her Arm'.[106]

Farouk's selfish and undignified pursuit of his private appetites made affinity with England's second Tudor monarch an inevitability. Mary Rowlatt, an informed observer of the Egyptian scene, commented that it was Egypt's misfortune to have been ruled in the 1940s by 'a mixture of Sultan Abdel Hamid [the last Ottoman sultan] and Henry VIII'.[107] In the *Daily Express*, Chapman Pincher claimed that Farouk's desire to divorce (and scapegoat) Farida had been because of her failure to produce a male heir. If the analogy to Henry VIII's desperate determination to secure his dynasty through divorcing his first wife, Catherine of Aragon, was not already obvious, the article was accompanied by the juxtaposed portraits of Farouk and 'Bluff King Hal'.[108]

In a provocative appraisal of popular attitudes towards the Abdication, Frank Mort has argued that some of the more sympathetic responses to Edward VIII's plight reveal the existence of emerging ideas of morality and sexuality which came into conflict with the ethical codes of the political and social establishment. This interpretation identifies the challenge to the Windsor model coming from affective cultures that were essentially 'modern'.[109] By contrast, a study of Farouk suggests that the inability of a 'domesticated' monarchy to achieve a secure and uncontested monopoly over the discursive terrain in which notions of kingship were articulated, comprehended and consumed derives from the resilience of older conceptions of majesty in popular culture. Public fascination with Farouk (and with the continued significance – in both folk memory and contemporary mass media – of lusty monarchs such as Charles II and Henry VIII whom he called to mind) reveals a surreptitious yearning for a more full-bodied image of the monarchy. The selfless duty and virtuous family life of George VI were undoubtedly widely admired, and there was genuine public grief and shock at his untimely death. However, his prosaic character never set hearts racing. Even the devoted monarchist Cecil Beaton found the king lacking in 'mystery and magic' when he photographed him in 1939, while one Conservative politician-cum-socialite (and lover of the king's brother, the Duke of Kent) despaired that George VI's court was 'moth-eaten… dour and glamourless'.[110] The heady rhetoric of the 'new Elizabethan age', which accompanied his daughter's accession and coronation in 1952–1953, quickly dissipated.[111] At the end of the 1950s one onlooker described the Windsors as 'a frightened, timorous monarchy hoping not to be noticed so that the death sentence may be delayed'.[112] By contrast, Farouk offered a tantalizing reminder of a now lost world, in which kings knew how to live like kings, and (perhaps even more critically) their subjects appeared willing to indulge them their private pleasures.

In Chapter 2, we considered how narratives of Farouk emancipated themselves from the confinement of the formal world of diplomacy and statecraft, and became incorporated instead within the discourses of modern celebrity culture. However, the consideration of Farouk's incorporation into British popular culture undertaken in this chapter requires us to cast a sceptical eye on claims for the efficacious and unimpeded advance of modernity in Britain between the late 1930s and mid-1950s. Farouk's affinity with both the boisterous music hall and roistering monarchs reveals the resilience of a much coarser, more vernacular, cultural milieu in mid-century Britain and the continued purchase (even if at the level of the fantasized and escapist) of the robust pursuit of masculine pleasures. Despite being both a foreign monarch and an international celebrity, Farouk was comprehended by ordinary Britons through highly localized cultural formations: the end-of-the-pier show, the bookie's corner in the local pub, the national service barracks, the worlds of amateur philately and cartophily, the bedroom romps offered by Whitehall farces or by mythologized cinematic renderings of the exuberant lives of Charles II or Henry VIII. The Foreign Office's attempt to keep Farouk at a distance from a British public that displayed not deferential respect but a politically disconcerting overfamiliarity had clearly failed. When Farouk went into exile in 1952, diplomatic efforts to control narratives of the now ex-monarch ceased. Not surprisingly therefore, the various geographical and temporal contexts through which Britons made sense of Farouk were to become even more extensive and unbounded.

4

# Exile or Tourist?

On 29 July 1952 the *Al Mahrousa*, the remodelled and refurbished Egyptian royal yacht that had been commissioned by the Khedive Ismail as long ago as 1865, weighed anchor in the port of Naples. Six years previously Farouk had put this luxury vessel at the disposal of King Victor Emmanuel III of Italy, who, having relinquished his crown in an ultimately doomed effort to secure the survival of his dynasty, was conveyed in maritime splendour to begin a life of exile in Egypt. In 1952, the now-republican government of Italy had returned the favour, offering refuge to Farouk after he was effectively deposed by a military coup on 26 July 1952. Farouk had left Egypt in haste, but not before he had time to gather his family and many of his possessions and load them onto the royal yacht. In addition to a total of 204 pieces of luggage, ammunition boxes filled with gold coins and whisky crates heavy with their content of ingots were allegedly disembarked on the Naples dockside, accompanied by gold accessories stripped from the ship's lavish interiors. The ship and its crew prepared to return to Alexandria, lowering the royal standard and running up, in its place, the flag of the Egyptian navy. Farouk was not there to witness this poignant moment. He had already transferred to the *Linda*, described in the British press as a 'gaudy little tripper ship', which took him on his onward journey, across the Bay of Naples, to the island of Capri.[1]

The stark contrast between the twelve-million-pound *Al Mahrousa* and the humble pleasure launch, with its cheap bar and sun roof crowded with regular holidaymakers, appeared as the ultimate hubris, a compelling encapsulation of Farouk's fall from grace. It also raised the somewhat impertinent question of how best to capture and categorize the now ex-king of Egypt. Was he an exile or a tourist? This remark may initially appear fatuous, since none of the vacationers who shared the cramped decks of the *Linda* with Farouk had gold bullion in their luggage or, as he was, were about to commandeer forty rooms in Capri's Eden Paradise Hotel. However, it is the contention of this chapter that the categories of both exile and tourist were important in framing understandings of Farouk after 1952 (and, in the case of the latter, even before he lost his throne). Moreover, the archetypes of the exile and the tourist had a not insignificant presence in the creation of the postwar landscape, both material and imagined. One was a product of the violent geopolitical disturbances created by the Second World War and the era of decolonization. The other was a symptom of mass affluence, increased leisure and rising expectations in both Western Europe and North America. Exile and tourism could be seen as 'opposite poles in the modern experience of displacement'.[2] In the case of Farouk, however, the exile and the tourist converged on a shared, highly specific, site: the Mediterranean. Farouk's Mediterranean was a celebrity pleasure zone, a playground for the new international *beau monde*. However, it was simultaneously becoming a popular destination for a new, more democratic, variety of mass tourism, associated with an often vulgar commercialization, and denigrated by old-style travellers for its boorishness and materialism. At the same time, these essentially modern understandings of the inner sea overlaid a long-established rendering of the Mediterranean as a domain of decadent hedonism, one which incorporated a mythologized past that encompassed everything from the debauchery of Ancient Rome to the raffish world of the *fin-de-siècle* Riviera.

I

Shortly before his abdication, Farouk purportedly remarked, 'In ten years time there will be only five kings left: the king of Hearts, Diamonds, Spades, Clubs and the king of England'.[3] Deposed and exiled monarchs were hardly unfamiliar to Farouk, even before he lost his own throne. During the Second World War, Egypt hosted the kings of Greece and Yugoslavia, who had both fled from German invasions of their kingdoms, and after the war, Farouk extended an invitation to settle in Egypt to the ex-kings of both Albania and Italy. In 1950 Farouk encountered a slightly different type of ex-monarch, the Duke of Windsor, while the two men were staying at the same hotel in Biarritz.[4] Within two years, Farouk was to join the confraternity of ex-kings that now lived out their aimless and purposeless lives in their European playgrounds. There were, it has to be said, a not inconsiderable number of them. The First World War had accounted for four emperors and six kings, and five more were eliminated during the Second World War and its aftermath. Some had given up their thrones to ensure the survival of their dynasties, but this strategy brought mixed results, and by the 1950s republican systems had become the norm across most of Europe, and, for that matter, increasingly in the Middle East as well. However, ex-monarchs were of greater symbolic, than they were of numerical, consequence. In the early 1950s, they provided a striking embodiment of the seismic changes wrought by the war, and a telling reminder of who and what was surplus to the requirements of postwar political and cultural reconstruction. In particular, the preposterous, desperate and even tragic lives in exile of the former kings of Romania, Albania and Yugoslavia, all received considerable (and largely unsympathetic) attention in the British press, their fates serving as proxy for broader patterns of transformative social and geopolitical change.

For these ex-kings, loss of official status was countered by the growing cultural power of celebrity. As one discerning commentator put it, 'Publicity is their vicarious kingdom, and the gossip columns are their gazettes'.[5] However, no longer subject to the accepted protocols and dispensations that applied to heads of state, former monarchs had limited control over the content and quality of the publicity generated by their often bizarre exiled existences. George II of Greece received little sympathy for spending most of his second period of exile in the company of his long-time English mistress, whom he had set up in a Belgravia townhouse. Ex-King Carol of Romania was mocked for continuing to assume the privileges of his former position, conferring titles and insisting that those who encountered him should bow or curtsey. Zog, the former sovereign of Albania, was similarly jealous of his former prerogatives, requiring visitors to the villa near Cannes, which served as his twenty-room kingdom, to continue to address him as 'Your Majesty'. The press therefore savoured reports in 1953 that Zog was being sued by the US government for back taxes on a Long Island estate he owned, but never visited. He ultimately paid up, but not before insisting that as a king, he was entitled to unconditional immunity from personal and wealth taxes. The following year the Egyptian government charged him with tax evasion.[6]

Given how much time they had on their hands, these deracinated Riviera villa-kings inevitably had a tendency to get into trouble. The least edifying of these ex-monarchs, by common consent, was Peter of Yugoslavia, whose spendthrift ways, and unprepossessing attempts to restore his finances, received comprehensive coverage in the British (and American) popular press. Despite his excruciatingly unsuccessful attempt to offer himself (via a Manhattan PR firm) for appearances with prestige clients, Peter continued his reckless approach to both love and money. In July 1953, a bounced cheque brought the bailiffs to his Paris apartment, from which they removed a mink stole, twenty-two pairs of shoes, twenty-eight dresses and even four petticoats and ten pairs of panties, all from the wardrobe of his wife, Queen Alexandra. At this time Peter and Alexandra were going through one of their periodic estrangements, this one caused by Peter's publicly flaunted affair with an American woman. Later in that year, the British press reported Alexandra had attempted suicide, in the hope that Peter would drop his divorce suit. The ex-queen's undoubted distress brought little sympathy for either her or her husband in the British press, which continued to regard the couple with a combination of prurience and unconcealed contempt.[7] The low esteem in which they were held took another battering when they attempted to restore their status and replenish their funds by publishing two independently authored memoirs (which, in Peter's case, was serialized in the *Sunday Dispatch*), each of which combined unsightly self-pity with an unsparing detailing of the less salubrious aspects of their marriage.[8] The *Daily Mirror*, the tribune of post-deferential postwar populism, openly revelled in Peter's fallen status, and disdainfully suggested he might do well to find himself a proper job: 'If anyone in Britain would like to make an offer – the quicker the better.'[9]

By contrast, a feature in *Picture Post*, 'Ex-King Farouk Says I Am Looking for a Job', was less much vindictive, possibly because Farouk's self-pity seemed to have fallen short of the self-absorption of Peter and Alexandra, and also because the ex-Egyptian monarch appeared to lack their impenitent sense of entitlement. For, whereas Peter continued to agitate for his restoration (with little hope of success, given the West's desire to retain Tito as a counterweight to the Soviet Union in the Balkans), Farouk seemed to have accepted his exile fate. Nevertheless, the tone of the article was no less facetious in its consideration of Farouk's fortunes in exile than British press coverage of other ex-monarchs. Farouk was allowed to articulate his insistence that he had been making serious efforts to curtail his expenses, by selling off his fleet of motor cars, pensioning off all but two of his army of retainers, and swapping his luxurious villa for a small apartment in Rome. However, his remark that he now needed to secure his income by getting a job elicited mockery and derision from the *Picture Post* reporter Jenny Nicholson. Farouk's job prospects, she contended, were handicapped by his 'unattractive appearance, few qualifications and a reputation for good living and irresponsibility'. His attempt to seek employment from the textile magnate Count Marzotto had been a disaster, since 'thorough shame, or habit', the ex-king had treated his job interview 'like an audience'. Nicholson suggested that Farouk might be better advised to become a museum curator or jeweller, given the knowledge and flair he had demonstrated in augmenting the Egyptian royal collections.[10]

Since she cited a positive valuation of Farouk's talent as a collector from an employee of Christies, Nicholson was not necessarily being wholly sarcastic here. However, it was clear that Farouk was subject to the same general disparagement that was directed towards the wretched and wearily wayward ex-royals who loitered around the Riviera, Parisian hotels and Belgravia's rented apartments. Coverage in May 1957 of Farouk's attendance at the Cannes wedding of the sister of ex-King Simeon of Bulgaria, whose guest list included an extensive array of exiled royalty, ensured he was inserted into a narrative of a post-royal existence characterized by asinine self-deception and aimless futility.[11] At a most basic level, Farouk suffered from guilt by association. As Geoffrey Bocca, an astute and judicious chronicler of 'kings without thrones' in the 1950s, declared, 'One king without a throne could command respect, sympathy, asylum and, where necessary, a hand out'. By contrast, a dozen ex-kings 'merely command a housing shortage, and invite laughter'.[12]

An investigation by the Rockefeller foundation entitled *The Refugee in the Post-war World* made clear that, while the term 'refugee' was often applied in everyday speech to anyone who had been compelled to abandon their home, the term was usually reserved for someone who was not merely homeless and uprooted but was 'a helpless casualty, diminished in all his circumstances'.[13] Such assertions did not deter Alexandra of Yugoslavia (in yet another regrettable display of ill-judged self-justification) from comparing her husband's status (as a deposed king with no place to go) in 1945 with the 'countless numbers of ex-prisoners of war, concentration camp victims, and stateless persons scattered desolately throughout Europe'.[14] Such dubious assertions of equivalence between ex-royals and the millions of Europeans uprooted by the Second World War who were classified as Displaced Persons (DPs), and whose continued suffering in refugee camps where disease and starvation were prevalent (and created a humanitarian crisis that extended to the end of the decade), were actually not entirely beyond plausibility. Ex-Queen Giovanna of Bulgaria was, at one point, obliged to seek assistance from the UN's International Refugee Organization.[15] However, overall, the experiences of privileged ex-royals like Farouk were very different from those of the millions of refugees who were such an important presence in the global landscape in the aftermath of the Second World War.[16]

Nor did Farouk's life after he left Egypt have much in common with those who participated in another critical category of postwar dislocation, the former colonial subjects who, as the formal edifice of empire crumbled, chose to seek a new life in metropolitan Britain. However, even if Farouk was hardly entitled to the status of either refugee or (im)migrant, his essentially stateless life after 1952 did exemplify broader motifs of estrangement and displacement that accompanied an era of refashioned geopolitics. Dislocation as a materially grounded condition has inevitably been a critical theme in the historical scholarship dedicated to the immediate postwar era.[17] However, it has also been increasingly employed at a more discursive level, especially in the field of postcolonial theory. Here, the attention is not just on the physical displacement and diasporas created as the European empires faded and faltered but on the forms of cultural and psychic alienation that accompanied decolonization and post-imperial immigration. Initially this scholarship focused on the unsettling consequences of migration from former colony to metropole, especially the ambiguities surrounding identity and hybridity that emerged as a consequence of resettlement.[18] However, it soon extended to encompass the outlook (albeit not entirely representative) of a number of white colonizers who also now felt 'out of place' – in both former colony and in metropolitan society – as the colonial order began to fall apart.[19]

How do we insert ex-kings such as Farouk into these broader narratives of postwar displacement? Given his failure to match the sociological and legal categories of refugee or migrant, maybe Farouk requires recourse to a more venerable, and usually more rarefied, genre of transposition: that of 'exile'. For much of the last half century, historians have displayed a notable lack of interest in political exiles, as opposed to migrants and other diasporic populations. Back in 1970, one observer noted that 'Historians generally dislike lost causes', and consequently had little desire to immerse themselves in the 'bitterness and futility' of exile politics.[20] However, the term 'exile' would appear to be a highly apposite appellation for Farouk's existence as an ex-king. As a discarded relic of a feudal order overthrown in favour of a self-consciously modernizing republic, Egypt's ex-king recalled the despondent royalists and aristocrats who fled France in the years after 1792.[21] In 1954, *Picture Post* published a poignant and sentimental portrait of the exiled Farouk and his young children's world of aimless privilege and deluded royal dignity in the confinement of their villa outside Rome which recalled descriptions of Louis XVIII's exiled court at Hartwell Hall.[22]

Of course, Farouk's determination that exile should not be allowed to curb his hedonistic proclivities meant he lacked the unconcealed melancholy of the exiled Bourbons (ironically they – at least temporarily – got their throne back. Farouk did not). However, the precedent of the Bourbon emigres suggests that popular understandings of Farouk as an ex-king might have been informed by romanticized visions of earlier figures who had been violently shunted from the centres of power and privilege to the despondent margins of history. The Bourbons were not the only illustration of the pathos and futility of exile available within the popular historical imagination. After all, Britain had been a place of refuge for other notable dynastic exiles over the previous century. There was the chronically ill Napoleon III in his Chiselhurst country house, alternately designing a new type of energy-efficient stove and impregnating local women. There was Xenia Feodorovna, cousin of the last Tsar, living out her long and lonely exile from Russia in a grace and favour apartment at Hampton Court. There was Haile Selassie, awaiting his return to the Ethiopian throne in a Bath townhouse, while laboriously writing his memoirs in Amharic.[23]

Such historical affinities, though, should not be allowed to obscure the contemporary (and specifically postcolonial) resonance of the notion of 'exile'. In 1960, George Lamming, the West Indian writer who had emigrated from Barbados to Britain ten years earlier, published a set of essays entitled *The Pleasures of Exile*. Lamming stressed the preference among diasporic Caribbean writers living in Britain for the term 'exile', as opposed to 'emigrant', since it implied their status as transnational intellectuals, rather than migrant labourers. More critically he argued that, as both the descendant of slaves violently transplanted from Africa to the Caribbean and a social category that was highly susceptible to feelings of alienation and exclusion in both the colony of their birth and their new metropolitan homeland, the West Indian intellectual had come to appreciate only too well that 'to be colonial is to be in a state of [perpetual] exile'.[24] Once again, any attempt to equate Farouk's exiled life of Italian villas and Riviera casinos with the disconnection, discomfort and racism that characterized the experience of West Indian writers in the 1940s and 1950s would clearly be ill-chosen.[25] However, what does seem common to these very different transplanted persons is a conception of exile that reflected the creation of a new global order.

In their own distinctive ways, both Farouk and Lamming, ex-king and colonial intellectual, represented a new type of global citizen, one who inhabited multiple locations and was identified with a multiplicity of cultural experiences. In the case of West Indian writers such as Lamming, this postcolonial cosmopolitanism produced new forms of subjectivity and self-identification. In Farouk's case, by contrast, this element is absent (or at least inaccessible to the historian). Rather, linkages between the paradigms of exile, postcolonialism and globalization in the context of Farouk may tell us something instead about the way metropolitan Britons made sense of their world in the era of decolonization. Popular interest in Farouk's life as a displaced ex-king might be seen to dramatize the sensibilities not of dislocated former colonial subjects but of their former rulers. Or to put it more boldly, media coverage of Farouk's exile may have been an exercise in psychological displacement, an unconscious disclosure of the melancholy, loss and dispossession that might have been expected to have accompanied the crumbling of Britain's empire, but which was rarely permitted within the public narratives surrounding imperial decommission in the postwar years.[26] An exiled king was inevitably both literally unsettled and discernibly unsettling.

## II

Ultimately, Farouk's life as an ex-king could not be confined within the despondent paradigms of exile, not least because many of the places he frequented after he lost his throne had already featured in the pleasure-seeking peregrinations he had undertaken in his final years as a monarch. In 1950, a protracted summer holiday, which extended from early August to mid-October, saw Farouk and his entourage pursue an apparently endless bachelor party, which took place in San Sebastian in Spain, San Remo in Italy, and the casinos of Biarritz, Cannes, Monte Carlo and Deauville. Farouk's thirteen-week honeymoon with his second wife Narriman in 1951 encompassed Capri, Rapallo, Venice, Switzerland and the Cote d'Azur. During his ten years as an ex-king, Farouk, who had initially accommodated himself and his family in a villa in the Frascati region outside Rome, regularly returned to many of the luxury resorts he had enjoyed as a spendthrift monarch. He also added an additional venue to his inventory of elite playgrounds: Deauville, the Bay of Naples, Monaco and the French Riviera were to be joined by the cafes and nightclubs of the Via Veneto, the infamous boulevard in Rome where he saw out his last years, and indeed the final hours, prior to his death in 1965. Critically, all these destinations were regarded in the 1950s as key sites in the performance and publicization of the leisure culture of the international *beau monde*. The arrival of significant numbers of Hollywood stars in European resorts allowed the fusion of New World glamour and Old World tradition into a cosmopolitan elite, which, while it operated its own forms of prestige and exclusivity, appeared to be more relaxed, open and accessible than established European high society.[27]

The apogee of this world of international travel, hotel lobbies, luxury villas and celebratory galas came in April 1956, when Grace Kelly married Prince Rainier of Monaco. Film stars Cary Grant and Ava Gardner and society notables

Aristotle Onassis and Conrad Hilton were among the 600 guests at this highly stylized (not to say contrived) merger of old-style European dynastic spectacle and Hollywood royalty, which took place in Monaco's Roman Catholic cathedral. Also present was Farouk, a regular at the Monte Carlo casino, who appeared to one British observer to be 'discouraged and lonely', slumped in his chair, and 'disinterestedly studying the programme of the service'.[28] Farouk's despondency is understandable, given that, as the former sovereign of twenty million people, he could hardly be expected to have enjoyed paying second fiddle to the inconsequential ruler of a toy European principality. However, Farouk's marginalization at the Rainier-Kelly wedding has symbolic connotations. At one level, it revealed that Farouk's full integration into the international smart set of the 1950s was incomplete and insecure. While he was to be found in many of the same locations as the celebrity jet set, his presence there may well have been interpreted not in relation to contemporary notions of glamour and mobility but with reference to narratives of privileged pleasure-seeking whose provenance went back to earlier periods in history. Moreover, it was equally the case that Farouk also called into question the exclusive identification of these locations with the rarefied worlds of fame, wealth and luxury, in both their contemporary and previous guises. The exiled king appeared to be responsible for (or at least an indicator of) a process of vulgarization and popularization in which the playgrounds of the rich and famous were obliged to coexist with the boorish imperatives of postwar mass tourism.

That Farouk's movement across the pleasure zones of continental Europe drew upon longer-established, not to say decidedly archaic, associations within the British imaginary is certainly pertinent in regard to the resort that was in closest proximity to British shores, namely Deauville. The Normandy seaside town had been developed as a resort by the Duc de Morny and Sir John Olliffe in the 1860s. Deauville's natural harbour was well-suited to accommodating the splendid yachts of its wealthy visitors, and by its boom years in the 1920s, the town had come to acquire a renowned racetrack, immaculately manicured golf courses, luxury hotels and a casino, and was hosting prestige motor shows and beauty pageants.[29] Farouk's twelve-day stay at a three-room suite in Deauville's Hotel du Golfe in August 1950 was notorious for the scale of the king's lavish entertaining and high-stakes gambling. Farouk's insistence that the holiday would demonstrate that he was actually 'a quiet-living fellow' was confounded by the fact that his swollen entourage included a coterie of senior army officers, countless bodyguards, the king's own cleaning and catering staff and two cabaret singers. Farouk also succeeded in having a large part of the beach cordoned off so that no pictures of him in his swimming trunks would appear in the press.³⁰ While such presumptive extravagance was inevitably attributed to Farouk's customary penchant for excess, it also corresponded with an already well-established identification of Deauville as a 'millionaire's playground', the resort of choice for the high rollers and thoroughbred owners of le haut monde. Indeed the Egyptian monarch was in Deauville at the very same time as the Aga Khan, a man whose gilded fortune dwarfed even that of Farouk.³¹ A 1956 profile of Deauville declared that it was 'the last of the rich man's resorts which gets by not on what the tabloids call glamour but on Class with a capital C'. Its grotesquely high prices kept the 'hoi polloi' at bay, and the resort made clear its long-established preference for the 'remaining maharajahs and princes who can still afford the traditional society migrations'. Moreover, unlike the more chic resorts of the Riviera, Deauville possessed a decidedly 'masculine, sporting, brandyish air'.³²

Deauville may have provided the model for Royale-les-Eaux, the fictitious northern French resort whose luxury hotels and gaming-tables Ian Fleming described with unabashed enthusiasm and empurpled prose in *Casino Royale*, the first James Bond novel, which appeared in 1953. While Bond's material self-indulgence and sexual licence might be seen to mark the dawning of a new cultural sensibility, critical analysis of Fleming's novels has highlighted that they might be best understood not as jet-age thrillers but as a refurbished version of the interwar adventure narratives of Dornford Yates and John Buchan, in which gentlemanly clubland heroes tackled a variety of continental villains and criminal syndicates.³³ Bond's accommodation in Royale-les-Eaux is in a five-star hotel, where he luxuriates in its furnishings of royal-blue curtains and carpets and 'brass-studied leather and polished mahogany', and dines in a grand restaurant with 'mirrored alcoves' and 'red sik-shaded tables' which had 'survived from the Edwardian days'. The town's casino, with its Negresco baroque fittings and vast chandeliers, secreted 'a strong whiff of Victorian elegance and luxury'. These wistful and nostalgic sentiments in *Casino Royale* (often overlooked by those anxious to establish Bond as a tribune of the rising 'permissive society'), an opportunity to retreat to 'more spacious, golden times', not merely registered Ian Fleming's reactionary and anti-egalitarian politics.³⁴ They also suggest that resorts such as Deauville continued to be identified not with contemporary (often Hollywood-derived) versions of wealth, status and glamour but with an older, more exclusive, vision of high society, in which princes and patricians remained socially pre-eminent. Farouk's sojourn in the Normandy resort revealed that the new international culture of celebrity emerged alongside, and in correspondence with, longer-established understandings of upper-class hedonism and social privilege.

While the resilience of the paraphernalia of princely privilege was undoubtedly more evident in the somewhat tweedy Deauville, memories and myths of elite waywardness in past times were no less significant in shaping popular perceptions of Farouk's regular visits to the resorts of the Cote d'Azur. The fact that so much of Farouk's well-publicized gallivanting took place on the Riviera meant that it inevitably recalled the rakish naughtiness associated with the progress of Edward, Prince of Wales (later Edward VII), and his retinue through the luxury hotels, casinos and card-rooms (not to mention a succession of professional *grandes cocottes*) of Cannes and Monte Carlo in the 1880s and 1890s.[35] If, by 1950, such sybaritic excursions were now beyond the means and stamina (and indeed offended the proprieties) of a decidedly insipid British royal family, the mantle of paramount monarchical excess on France's Mediterranean shore had clearly passed to Farouk.

Monte Carlo, in particular, had, from the last decades of the nineteenth century, become notorious among the British public for its purported sin and depravity. In 1905, Sabine Baring-Gould, in a censorious mode that befitted the lyricist of the hymn 'Onward Christian Soldiers', declared Monte Carlo to be 'the moral cesspool of Europe', an 'earthly paradise' that had unfortunately been given over to 'harlots and thieves'.[36] Those whose inclinations were prurient, rather than prudish, eagerly consumed salacious tales – real and fictional – of women of easy virtue, spectacular losses at the gaming tables and dishonourable suicides. Monte Carlo in the *belle epoque* became a byword for upper-class sleaze and irresponsibility, the playground of princes, courtesans, wealthy plutocrats, gold-diggers and publicists, its summer season providing endless copy for newspaper gossip columns and sensationalist journalism. Popular novelists were equally attracted to its sybaritic licentiousness, E. Phillips Oppenheim regularly using it as an exotic backcloth to his suspense fiction. His *Mr. Grex of Monte Carlo* opens with a gushing description of its 'fantastically brilliant' casino (frequented by 'a beautiful Englishwoman who was a duchess but looked otherwise' and 'an equally beautiful Frenchwoman, who looked like a duchess but was – otherwise') that would have put Ian Fleming to shame.[37] Monaco attempted to refute accusations of crassness and immorality by surrounding its casino with galas, regattas, opera and other artistic events. Nonetheless, up to 1914, it retained is reputation as the most secure resort in Europe in which to pursue an illicit holiday. As Somerset Maugham succinctly phrased it, 'Monte' was 'a sunny place for shady people'. By the late 1940s, Monaco had become increasingly staid. A visitor in 1954 bemoaned that, not merely was the resort tainted by wartime collaboration with the Nazis, but 'all the old atmosphere of sin and voluptuousness had gone'. However, from the mid-1950s, the patronage of an increasing number of wealthy American businessmen and celebrities, reinforced by some well-chosen re-investment from both Prince Rainier and Aristotle Onassis, revived the resort's reputation for high living.[38]

Farouk and his entourage were a regular presence at the Monte Carlo casino, and at the resort's sumptuous Hotel de Paris, where he would frequently arrive without advance notice, often requiring the management to expel existing guests, so that he could occupy his favourite suite.[39] Farouk's ruthlessness at baccarat and chemin-de-fer, and ability to draw on apparently infinite supplies of capital, singled him out as one of those elite gamblers who was able to meet the casino on an equal footing. As one fellow player recorded, 'With a big cigar in his mouth, his face set suitably in a sphinxlike expression, a bottle of Perrier water at his side, he plays until he wins $50,000 or until the casino closes, whichever comes first'.[40] With his preference for high-stakes games (and his – possibly undeserved – reputation for flirting with the women he encountered across the green table tops), Farouk's stays in Monaco seemed more redolent of

**Figure 5** Farouk with his mistress, Irma Minutolo, at a Monte Carlo casino, 16 February 1954 (Keystone/Getty Images).

the grand and raffish era of Edward VII and his plumed women – the 'old ton' – than they were of the comparatively tamer Monte Carlo of Grace and Rainier, whose social round was comprised of Red Cross charity galas attended by Cary Grant or David Niven, and whose casino ante-rooms now hosted fruit machines and dice tables, installed to attract American tourists.[41]

Indeed Britons might have comprehended Farouk's high-rolling reincarnation of a *fin-de-siècle* grand boulevardier through the folk memory of Charles de Ville Wells, whose phenomenal winning streak in 1891 was immortalized through the song, written by Fred Gilbert, 'The Man That Broke the Bank at Monte Carlo'. First performed by the music-hall star Charles Coborn, this rollicking ditty remained popular into the mid-twentieth century, inspiring (or at least featuring in) a number of feature films.[42] If Farouk's sojourns in Monte Carlo aligned him with a mythologized pre-1914 gilded age, he was not entirely a stranger to the more contemporary glamour of the 1950s Riviera. It is true that he had little to do with St. Tropez, which had emerged by the end of the decade as the new hotspot of the Cote d'Azur, a resort which prioritized (through its association with Roger Vadim, Brigitte Bardot and Claude Chabrol) a new form of exclusivity focused on youth and the lionization of the carefree, the casual and the cinematic.[43] However, Farouk did divide his time on the Riviera between Monte Carlo and Cannes, and he spent an increasing amount of time at the latter's casino after 1959, when his adoption of Monegasque citizenship had the unfortunate corollary of debarring him from the Monte Carlo casino.

Cannes shared Monte Carlo's racy reputation before the First World War, but by the 1950s it increasingly catered to those with a modest amount of money to burn, rather than the millionaires and grand English notables it had hosted a half century before. Conversely, the international Cannes film festival (launched in 1946) created an association between the resort and the glitz of Hollywood, as beautiful movie stars paraded on its beach before a frenzy of flashbulbs. While Farouk eschewed both the beach and the lavish parties that accompanied the festival, in favour of playing against movie moguls Darryl Zanuck and Jack Warner at Cannes' Palm-Beach casino, this did not preclude ambitious agents from contriving to have Farouk photographed in the company of an aspiring, bikini-clad, starlet.[44] The worlds of Farouk and Hollywood also overlapped on Italy's Mediterranean shore. The rugged islands of the Bay of Naples may have lacked the grandeur and glitz of the casino resorts of the Cote d'Azur, but their natural clarity of light and blue waters made them an incomparable picture postcard backdrop for glamorous film stars. Capri, where Farouk spent both his honeymoon and his first days in exile, had increasingly become a playground for wealthy Americans and both Hollywood and European movie actors.[45]

The closest intersection between Farouk and the pleasure zones of the postwar *beau monde* ultimately came to be, however, not the sun-dappled shores of the Ligurian and Tyrrhenian seas but the nightspots of Rome's Via Veneto. Here, narratives of Farouk's carousing were fashioned and framed by understandings (and media forms) that, far from looking back to the *belle epoque*, were distinctly contemporary, and, indeed, were intrinsic to the creation of postwar celebrity culture. For Farouk (together with the models and would-be actresses who sought to gain attention by publicly cavorting with the ex-king in the cafes and nightclubs of this glitzy enclave of the Eternal City) was a prominent figure in the culture of excess and exposure that constituted the so-called *dolce vita*. In the course of the 1950s, the Via Veneto, which offered elegant shops and cafes by day, and a palpitatingly promiscuous nightlife once the sun went down, became a place for the rich and famous to see and be seen, an opportunity for celebrities to show off both themselves and their equally flashy companions. Venues such as the Café de Paris and Harry's Bar, outside of which were parked rows of big-ticket sports cars, became the haunt of an ostentatious mix of super-rich playboys, film stars, deracinated aristocrats, aspiring starlets, escort girls and gigolos. The Via Veneto encouraged a new form of celebrity journalism, more aggressive and intrusive than that which operated in Hollywood, where the film studios still found it much easier to prevail on the media not to publicize the indiscretions and improprieties of its leading stars.[46]

Exiled Farouk was a Via Veneto regular, his larger-than-life appetites matching the profligacy, not to say debauchery, of Rome's celebrity goldfish bowl. The British press seized on reports of 'predatory females' offering bribes to the doormen at fashionable Rome night-spots in order to get an introduction to the ex-king, and noted his nightly presence at the bar of the Excelsior Hotel, which became a notorious pick-up joint for the well-heeled and well-known.[47] One of the most distinctive features of the high life of the Via Veneto (and its primary contribution to the development of postwar celebrity culture more broadly) was the emergence of the paparazzi, the youthful freelance photographers who cruised along the boulevard in their Vespas, ready to snap unsuspecting celebrities, as they emerged from a hotel, restaurant or nightclub. Farouk featured prominently in the notorious sequence of unseemly brawls between a number of celebrities (which included not merely the ex-king and his bodyguards but also the actors Ava Gardner, Anthony Franciosa, Anita Ekberg and Anthony Steel) and gangs of scooter-riding photographers which took place on the torrid night of 14/15

August 1958. The paparazzi had approached Farouk and his entourage at his pavement table outside the Café de Paris. Farouk usually appeared to welcome the attentions of the paparazzi, but, on this occasion, the ex-king was startled by a flash bulb set off in his face. Possibly believing it to be an assassination attempt (thereby neatly conflating the worlds of celebrity and politics), Farouk hurled himself at the offending photographer, Tazio Secchiaroli. The unprepossessing images of toppled tables, flying fists and a shattered camera, captured by another photographer, have been regularly credited with establishing Secchiaroli's reputation as the most famous *paparazzo* of them all.[48]

**Figure 6** Farouk shields himself from a paparazzi photographer at a Rome restaurant (Bettmann/Getty Images).

Secchiaroli was an advisor on *La Dolce Vita*, the film in which Frederico Fellini presented the high life of the Via Veneto as ultimately worthless and soulless, a debased culture where morality was subsumed by materialism. It is possible that those Britons who watched Fellini's film (and the film's exposure certainly reached well beyond the select audiences who normally patronized continental art house film in Britain in the late 1950s) might have come to understand Farouk's years on the Via Veneto in a context provided by Fellini's uncompromisingly critical prism.[49] Sordid stories of aspiring female film stars 'with fortunate figures' forced to 'draw haphazard attention to themselves' by becoming companions to 'dissolute princes' they had met on the Via Veneto had certainly become something of a cliché in the British press.[50] Others might have placed Farouk's Roman nightlife in the context of the Wilma Montesi scandal, which was widely covered in the British popular press between 1953 and 1957.[51] The discovery of the body of a half-undressed young woman on a beach near Rome led to a series of allegations which demonstrated that the newfound glamour of the Via Veneto overlay a sordid world of sex, drugs, corruption and even murder, among Rome's social and political establishment.[52] While even the most fanciful and sensationalist press coverage of the Montesi affair never sought to establish Farouk as one of its protagonists, its exposure of the more unsavoury aspects of Italy's capital after dark might well have invested narratives of the ex-king's residence in Rome with an insalubrious element that had been much less evident in earlier descriptions of his private pleasures. Far from securing him a place among the beautiful people, Farouk's final years in Rome ensured the dominant image of his final years was of a balding, corpulent lecher, gracelessly attempting the rumba in the less than edifying company of pin-up girls or his favoured brassy Neopolitan mistress, Irma Capece Minutolo.

With the major exception of Deauville, what all of Farouk's pleasure zones had in common was their location on, or adjacent to, the Mediterranean. It has generally been accepted that the Cold War created a new international system in which the Mediterranean as a single unit was to be dismembered and superseded by a number of alternative zones of demarcation, such as Southern Europe, North Africa and (most significantly of all) the Middle East. However, in cultural – as opposed to geopolitical – terms, the eclipse of the unitary Mediterranean should not be overexaggerated. Farouk, who, even before he lost his throne, enjoyed the diversions of the Riviera and Italy, while possessing little affinity with the peasant *fellahin* of the Upper Nile (let alone the black Africans for whom he publicly recorded his contempt) presumably required little persuading that Egypt was better understood as the south shore of the Mediterranean that it was as part of the African continent. On the eve of Farouk's extended jaunts on the Riviera and Capri, the French historian Fernand Braudel had published his classic magnum opus *The Mediterranean and the Mediterranean World in the Age of Philip II*, in which he identified the inner sea as a single unit of 'creative space', its populations intrinsically connected by sea-routes and trade, but, even more fundamentally, sharing a common rhythm of life which transcended nation, region and even religion.[53]

For all its achievement as a work of profound scholarship, Braudel's book could have been better timed. The first Arab-Israeli War (which had just concluded) and the emerging crisis of colonial governance in French Algeria suggested that the commonality of olive groves, dazzling blue water and vivid sunshine might not be insufficient to overcome religious and political distinctions among the various communities who inhabited the Mediterranean's many shores.[54] However, British audiences in the 1950s may have still been particularly attuned to thinking about the Mediterranean in unitary terms. The reason for this was that narratives of British participation in the Second World War had appeared to grant the Mediterranean a common history once again. The British high command, often to the consternation of their American allies, had viewed the Mediterranean as an integrated and comprehensive theatre of war. British sailors, soldiers and airmen sought to attain pan-Mediterranean supremacy against Italy, Vichy France and (increasingly as the war dragged on) Germany, in a series of interconnected campaigns in North Africa, Syria, Greece, Crete, Malta and mainland Italy.[55] The Eighth Army's long, regularly stalemated, advance between 1942 and 1945, first beside the North African coast from Egypt to Tunisia, and then along the rocky spine of Italy from Salerno to Trieste, emblematized this unitary Mediterranean experience during the war.[56] Wartime service in Egypt, Libya, Tunisia, Greece and Italy gave many ordinary Britons access to the classic sites of the Mediterranean Grand Tour and others were encouraged to experience a common Mediterranean culture vicariously in the 1950s through the novels and travel writing of Lawrence Durrell or the cookbooks of Elizabeth David.[57] Such understandings undoubtedly framed narratives of Farouk's peripatetic journey from Cairo to Capri, from Alexandria to Antibes, both familiarizing and naturalizing them, even if the specific contexts were obviously decidedly different.

Farouk's association with the Mediterranean in the 1950s ensured that the latter's contemporary identification with affluent leisure or celebrity hedonism coexisted with the continued pertinence (and indeed reaffirmation, through the medium of feature film) of hoarier understandings of the supposed attributes of the inner sea and its peoples. Generations of privileged Britons (initially aristocratic, but, from the second half of the nineteenth century, joined by increasing numbers of middle-class travellers) had been infatuated with the Mediterranean's landscape, history, art and literature (although less so with its current inhabitants).[58] There is no exaggeration in the claim, made by the author of an extensive survey of Victorian and Edwardian visitors to the Mediterranean, that 'the journey south was a rite of passage' for many nineteenth-century Britons. The possibilities of edification and improvement inevitably motivated discerning travellers to explore the Mediterranean's seemingly boundless treasury of art and ruins. Some visitors sought a simplicity and freedom they believed had been abandoned in the restless, feverish urban milieu of northern Europe, while others found in the distinctive features of the Mediterranean, especially the prevalence of the olive tree, the familiar landscapes of the Bible.[59]

However, the Mediterranean also appeared to be a place where piety was obliged to defer to paganism. Luigi Barzini, a distinguished Italian journalist and politician, introduced his native land to English-speaking audiences as 'one of the last countries in the western world where the great god Pan is not dead,... where Christianity has not deeply disturbed the happy traditions and customs of ancient Greece and Rome'.[60] The association of the Mediterranean with the moral turpitude and hedonistic debauchery of Ancient Rome was not confined to those in possession of a classical education, having been popularized in bestselling novels such as Edward Bulwer-Lytton's *The Last Days of Pompeii* in the mid-nineteenth century and Robert Graves' *I, Claudius* a century later.[61] Moreover in the 1950s the cruelty, despotism and even sexual perversion of the Roman Empire (and its replacement by a new – Christian and liberal – order) took centre stage in a series of epic films, mostly made in Hollywood, but popular with British audiences: *Quo Vadis* (1951), *The Robe* (1953), *Demetrius and the Gladiators* (1954), *The Silver Chalice* (1954) and *Ben-Hur* (1959). The potential political allegories offered by these cinematic narratives of Ancient Rome – their ability to refract intimations of not merely the Cold War but of decolonization and the emergence of the civil rights movement in the United States – have been effectively unpacked by scholars.[62] It is certainly true that, in one case, the film *Quo Vadis*, their value as parables of the decline of the British Empire and the emancipation of its colonial subjects was reinforced by the casting of the British actor Peter Ustinov as an outrageously depraved Nero. While Ustinov failed to acknowledge any contemporary parallels, his Oscar-winning turn as the plump, spoilt and lascivious Roman emperor might well have brought Farouk to mind among British audiences. The potential similarities certainly registered with cinemagoers in Egypt itself, where Nero's appearance on screen was met with ribald cries of 'To Capri! To Capri!'[63]

Indeed Capri proved to be the primary site on which Farouk straddled novel and established renderings of the Mediterranean as a zone of hedonistic extravagance. Norman Lewis, serving as an army intelligence officer in recently liberated Naples in 1944, compared the Tyrrhenian island idyll to hashish, proven as it was 'to bring out the demon, whatever its nature, lurking at the bottom of the human personality'.[64] Capri had been notorious for its depravity and transgressive pleasures since antiquity. It possessed the ruins of the cliff-top villa in which the emperor Tiberius (if his prominent detractors Tacitus and Suetonius were to be believed) had sated his perverted appetites, before throwing his degraded victims into the sea. Its Grotto delle Felci was reputed to have hosted a Priapic cult and the island's caves were allegedly a regular venue for Roman orgies.[65] Fortunino Matania, the Italian artist and illustrator who was popular with British audiences into the 1950s (despite remaining unapologetically wedded to the traditions of Victorian aestheticism), included, among his portfolio of salacious images of the bacchanalian roisters of ancient Rome, a grotto on Capri, populated with his habitual voluptuous female nudes.[66] Farouk's stays on Capri, although accompanied by gargantuan hotel breakfasts and luxury spending, offered the press little in the way of carnal diversions, not least because he was accompanied by Narriman (and, in 1952, by his children). However, the fact that, while on Capri, Farouk shunned the nightclubs and ensured he was not seen with any woman other than his wife failed to prevent sordid scandalmongering (widely disseminated, if rarely put into print) that Farouk intended to decorate his suite in Anacapri's Eden Paradiso hotel like an Arabian Nights harem, or that he had hosted 600-person orgies on its rooftop.[67] Such flights of salacious fancy ensured that Farouk had been seamlessly assimilated into the island's long history (or more accurately mythology) of high-living and sexual indulgence.

However, at the very time that Farouk became a prominent visitor, Capri became associated with more contemporary transcriptions of illicit pleasure. In the 1950s, its rugged coastline and transparent blue water provided a dramatic backdrop for the wild parties, steamy romances and tempestuous affairs (not forgetting their tanned bodies and fashionable summer wardrobes) of Hollywood stars such as Rita Hayworth, Errol Flynn and Elizabeth Taylor.[68] Capri's enchantments also brought British screen stars to the island, although, lacking the funds of their American peers, their presence was less about taking the opportunity to let their hair down and more about working on location. Farouk's honeymoon on the Tyrrhenian 'isle of gay escape' in 1951 came on the heels of the release of two British movies set on Capri, *The Golden Madonna* and *That Dangerous Age*. The latter was a mildly histrionic love triangle drama involving a convalescing English barrister's wife, whose reunion with a former lover is compromised by the fact he is now courting her step-daughter. The film clearly acknowledged, even if in muted and circuitous form, contemporary anxieties about marriage and divorce in metropolitan Britain, even if it also seemed to imply that the disclosure of such matters might prove easier in the environment of an island paradise renowned for its carefree, sultry sensuality.[69]

## III

Moreover, long regarded as a refuge for prominent gay and lesbian artists and writers, Capri was an obvious destination for the likes of novelist Robin Maugham, who had been discomforted by the increasing (state and media) victimization of male homosexuals in Britain in the years immediately after 1945. Maugham came to Capri at the invitation of writer and (homo)sexual hedonist Norman Douglas, who had resided on the island since the 1930s.[70] While Farouk had no direct connection with Capri's not-so-secret queer history, it could be posited that British press interest in the king's partying on the island was an exercise in re-heterosexualizing Mediterranean decadence, in order to mitigate its potentially disruptive challenge to the protocols of normative, mediatized sexuality in Britain at this time.

Not all of the more contemporary renderings of Capri's reputation for wealthy relaxation and sexual indulgence were entirely positive. By the early 1960s, Capri was associated with vacuous materialism in Godard's caustic film *Contempt*, and it served as the final residence of the appallingly hollow and narcissistic Diana Scott in John Schlesinger's savaging of the jet set, *Darling*.[71] However, if observers chose to yoke Farouk to the more negative connotations of Capri, these were less about the moral emptiness of fame, wealth and privilege than they were about the island's increasing exposure to commercialized mass tourism. In the late 1940s, continental Europe had been a leisure destination beyond the means of all but the well-heeled, but in the 1950s there was a dramatic increase (reaching two million, twice the prewar peak, in 1958) of Britons travelling abroad for their holidays. If the introduction of tourist class on airliners in 1952 was the most notable marker of the dawning of the age of mass tourism, most British holidaymakers in France, Spain, Switzerland and Italy adopted the cheaper options offered by the motor-coach, the bicycle, hitch-hiking or youth hosteling.⁷² Many of these tourists were visiting places in proximity to the wealthy playgrounds frequented by Farouk.

There is an arresting juxtaposition in the pages of both the *Daily Mirror* and *Picture Post* in the early 1950s between features about Farouk's antics in Italy and the Riviera and advertisements (economically priced, as befitted their readers) for holidays in the vicinity of those very same locations. Global Tours offered a coach tour of 'romantic Italy' for sixty-five guineas.⁷³ The Ramblers Association promoted more modestly priced stays in Rome and Capri.⁷⁴ Capri also featured on the itinerary of Thomas Cook's 'Ideal Tour of Italy' while, in 1953, the Belgian Sabena Airlines, claiming that 'continental holidays are cheaper this year', listed a service from London 'to Naples (for Capri)' for £51.⁷⁵ For six pounds less, one could avail oneself of the Elizabethan Coach Tours' excursion to 'The Three Rivieras'.⁷⁶ There were also plebeian independent travellers, like the couple who hitch-hiked to the Riviera on a five-pound budget in 1954.⁷⁷ The democratization of the Grand Tour brought a completely new type of visitor to Farouk's favourite resorts. Deauville was exceptional in debarring the 'rucksack-trudgers'. By, contrast, the French Riviera was, to the mind of a seasoned observer, Geoffrey Bocca, becoming 'an overpopulated Coney Island', overrun by plebeian visitors who preferred to pitch a tent in a field outside Cannes rather than check in at the Carlton. (The worst offenders, Bocca maintained, were Scots and Germans, 'thumbing lifts with propitiating leers, long expanses of hairy leg between short shorts or kilts and dirty tennis shoes'.)⁷⁸

Peter Wildeblood provided a sketch in 1951 of the 'train-loads and plane-loads' of 'ordinary' Britons vacationing on the Cote d'Azur. Kings and millionaires now rubbed shoulders with 'blameless mothers from Balham' bursting out of their bikinis and 'quiet City typists parade on the Croisette in outfits that would stop the traffic on Ludgate-hill'. Indeed Wildeblood was convinced that the balmy sunshine was transforming traditional British sartorial caution. The reporter struck up a conversation in the lobby of the Carlton in Cannes with a businessman from Leeds who, 'in a black linen chemise emblazoned with starfish, stretched out a sandalled leg luxuriously'. 'At that moment', Wildeblood casually noted, 'King Farouk passed by'.⁷⁹ It wasn't just in hotel lobbies that holidaymakers and monarchs converged. In 1951 the yacht carrying Farouk and Narriman to their honeymoon on Capri was initially unable to dock, when its berth on the island's marina was snatched by a tourist pleasure steamer carrying day trippers from Naples.⁸⁰

For those hostile to commercialized mass tourism, there seemed to be an implication that Farouk was not simply a witness to but was an active agent in the vulgarization of once rarefied and exclusive Mediterranean travel. In particular, the debasement of Capri by popular tourism was explicitly attributed to Farouk's apparently coarsening presence. In 1959, Nicholas Blake (the pseudonym of writer Cecil Day-Lewis) published the eleventh mystery novel to feature poet and amateur detective Nigel Strangeways. Strangeways is on a cruise ship, travelling around the Aegean, when he encounters the mysterious widow Melissa Blaydon. At first meeting, Blaydon appears vacuous and artificial, her conversation consisting largely of 'name dropping' and the enumerating of all 'the places she had lived in and visited'. She knew Cannes well, found the shops of Rome 'absolute heaven' and was familiar with Greece, at least in regard to its status as 'the birthplace of the Onassis brothers'. However, she had less positive things to say about the Bay of Naples. 'Capri', in her estimation, 'had been ruined since Farouk went there'.[81]

Five years previously, S.P.B and Gillian Mais, an upper-middle-class British married couple, had published a decidedly grumpy account of their 1951 summer excursion to Italy. Possibly setting themselves up for disappointment and distress, they had made the rash decision to visit 'colourful and exotic' Capri in August, a time when, as they irritably conceded, the island was 'much too crowded and much too hot'. Mr. Mais disparaged the 'milling crowds' who thronged the piazza in Capri as reminiscent of those 'who jostle one another up and down the pier at Southend or on the front at Brighton', and compared the shoddy goods sold on its souvenir stalls with those to be found in Margate or Blackpool. Mais reserved particular contempt for the restaurant-cum-bathing pool on Capri owned by Gracie Fields, where Farouk, shortly before the Mais' visit, had spent some of his honeymoon: 'Gracie Fields, as we all know, comes from Rochdale. The crowd that I saw bore a strong resemblance to the crowds from Rochdale who enjoy their wakes [week holiday] at Blackpool'. In one of Capri's 'squalid' shops, Mais was offered 'an oil painting of an octopus done by an artist who had just sold a similar picture to the then King Farouk of Egypt'.[82]

The analogies to popular British seaside resorts also coloured newspaper descriptions of the deposed king's first days and weeks in exile, spent on Capri. Farouk, relaxing at Gracie Fields' Song of the Seas restaurant, was described as sitting 'shirtless in old grey flannel slacks on Capri's version of Brighton beach… eating chocolate ice-cream and sucking pop through a straw'. The ex-king, Narriman and his three daughters disported themselves 'almost as trippers'.[83] Society columnist Eve Perrick reported a comment overheard in an upscale London restaurant that what was most deplorable about Farouk's cavorting on the Tyrrhenian island in the high summer of 1952 was his failure to recognize 'how massively unsmart Capri is at this time of the year'. Given that Farouk's precipitate flight from Egypt had obviously left him with little opportunity to choose the timing of his visit to Capri, one can only assume the remark was made in jest.[84] However, the condescending quip was clearly testimony to how far Farouk had come to be identified with the lowbrow, not to say boorish, predilections of the postwar tourist.

Indeed this association of Farouk with a modern, democratic, conception of leisure and travel led to him becoming a tourist attraction in his own right. Gordon Cooper's *A Fortnight around the Bay of Naples*, published in 1955, was

**Figure 7** Farouk and Narriman on Capri, August 1952 (Photo 12/Universal Images via Getty Images).

one of a series of guidebooks for British vacationers on relatively modest budgets (hence its recommendation to its readers to avoid luxury hotels dominated by American visitors). It was largely scathing about Capri, conceding that it was delightful if one could get away from the crowds, but that a short visit as part of a conducted excursion was likely to leave the unbecoming impression of 'a cheap, flamboyant Blackpool'. Gracie Fields' restaurant and swimming pool was deemed underwhelming and overpriced. However, as Cooper grudgingly acknowledged, 'of course, you don't go there so much to bathe as to mingle with film stars and, possibly, ex-King Farouk'.[85]

Holidaymakers who spotted Farouk and Narriman often endeavoured to take a photograph, although this led to several well-publicized incidents in which the king (or, more generally, one of the fearsome Albanian bodyguards who accompanied him) either confiscated the unfortunate tourist's camera or ripped out the offending spool of film.[86] More fortunate was Earl Wilson, a theatre-critic-turned-amateur-photographer who deliberately travelled to Deauville to photograph Farouk. Wilson approached Farouk in a hotel lobby and succeeded in having him pose for a photograph by interesting the king in the instant printing function the camera (a polaroid pathfinder) possessed. Farouk was apparently highly accommodating, and even made suggestions of where he should stand for best effect.[87] Farouk's value as a tourist attraction did not go unnoticed by the more inventive and entrepreneurial inhabitants of the resorts he frequented. A feature on Farouk's 1952 stay in Capri concluded that the ex-king was 'just another exploitable asset' for the island's hoteliers, souvenir sellers and tour guides. Within days of the ex-monarch moving into his suite in the Eden-Paradiso, someone had crudely carved, into a plastered wall below the hotel, an arrow pointing upwards, accompanied by the appellation 'To Faruk, 3 min[utes]'.[88]

In his first weeks in exile on Capri in 1952 *Picture Post* had speculated that Farouk's absence from Egypt might be short-lived. It attributed his expressed desire to reside in Italy to the fact that Rome was 'only five hours flying time from Cairo' and a nation like Egypt which 'can stage-manage a 48-hour coup d'etat this year, might one day stage-manage a 24-hour one'.[89] In fact when Farouk died in 1965, the nationalist regime which had overthrown him was still definitely in power, and Egypt's former king had become a forlorn, if not altogether tragic figure, still living a life of luxury, but now prematurely aged and surrounded by a shrinking coterie of nonentities, call girls and hangers-on. Farouk had spent his last years in the cafes and nightclubs of the Via Veneto, but their glamour and notoriety had also faded by the early 1960s. The demise of Rome's *dolce vita* had been less a consequence of Fellini's blistering cinematic critique of its narcissistic amorality and more a product of the fact that the beautiful and the shameless had found alternative playgrounds, their place taken by middle-aged tourists content with decidedly ersatz versions of the debauched pleasure-seeking that had characterized the Via Veneto in the 1950s. One observer concluded that the Via Veneto now looked like an inland version of a cheap seaside resort.[90] To the end of his life, Farouk continued to be comprehended through the (nominally contradictory) discourses of privileged leisure and tawdry mass tourism. By contrast, there was little appetite to address his death in terms of the despondent homilies of exile, futility and loss. Farouk's Capri, Cannes and Rome could hardly be compared to the melancholy settings of Ovid's Tomis or Bonaparte's St. Helena.

Without sounding unduly callous, any sympathy for the deposed king was inevitably compromised by the fact that, to the very end of his life, he continued to live a life of self-indulgent excess. In the aftermath of his fatal collapse in the Ile de France restaurant in Rome on the night of 17 March 1965, outlandish stories of Farouk's last hours rapidly circulated. He had enjoyed a hearty meal of a dozen oysters, a lobster Thermidor, a double portion of roast lamb with fried potatoes and a large helping of trifle. Having completed his meal, he had slumped in his chair, just after lighting an enormous cigar. He was in the company of his new girlfriend, a hairdresser, Annamaria Gatti. Or, other reports insisted, he was with his other new amour, movie starlet Sonia Romanoff, whom he had recently presented with a mink stole. The exact details remained a matter of speculation and contestation.[91] However, what all the stories about Farouk's death alluded to were the self-evident extravagance of his appetites: for conspicuous consumption, for food, for women. It is to this preoccupation with excess in representations of Farouk (and what it might tell about the changing priorities of British culture between the 1930s and 1960s) that we now turn.

5

# Excess

The opening, if somewhat contrived, was undoubtedly dramatic. A Captain of the Guard broke the heavy red seals on the door to the Koubbeh Palace, and ushered in the select group of reporters who had been granted an opportunity to look around Farouk's winter residence, abandoned only a few weeks previously, in the wake of the king's flight into exile. Among the visitors were Walter Farr of the *Daily Mail* and Alan Whicker of the *Daily Mirror*, who avidly detailed for their readers back in Britain both the fabulous wealth and the ostentatious kitsch they encountered in the 250-room palace. The highlight of their tour was unquestionably the Royal Treasury, entered through four-inch-thick steel doors, supplemented by an advanced security system 'emitting invisible rays'. Whicker was informed that Farouk had taken both the keys and combinations for his myriad safes into exile, and it had only been possible to open them after weeks of painstaking effort by 'an Armenian cracksman'. A twelve-foot-high safe contained drawers of neatly arranged bank notes, coins and gold medals, while there were crates of Sevres dinner services, diamond-studded cocktail glasses and scores of boxes of 'bejewelled trinkets'. Whicker, finding that conveying this superabundance of treasure was impossible to confine to a single analogy, offered two: Farouk's Treasury simultaneously recalled a 'floodlit, soft-carpeted Aladdin's cave' and the interior of 'a Bond Street jewellers'.[1]

Farouk's private rooms in the Koubbeh offered up even more evidence of the former king's luxurious lifestyle, but also testified to the essentially dissolute and sullied nature of his profligacy. His wardrobes heaved with elaborate uniforms and 2,000 silk shirts. His closet drawers yielded up 1,500 silk ties and hundreds of bottles of perfume. On Farouk's study desk, Walter Farr counted fourteen paper knives, each with a diamond-studded handle, and, on opening its drawers, found them stuffed with countless gold fountain pens. However, it was Farouk's ostensibly less financially valuable personal effects (items that one of the guides dismissed as 'utterly useless' or 'simply disgusting') that Farr's report chose to dwell on. He was shown a large collection of keys to flats and hotels in Cairo, many of them with a label bearing a woman's name. There were cupboards full of what a guide identified as Farouk's 'love charms', an aphrodisiac cornucopia of 'weird medicaments, powders and potions'. The king's 'gambling room' contained not merely solid silver roulette wheels and diamond-encrusted dice but 400 packs of gilt-edged playing cards, every single card bearing an image on the reverse of a semi-clothed pin-up girl. In one of his six luxury bathrooms, towel rails took the form of 'modeled girls' legs standing out from the wall', and in several apartment rooms were 'hundreds of magic-lantern devices showing slides of bathing beauties'. Finally, there was a cabinet containing a copious number of glasses in 'the shape of dancing girls'.[2]

What was shown to visitors to the Koubbeh palace in August 1952 therefore registered the apparent interdependence of the luxurious and the licentious, the lush and the lascivious. Juxtaposing the plush and the priapic, press coverage of the opening of Farouk's private rooms emphasized the intrinsic links between his colossal wealth and his concupiscent appetites. This is not to say that narratives of Farouk's propensity for overindulgence necessarily required the extravagantly rococo settings of his royal palaces. They could just as easily be articulated in the terms of a flabby, dissipated profligate, cavorting with starlets on beaches and call girls in nightclubs, gambling huge sums in casinos, and devouring meals of Brobdingnagian proportions in exclusive restaurants. However, the association of Farouk with a culture of excess was not merely a reflection of the king's own personality and proclivities. Stories about Farouk's high-living dramatized developments in metropolitan Britain, notably the emergence of new sexual standards and anxiety over the impact of increased affluence. It ultimately proved impossible to attribute Farouk's outrageous lifestyle exclusively to the idiosyncratic traits of the fantasized 'oriental potentate', who (if he existed at all) was extant at a distinct remove from the material and moral universe of ordinary Britons. Rather than being interpreted through the discourses of orientalism, Farouk's pleasure-seeking was, in part, comprehended in Britain through a filter created by the puritanical and egalitarian imperatives of post-imperial Arab nationalists. Far from a figure confined to a rarefied and singular world of wealth, exoticism, fame and privilege, Farouk's amorous escapades were discerned through changing attitudes to sexuality among the wider public in Britain which emerged during the 1940s. Similarly, his corpulent body and susceptibility to kleptomania dramatized what many Britons saw as the moral and social pitfalls of increased material prosperity in the 1950s.

# I

The Koubbeh was only one of a number of lavishly appointed royal residences in Farouk's Egypt. It served primarily as Farouk's private lodgings in Cairo, his official residence in the city being the even grander Abdin palace, which, while it was furnished to accommodate the king and his family, was primarily used to host public ceremonies, formal banquets and official receptions. The upkeep of Abdin's 500 rooms strained even the three quarters of a million pounds allocated to the palace each year by the Egyptian Ministry of Public Works. Sumptuous carpets, alabaster statues, old master paintings mounted with solid gold frames, enamelled clocks, crystal bannisters, a wine store with bottles going back to the Napoleonic era, a purpose-built theatre, a 27-room library containing 150,000 rare volumes and a private military museum: all of these were to be found within the walls of the palace that had been built – in a dazzling mishmash of *belle époque* and arabesque styles – by the Khedive Ismail in the 1860s. The Abdin's grounds were home to the royal garage, which housed around 200 vehicles, mostly Cadillacs, but also Farouk's distinctive Bentleys and Rolls-Royces, which were always coloured red, so that the notoriously rubber-burning monarch could be assured of not being pulled over by the Cairo police. One large Cadillac was furnished with two beds, a cupboard, a radio communication system inspired by Hollywood police movies and an air-conditioning unit. This car was regularly accompanied by a smaller vehicle, which served as a mobile kitchen. In Alexandria, Farouk's official summer residence was the Ras-el-Tin, with its opulent throne room and gardens planted with rare flowers specially imported from Holland. However, Farouk's sojourns in Alexandria were normally spent at his 'fun palace', the Montazah, a five-storey-high palazzo with its distinctive Tuscan bell-tower and grounds containing a herd of a hundred gazelles and a variety of follies, including a Palladian temple and copies of London Bridge and a Nantucket lighthouse. Farouk's four major palaces were supplemented by several smaller residences and rest-houses. Most notorious among the latter was the Auberge des Pyramides, which Farouk commissioned himself in 1942 to serve as a private night-club and cabaret outside Cairo, and which was gaudily furnished with marble and alabaster in the pharaonic style.[3]

Farouk's palaces disclosed a level of material opulence that was undoubtedly mindboggling. While most of the palaces were the property of the Egyptian state, and not the monarch in his personal capacity, these sybaritic pleasure domes were clearly fitting abodes for a man whose personal fortune at the time of his deposition was calculated at around $50 million.[4] In what particular ways, though, did Britons make sense of Farouk's colossal accumulation of treasures and luxuries? What were their other reference points when they encountered this world of extraordinary extravagance in the detailed accounts of Farouk's possessions and lifestyle in newspapers, illustrated magazines and newsreels? An appreciation of contexts and contingencies is obviously indispensable in answering such questions. Take, for example, British press coverage of Farouk's two weddings. When the king married Farida in 1938, newspaper reports brimmed with effusive descriptions of the bride's trousseau of forty-five silver lace and satin gowns (the products of several venerated Parisian ateliers), the twelve-foot-high wedding cake in the shape of a Palladian rotunda, the three-strand diamond necklace Farouk presented to his new queen, the protracted fireworks displays over the Nile, the huge flower parade and the hundred tonnes of lamb donated by the king that was barbecued to feed 100,000 of Cairo's poor. Awe at the scale of the wedding celebrations was accompanied by a positive portrayal of the glamorous young couple as an embodiment of the promise of a new reign, a symbol of Egypt's emergence (under continued British tutelage) as a modern, prosperous independent nation.[5]

Coverage of the celebrations accompanying Farouk's wedding to his second wife, Narriman, in 1951 was equally enthralled, offering details of the bride's diamond-studded gown (and shoes), the 4,000 soldiers who composed her guard of honour and the magnificently bejewelled and gorgeously uniformed guests at the reception.[6] However, by this point, the propitious ambience of Farouk's first years on the throne was a distant memory, and his extravagance was no longer validated as a requirement of maintaining royal status and prestige, but was instead attributed to the king's personal proclivities. In 1938 the press had respected the young couple's privacy during their brief honeymoon.[7] By contrast, in 1951, detailed daily intelligences of Farouk and Narriman's outrageously lavish four-month European honeymoon were provided, cataloguing the king's gifts to his bride of priceless jewels and *haute couture*, the fleet of Rolls-Royces that conveyed the couple from their luxury yacht to their luxury hotel suites and (a feature that was particularly appealing for the illustrated press and newsreels) the fact that all sixty members of the honeymoon party sported identical uniforms composed of blue blazers, white trousers or skirts and yachting caps.[8] Even if the wedding had necessitated and permitted appropriate pomp and pageantry, the subsequent honeymoon appeared to merely reinforce Farouk's reputation for private profligacy.

That said, it would be unwise to assume that we have the ability to definitively establish how these representations of Farouk's wealth and extravagance were received by those who consumed them. Responses most likely ranged across a broad spectrum – all the way from indignation to indulgence, or even on to indifference. Some inevitably found Farouk's wealth obscene, given he ruled a nation in which millions of his subjects lived in acute poverty. During the war, the poet Keith Douglas, who possessed an instinctive loathing for Farouk, wrote of a half-blind female pauper he observed in Egypt, 'her beauty, succumbing in a cloud/of disease, disease, apathy, My God/the king of this country must be proud'.[9] However, others might have been less judgmental, and even more forbearing. That kings got to live in sumptuous palaces and travel in luxury yachts was not an affront: it was merely a self-evident fact of life. An innovative study of the apparently incongruous relationship between widespread resentment of social inequality and popular support for the British royal family in the twentieth century pointedly reminds us that people who were 'neither wealthy, nor privileged, nor leisured' have 'identified with, and enthusiastically supported' a monarchy that appeared to embody all three of these qualities. The explanation for this apparent inconsistency in popular attitudes is that royalty was entitled to the trappings of wealth and privilege as compensation for being obliged to maintain an official life of rigid protocol, stultifying repetitious ceremonial and tediously irksome public appearances.[10] Clearly this model, which carries conviction in regard to ordinary Britons' perception of their own monarchy, has limited application in the case of Farouk. With the exception of the opening months of his reign, reporting on Farouk's official (as opposed to personal) life would have provided the British public with meagre evidence of any commitment to those nostrums of duty and service which had become so central to contemporary understandings of the House of Windsor. Farouk saw nothing contractual or compensatory about his gilded life. For him, the accumulation – and enjoyment – of treasures and luxuries was implicitly accepted as a (birth)right.

Even if he had been more diligent and conscientious in his public duties, Farouk's staggering fortune and untempered high-living clearly put him in a different league to his contemporaries among the European monarchs. Is it possible, then, that he might have been more likely to be compared to his peers in the Arab and Islamic worlds, a cluster of latter-day 'oriental potentates', who possessed vast fortunes and lived lives of exuberant panache? An obvious pairing might be with another Middle Eastern monarch who, like Farouk, was labelled a 'playboy'. Hussein bin Talal, king of Jordan from 1952, had attracted the attention of the British press from his days as a cadet at Sandhurst, during which time he was regularly spotted speeding off in his Lincoln convertible at the weekends, to sample London's high life in the company of a variety of socialites and debutantes. In the mid-1950s, Hussein enhanced his reputation as a charismatic playboy, displaying a penchant for exclusive (and often dangerous) sports such as aerobatics and water-skiing, and (after his first marriage collapsed in 1957) being regularly photographed in the company of glamorous models and actresses. The British press was no less captivated by Jordan's young monarch when, in 1961, he appeared to put an end to his bachelor lifestyle by marrying a nineteen-year-old English clerk, Toni Gardner.[11] However, Hussein differed from Farouk in several respects. It was not merely that his youth (he was fifteen years younger than Farouk) and debonair good looks gave him a romantic aura which the balding and bloated Farouk of the 1950s clearly lacked. More critically, as he disclosed in his memoirs, Hussein appreciated the vital importance of exercising 'the self-discipline I would need to keep my throne', aware that ostentatious displays of frivolous high living by their dynastic rulers did not go down well among the Arab masses. 'I had', he declared, 'seen enough of Europe… to know that its playgrounds were filled with ex-kings, some of whom had lost their thrones because they did not realize that the duties of the monarch are all-embracing'. The Jordanian monarch's aspiration not to become 'a permanent member of their swimming parties in the South of France' was undoubtedly reinforced by the unfortunate precedent of Farouk's failure to publicly conceal, let alone curtail, his appetites.[12]

Those familiar with the tabloid preoccupation in the 1970s with 'sexy sheikhs' and their wild-spending ways among the gaming tables and escort agencies of Mayfair might assume that the rulers of the oil-rich Gulf states offer the most obvious parallel to Egypt's debauched monarch.[13] In fact, during the 1950s, the British public were only just becoming aware of the astounding wealth of the kings and princes of Saudi Arabia, Kuwait, Qatar and Bahrain. In 1951, as the crisis initiated by Iran's attempt to wrest control over its oilfield from British control intensified, one newspaper still felt obliged to draw its readers' attention to the fact that petroleum could also be resourced from Saudi Arabia. 'Not all the oil in the Middle East', it averred, 'is in Persia'.[14] In 1953 a short-lived confrontation between Britain and Saudi Arabia, arising from the latter's territorial dispute with Oman over the Buraimi oasis, led to increased press interest in the Saudi ruler Ibn Saud, further promoted by the venerable monarch's death later that year. A profile in the *Daily Mirror* presented Ibn Saud as a fusion of old-style desert chieftain and multi-millionaire spendthrift, surrounded by 'camels and cadillacs, eunuchs and refrigerators', and living in a 'forty room harem' equipped with 'short-wave radio'. At the time of his death, the British press calculated that his earnings from Saudi oil extraction were in the region of £30 million but were even more impressed by the king's convoluted – and polygamous – marital history, encompassing his 200 wives and 64 male children.[15] In the same year, the rapidly swelling fortunes of the Gulf sheikhs, 'floating in oil royalty cheques', were noted by *Daily Mail* correspondent Noel Monks, who provided details of six 'Arabian Nights palaces' being built across the Gulf states, for a total cost of £10 million. Each one apparently contained 'air-conditioned harems, platinum and gold fittings and expensive furniture flown from Europe'.[16] However, in the 1950s British imaginary, the oil sheikhs were rarely conflated with Farouk. They appeared remote and mysterious, and lacked the immediate recognition and familiarity that surrounded Egypt's ruler. Moreover, for all their wealth (and wives), the Gulf rulers retained a stern and austere puritanism that set them apart from the frolicking Farouk. British readers were informed in 1952 that the sheikh of Kuwait had deemed posters featuring the Venus de Milo 'indecent' and banned them.[17] They could be confident, though, that such public declarations of war against the sensual and the voluptuous were unlikely to receive much sympathy from Egypt's 'king of parties'.

Rulers in the Muslim world beyond the Middle East might have provided more substantial comparisons with Farouk. The princes of the Indian subcontinent, with their prodigiously ornate palaces, and proclivity for dazzling ceremonial, colourful dress and iridescent jewels, were prominent in British imperial iconography during the interwar years. Moreover, those maharajahs who spent extended time in Britain, whether cheering on their horses at race meetings or carousing in Mayfair, featured regularly in the society pages and gossip columns of British newspapers. In the late 1930s, the Tenth Nizam of Hyderabad was widely credited with being the wealthiest man alive, a generous benefactor to his subjects, but also a prince who used a 185-carat diamond as a paperweight.[18] However, the termination of the Raj in 1947 not merely seriously reduced the political and pecuniary power of the Indian princes. It also made them less visible – and frankly less noteworthy – to British audiences. It was to be a *non-territorial* South Asian potentate whose name recognition between the 1930s and 1950s bore comparison with Farouk's.

Sir Sultan Mahomed Shah, the forty-eighth Imam of the Nizari Ismailis, was much better known as the third holder of the honorary title of Aga Khan. The majority of the British public were – understandably – probably a little hazy in regard to the precise details of the Aga Khan's complex provenance and contemporary status. One magazine profile contrasted the Aga Khan's background, 'tinged with the Eastern Romance of The Thousand and One Nights' with his current life in his modern villa in Cannes, and his regular appearances 'playing golf at Deauville or Le Touquet'.[19] Born in Karachi in 1877, the Aga Khan possessed both Fatimid and Qajar ancestry, while his professed descent from the Prophet made him the global leader of a branch of Shia Islam. While he became an important protagonist in Anglo-Indian politics in the first three decades of the twentieth century, he led a decidedly peripatetic life, frequently travelling across Africa and Asia to receive the homage (and to seek improvements in the welfare) of the Ismaili community, before returning to his residences in Switzerland and France. Nevertheless, his Eton and Cambridge education produced a sentimental attachment to Britain, and his record-breaking run of five triumphs – his jockeys wearing his distinctive green-and-chocolate-hooped livery – at the Derby made him a household name by the late 1930s.[20]

More specifically, the Aga Khan became a byword for sensational wealth. At his 1937, 1946 and 1954 jubilees, his Ismaili followers demonstrated their appreciation by weighing their Imam in, respectively, gold, diamonds and platinum, in ceremonies widely reported in the press and in Pathe newsreels. The 1946 jubilee celebrations took place in front of a crowd of 100,000, and the value of the diamonds in the counterweight to the Aga Khan's 234 pounds was reputed to be in excess of three million dollars. Such overt displays of wealth must have seemed almost unreal to British audiences, ground down by rationing and shortages.[21] Media coverage, especially the gossip column inches devoted to his colourful personal life, notably his four marriages (including one to a Parisian dressmaker and another to a former Miss France) presented the Aga Khan as a likeable *bon viveur*, a unpuritanical connoisseur of fine food and charming ladies' man.[22] However, it was also agreed that he was clearly able to combine a regular presence in the winner's enclosures at Epsom and Newmarket with a unqualified commitment to international welfare and social reform (including a term as president of the League of Nations), and a dignified contribution (confirmed by his elevation to the Privy Council) to Britain's diplomatic relations with the Muslim world. Within the Foreign Office, it is quite clear that British diplomats heartily longed for Farouk to be less like himself, and more like the Aga Khan.[23]

The Aga Khan had been a regular visitor to Cairo from the days when Lord Cromer was still at the Residency, and he was a close acquaintance of both Farouk's father, King Fuad, and several prominent figures in Egyptian and court circles. The Aga Khan provided a judicious, not to say sympathetic, portrait of Farouk (whom he first met as an adult on a visit to Egypt in 1945) in his 1954 autobiography. The Aga Khan believed that the king suffered from an inferiority complex, largely because the British compounded the emotional deprivation he suffered at the hands of his parents by failing to allow him to complete his education, and restricting his social world to a small coterie of 'ill-educated flatterers'. He also commended Farouk for his piety (encapsulated in his aversion to alcohol) and his patriotic pride. In the Aga Khan's opinion, Farouk was 'an Egyptian from the crown of his head to the soles of his feet, resenting hotly any suggestion that Egypt has been inferior to any country or people in the world'. Such positive valuation of Farouk was rare by this point. Mindful of his dramatically increasing girth, most observers tended to take the king's measure horizontally, rather than vertically. Indeed, even the Aga Khan was unwilling to ignore Farouk's all-too-obvious defects: the gambling, 'the long, aimless hours wasted in seeking distraction in cabarets and night clubs', his life of 'sad and purposeless vacuity'. The Aga Khan met Farouk again in Deauville in 1951, when he noted the king's growing fatalism, which, he insisted, did not augur well for the future of his throne.[24] However, empathy and understanding did not equate to affinity, and the Aga Khan did little to dispel a dominant understanding among the British public that Farouk and himself offered very different versions of wealth and dynastic power.

## II

In fact it was the Aga Khan's son, Ali Salman, popularly known as Aly Khan, who found himself more regularly – and feasibly – compared to Farouk. A decade older than Farouk, Aly was a notorious man-about-town, whose rakish lifestyle was already well known within the British social establishment in the 1930s, a decade in which he pursued affairs with such high-profile lovers as the Duchess of Argyll and Thelma Furness (who was simultaneously involved with the Prince of Wales) and was named as a co-respondent in the 1935 divorce suit between Loel and Joan Guinness. Aly went on to marry Joan in 1937 and his reputation appeared to have rallied as a result of an efficacious record as both a soldier and a military intelligence officer during both the North African campaign and the Allied liberation of southern France.[25] However, in 1943 the Foreign Office intercepted a letter sent by Joan Aly Khan to her father-in-law, the Aga Khan, which disclosed difficulties in her marriage, including Aly's continued womanizing. Fearing the impact on Muslim opinion if the contents of the letter became public, the letter was passed to Lampson in Cairo, who informed Joan that, if she still felt the need to say anything to the Aga Khan, he would allow her to use the embassy's enciphered telegram service.[26]

After 1945 (in a striking parallel to Farouk) Aly Khan's reputation as a millionaire playboy and latter-day Casanova was no longer contained within the exclusive domain of the social and political establishment. Newsreels and newspapers reported on Aly's exploits as a 'gentleman jockey' (riding his own horses to victory), his predilection for expensive sports cars, the luxury fittings of his private aircraft and the fact that he always appeared to be in the company of the most beautiful, glamorous and well-connected women of the day, most notably Pamela Churchill. While press coverage often adopted the language of euphemism, it was clear that Aly, while undoubtedly charming and generous, was a womanizer of the most blatant type. In 1948 he began a highly publicized affair with Hollywood star Rita Hayworth, despite the fact both of them were still married to other people. Once they were free, in May 1949, Aly and Hayworth married, in a grandiose celebration on the French Riviera, during which guests enjoyed 600 bottles of champagne, 40 lobsters and 50 pounds of caviar, a feast that even Aly's father regarded as both excessive and gauche. Inevitably, given that Aly Khan might well have deserved his reputation as the most promiscuous man in Europe, the marriage collapsed (in the full glare of the media spotlight) within a matter of months.[27]

The worlds of Aly Khan and Farouk certainly overlapped. Deauville, the playground of wealthy princes, was a popular destination for both men, and Farouk's infamous sojourn at the French resort in 1950 incorporated a lavish party that Aly and Hayworth also attended.[28] However, it was to be in the world of popular entertainment that the most lasting conjunction of Aly and Farouk was to be realized. In 1955, Noel Coward, finding that postwar British audiences had less appetite than their pre-1939 predecessors for his drawing-room comedies, looked for new ways to support his taste for the finer things in life. The Master accepted the offer to perform a one-man, twice-nightly, cabaret show at the Desert Inn, Las Vegas. The ultimate success of this enterprise (further boosted by the LP live recording made of Coward's routine) was definitely not predetermined. Coward's elevated, not to say effete, style seemed poorly suited to audiences that had come to Vegas largely to gamble, and were generally content with undemanding singing and comedy acts such as Abbe Lane and Red Skelton. Coward's response was to emphasize the risqué and contemporary aspects of his act, by reworking both his own material and the songs of other composers.[29] The lyrics to Cole Porter's 'Let's Do It' were almost completely rewritten, in order to include a series of topical stanzas featuring, among others, Liberace and Ernest

Hemingway. Coward's innuendo-saturated rendition also yoked together two other prominent personalities:

> Monkeys, every time you look do it
> Aly Khan and King Farouk do it
> Let's do it
> Let's fall in love[30]

Such assertions of the essential commonality between two womanizing princely playboys were not allowed to go uncontested. Celebrity hostess Elsa Maxwell unfavourably contrasted Aly Khan's 'romantic allure', 'magnetism' and 'animal vitality' with Farouk, 'one of the most repulsive creatures God ever created'. Aly Khan, for all his coquetries, was a gentleman, 'a word that will never be applied to ex-King Farouk… the most horrid specimen of so-called royalty of the last century'.[31]

What Aly Khan and Farouk did have in common was that their notoriety was invested with highly particularized spatial associations. Press coverage of Aly's relationship with Rita Hayworth might have been expected, even if insidiously, to have traded in the discourses of racial fear and miscegenation. Instead, the media chose to reference their affair in terms of its setting in the 'sinful' Mediterranean (or more specifically, the Riviera). Here was an imagined space where moral laxity went apparently unchecked, a conviction seemingly confirmed by the fact that the Inner Sea was also to serve as a backdrop for the equally scandalous affair between Ingrid Bergman and Roberto Rossellini, which became public knowledge in the winter of 1949–1950.[32] As with his fellow Muslim Farouk, situating sexual scandal in a Mediterranean context ensured that understandings of Aly Khan's sexual adventures were to substitute place for race. The uneven application of orientalist tropes to Farouk has been noted previously in this book. In regard to responses to his sexual exploits, there was only limited resort to myths of oriental potentates and their harems or the template of the light-skinned woman in the clutches of a ruthless desert tyrant, both of which had been alive and well as recently as the 1920s, if the popularity of Rudolph Valentino's performance in *The Sheik* and the sentiments expressed during the notorious trial of Marguerite Alibert are anything to go by.[33] Nor, for that matter, was Farouk aligned with more contemporary genres of racialized sexual anxiety which dramatized both the crumbling of imperial hierarchies abroad (revealed in the Seretse Khama case) and the impact of Commonwealth immigration on metropolitan Britain (in the moral panics surrounding mixed-race children).[34]

The reason for this may be that, as a consequence of the loosened sexuality promoted by the Second World War, it became increasingly difficult to maintain the conceit of the virtuous and self-disciplined Briton sustaining their authority over the capricious oriental, enslaved by his unruly passions and lusts. Yasmin Khan has drawn attention to how nationalists in the Indian subcontinent were able to contest British notions of racial superiority by drawing attention to the errant sexual behaviour of married memsahibs, whose husbands were away at the front.[35] Cairo had long enjoyed a reputation for debauchery among the British and Egyptian elites, but the specific contexts of wartime further eroded the proprieties of self-denial and sexual continence. For Egypt's temporary wartime population of diplomats, soldiers and imperial administrators, both the loneliness created by distance from family and home (exacerbated by apparently limitless opportunity and temptation) and the ever-present possibility of physical annihilation critically destabilized codes of imperial virtue.[36]

In the overheated environment of sexual immoderation which characterized wartime Cairo, Lampson was not merely preoccupied with growing evidence that Farouk was pursuing a number of extramarital affairs. The ambassador was equally obliged to attempt to rein in some of the more recklessly amorous members of Cairo's British elite. For almost two years Lampson fretted over the possibility that the portrait painter Simon Elwes was having an affair with Queen Farida.[37] In 1942 he personally admonished Anne Rendel, the daughter of a prominent British diplomat, for her scandalous behaviour.[38] In 1943, Lampson was obliged to ship the Duke of Roxburghe out of Egypt, after 'Bobo' had become romantically involved with a South African female auxiliary whose husband was a POW in Germany.[39] The most notorious affair to come to Lampson's door was the adulterous relationship between Walter Monckton, the director of British propaganda in the Middle East, and 'Pistol Mary' Newall, the flamboyant and curvaceous head of the female Motorised Transport Corps.[40] Given the regularity of these breakdowns in imperial discipline, it would have required a hypocrisy of monumental proportions to have singled out Farouk's infidelities as a consequence of his status as a degraded colonial 'other'.[41]

How then were Farouk's sexual adventures comprehended? During the war years, the answer to this question largely requires attention to those who encountered him, or knew of him, within the military and political infrastructure the British had assembled in Egypt. Newspaper readers back in Britain presumably continued to see him as they had before 1939, as a happily married man with a glamorous wife and young daughter to whom he was devoted. However, for those in the know, Farouk seemed to have embraced the war years as an opportunity to embark on a career of shameless philandering that was to persist to his dying day. After his humiliating confrontation with Lampson at the Abdin palace in February 1942 had exposed the reality of his limited authority in a state of which he was nominally the head, the king sought consolation in the pleasures of the flesh. Farouk's first significant extramarital affair was with Princess Fatma Toussoun, who was his cousin by marriage. In November 1942, Lampson's diary recorded the rumour that Farouk had got Toussoun 'in the family way', and gleefully passed it on to the foreign secretary.[42] Toussoun was the first of a succession of 'official mistresses' during the war years, followed by the Alexandrian Jewish divorcee Irene Najjar and the British cipher clerk Barbara Skelton. These women were supplemented by various chorus girls, belly dancers and prostitutes procured from the Cairo nightclubs and tonier brothels by his devoted aide Antonio Pulli, the latter credited by Lampson with expanding the King's amatory repertoire.[43] Farouk's newfound reputation as 'king of the night' was common knowledge among the British establishment in Cairo, and – judging from the ribald songs they sung about him – among ordinary British troops stationed in Egypt.[44]

Some wartime stories about Farouk's libertine proclivities suggested the king possessed a strong sense of both male sexual entitlement and royal prerogative. As a consequence, he became notorious for his blatant propositioning, carried out with little regard to the feelings, or even status, of the women he attempted to seduce. He was alleged to have made moves on Princess Ashraf, the sister of his brother-in-law, the Shah of Iran, while Lampson had little doubt that a story relayed to him about Farouk's clumsy attempt to proposition the exiled Princess Irina of Greece in her own bedroom was entirely credible. Lampson also shared with Eden gossip about Farouk's pursuit of an American Red Cross employee identified as 'Miss Winsloe'.[45] Memoirs of both British and American women who worked in the extensive Allied military intelligence apparatus which operated in wartime Cairo suggest that fending off the unsolicited attentions of Egypt's priapic monarch was something of an occupational hazard, especially for young American blondes, who were reputed to be Farouk's favoured victims. British cipher clerk Irene Gurney Orr recalled encountering the 'heavy-lidded' Farouk at the Auberge de Pyramides, where he 'seemed to mentally undress you', and, if a young woman on the dance floor caught his eye, he would 'send his equerry to request that she dance with him'. Laura Tuckerman, an officer for the American OSS, remembered being covetously followed by Farouk around the room at a reception at the US embassy. Her colleague Josephine Britton was obliged to go nightclubbing in the company of virtually the whole OSS Cairo station in the vain hope that their presence might oblige Farouk to desist from constantly asking her to dance with him.[46] Farouk's roving eye became a staple ingredient of the folklore – and subsequent mythology – of wartime Cairo. A popular history of Shepheard's Hotel detailed an incident when Farouk was dining there and noticed an attractive young woman guest. The next day, a palace equerry appeared at the hotel desk and insisted on viewing the register in order to ascertain the identity of the mystery woman. When the hotel's Swiss clerk refused to concede to this act of blatant *lese-majeste*, he was told to pack his bags and was then escorted to the Cairo rail station.[47]

However, stories about Farouk's colourful love life were not exclusively narrated in terms of the insalubrious behaviour of a lubricious sexual marauder. Barbara Skelton, the cipher clerk who became Farouk's lover in 1943, was eager in her memoirs to dispel notions of the king as a debauched satyr. She presented Farouk as endearing rather than sinister. He was not merely charming but attentive and solicitous, treating Skelton with genuine courtesy. Rather than boasting of his sexual conquests, Farouk appeared sentimental and 'incredibly sweet', an almost childlike figure, prone to holding hands and cuddling in the palace screening room, and hosting dressing-gown parties on the roof of his palace. Skelton conceded that her relationship with Farouk was no grand passion, and that he had limited skills as a lover, but she described their relationship in affectionate terms. Far from being a victim of Farouk's unwarranted advances, Skelton presented herself as a willing and active agent in their affair. This should come as no surprise, given Skelton (the daughter of a civil servant who married a Gaiety girl) was something of a femme fatale, who had actively pursued romantic relationships with a number of prominent literary and intellectual figures, as well as being a model for the designer Schiaparelli. In the world of orientalist fantasy, lusty Arab potentates seduced innocent young white women and then imprisoned them in their harems. In Skelton's story, by contrast, Egypt's ruler appeared little more than an accessory to (although, of course, also a beneficiary of) the unfettered sexual standards of metropolitan bohemians, many of whom had gathered in wartime Cairo, and had found the specific contexts of time and place had created a decidedly permissive environment for sexual adventure. Skelton, after all, had already lived an extensive life of sexual experiment and self-discovery, long before she drifted into Farouk's line of vision during an evening out at the Auberge des Pyramides.[48]

By the late 1940s, Farouk's libidinous reputation was no longer confined to military and diplomatic circles in wartime Egypt. The popular press ensured that its readers were kept abreast of the panoply of women Farouk pursued with varying degrees of perseverance and success. While such stories often presented Farouk in an unprepossessing, or even preposterous, light, they were generally congenial and indulgent in tone. They were deficient in the intimate details present in wartime rumours and gossip, and were willing to leave a great deal to the reader's imagination. They certainly lacked the graphic physical details – and prurient emphasis on fetishism and perversity – that became prominent in narratives of Farouk's sexuality which appeared in the years immediately after his death in 1965. Nevertheless, they certainly reflected the more relaxed approach to the subject of sexual knowledge, which came to characterize the British popular press after 1945. Stories about the 'king of the night' were certainly not free from casual sexism, a continued commitment to notions of sexual difference or the objectification of women as sexual playthings. However, they conformed to a new media standard which presented taking pleasure in sex as a natural imperative for both men and women. Sex had also become a critical element in the mass media's creation and promotion of celebrity. If readers might have tired of stories of Farouk's philandering, newspapers attempted to refresh their narratives by shifting focus from Farouk the pursuer to Farouk the pursued. By the mid-1950s, there was no shortage of young aspiring actresses or socialites who took the opportunity of being seen with Farouk as a means to attract media attention, even at the risk of being mocked as 'chubby chasers'. Studies of the British press in the decade immediately after the Second World War have emphasized how newspapers legitimized their increased attention to both sexuality and the private lives of public figures through the simultaneous deployment of two, ostensibly discordant, media strategies: moral censure and titillation.[49] In the case of press coverage of Farouk, the latter was definitely much more in evidence than the former.

While the changing culture of mediatized sexual knowledge in 1940s and 1950s Britain was critical in evaluating how Farouk's carnal appetites were represented and comprehended, it is important to appreciate that the British press was not the sole author of the scripts of personal excess which surrounded him. In particular, media coverage of the public display, and subsequent auction, of the contents of Farouk's palaces in the immediate aftermath of his fall from power projected an image of Farouk that accorded with that being promoted by the Free Officers: Egypt's new republican rulers. The opening of the doors of the Koubbeh palace to journalists in August 1952 was only the first of many opportunities to appreciate the scale of Farouk's colossal accumulation of treasure and to view material evidence of his irrepressible pleasure-seeking, all under the careful surveillance of an army guide, who missed no opportunity to remind visitors of the selfish prodigality of the former monarch. By 1953, the Free Officers had decided to sell Farouk's gargantuan collections of *objets d'art* and personal possessions by public auction. Sothebys was given responsibility for the sale, taking the best part of a year to catalogue all categories, encompassing as they did coins, precious stones, paintings, stamps, snuff-boxes, paperweights, clocks and watches, silver and glass, and a range of Faberge objects. Both Sothebys (no stranger to selling treasures at stratospheric prices) and the British press readily resorted to hyperbole when sharing details of the royal collections, comparing the sale to the legendary auction of the contents of Versailles by the French republic in 1793.[50] There was extensive coverage of the auction itself, which took place at the Koubbeh palace over several weeks in March 1954.

Amidst all of Farouk's lavish possessions, many journalists were particularly intrigued by the 'Secret Museum', a locked and barred room of the palace which had been made into a repository for Farouk's pornography collection, only accessible to the privileged few who bid over £5,000 at the auction. Most press features referred to the contents of the 'Secret Museum' in euphemistic terms, *Picture Post*, for example, contenting itself with a photograph of an Egyptian officer peering through the steel grille installed at the entrance to what was identified as 'Farouk's *most* private and personal collection'.[51] However, speculation inevitably abounded. Some who had availed themselves of the opportunity for a pornographic peek claimed that what lay inside the 'Secret Museum' was decidedly tame, largely composed of badly executed risqué paintings of neo-classical nudes and scores of American pin-up photographs.

An employee of Sothebys, who was required to compose an inventory of Farouk's more esoteric possessions, in his working notes disclosed more details of Farouk's collections of erotic postcards, 'amber phalluses, bronze love scenes, pornographic cocktail glasses, and corkscrews in every sexual shape that the craftsman could devise', in a tone that suggested he was more appalled by Farouk's execrable taste than he was by the former monarch's apparent sexual depravity. The auctioneer found that, in the midst of various studies of erotic coupling rendered in gold, marble, alabaster and ivory, there were several 'cheap plastic nudes with jokes like "Is that Fanny Browne" written across them, and also drinking mugs in the shape of torsos'.[52] This reference to the presence among Farouk's possessions of objects that were reminiscent of the vulgar kitsch to be found in the shops of plebeian British seaside resorts might suggest additional reinforcement of claims made in a previous chapter about the affinity between representations of Farouk and the coarser aspects of British popular culture.

**Figure 8** Farouk's 'Secret Museum' (ZUMA Press Inc./Alamy).

However, undue attention to the 'Secret Museum', while it might have reflected the prurient voyeurism of the British press, was not unwelcome to Egypt's new rulers, keen to discredit both Farouk and the quasi-feudal social system, of which he was the apex. In the years between 1952 and 1954, the Free Officers commissioned a number of uncompromisingly didactic publications in the English medium which were intended to foster the notion that Farouk was a debauched spendthrift. Rashed El-Barawy, a history professor at Cairo University, attempted to justify the 1952 coup to Western audiences by detailing Farouk's unconstitutional acts and by presenting him as the hated symbol of an antiquated and oppressive social order. However, El-Barawy also took time away from a focus on the king's public and political failings to highlight that Farouk's 'personal conduct' had reached 'scandalous proportions'.[53] Major Mahmoud El-Gawhary was tasked with describing Farouk's former palaces in order to expose the monarch's 'unimaginable life of luxury during which he sucked and drained the wealth of the country which the Liberation Movement had at last saved and returned it to the people'. In the Koubbeh palace, according to El-Gawhary, a plethora of 'fearful things', including a collection of whips: 'Nobody knows on whom such contrivances were applied', had been discovered. The ex-king's bedroom, he confidently averred, 'reflects his character':

> This is what is found there: a collection of large size albums containing sexual pictures, trivial post cards and magazine covers... His private cupboard contains a collection of detective stories, playing cards bearing indecent pictures, perfume bottles, anaesthetic ampules and a box containing a large number of injections. Amidst this maze of things Farouk used to retire. One of the strange items found among his collections is a pair of spectacles which, when used, shows the lower part of anything viewed. The ex-king usually wore them when he wanted to eye a lady without letting her notice his glance. This really shows that the owner of such a mélange was a restless, disturbed person.[54]

While British press and newsreel coverage lacked the earnest puritanism and anti-monarchism of Egypt's new rulers, it nevertheless served to ventriloquize the image of Farouk that those who had deposed him sought to convey to the rest of the world. British audiences, astounded by the scale of Farouk's overindulgence revealed by the confiscation of his palaces, were unlikely to have realized that this extravagant exposition of his debauchery had been curated and choreographed by the Free Officers. There is an irony here, given that Britain and Egypt's new military leaders were beginning a drift towards confrontation that would culminate in the 1956 Suez debacle.

## III

The auction of Egypt's royal collections also raised the issue of the dubious provenance of some of Farouk's treasures. In February 1954 one of the trustees of St. Michael's College, Tenbury Wells, contacted the *Birmingham Post* with a story that revealed an unexpected, albeit tentative, connection between Egypt's notorious ex-king and a minor provincial boarding school, known to musical aficionados for its choral tradition, but otherwise a fairly innocuous institution. The school had been founded in the mid-1850s by Frederick Ouseley, a composer and musicologist, but also the son of Britain's ambassador to Persia in 1810–1814. The younger Ouseley inherited from his father a gold-enamelled plate that the latter had received from the Persian government. The plate was housed at the school, but mysteriously disappeared at some point in the opening decade of the twentieth century. However, an eagle-eyed reader had spotted a dish matching the description of the lost heirloom in the catalogue volume pertaining to 'silver and silvergilt, together with some gold' prepared by Sothebys for the auction of Farouk's palace collections. 'We have no idea how he acquired it', declared a dumbfounded member of the school's staff.[55] If no definitive answer to this question was immediately forthcoming, it cannot be denied that Farouk's passion for augmenting his royal and personal collections appeared to amount to kleptomania. Two of his wartime lovers, Irene Guinle and Barbara Skelton, later recalled that wealthy Egyptians who hosted the monarch found it expedient to hide from view their treasured possessions, since the next morning a truck might arrive from the palace, ready to be loaded with any items (which extended to priceless paintings, grand pianos and crystal chandeliers) from their homes that Farouk had taken a fancy to. The king's predatory instincts also extended to removing jewels from the necks and bodices of wealthy women, thanking them for making a gift to the royal collections. Guinle also claimed that Farouk pilfered from her a gold cigarette case that had been given to her by Randolph Churchill, who, in turn, had originally received it as a twenty-first birthday gift from his father, Winston. To Guinle's mind, Farouk's kleptomania complemented his gauche pursuit of women: 'If he wanted something, he went after it, the way he went after me.'[56]

An American who had been showing Farouk a new type of electric razor was flabbergasted when, after asking if he could make a closer examination, Farouk nonchalantly pocketed the gadget.[57] Farouk also allegedly took lessons from Egypt's most accomplished pickpocket, to whom he proved an admirably effective pupil. Rumours spread in 1944 that Farouk had taken the opportunity presented by the desire of the exiled Shah of Iran to be buried at a mausoleum by the Nile at Aswan, to remove the Shah's fabulously jewelled belt and sword from his coffin, prior to internment. While, even Lampson, never shy in recording gossip about Farouk's more outlandish behaviour, failed to sanction this particular rumour, his embassy staff determined that many stories of Farouk's magpie tendencies (furthered by varying degrees of coercion) could be definitely verified. Lampson was informed that Farouk had raided a sequestered German bookshop at the outbreak of war, and had appropriated both a collection of swords belonging to George Lotfallah and the private armoury of Mahmoud Khairy Pasha. In the latter case, Khairy was obliged to accommodate the king's wishes, after Farouk threatened to terminate the royal pension paid to Khairy's wife, Princess Kadria.[58]

Farouk's belief that he was entitled to take whatever he wanted might be constituted as simply a manifestation of his hereditary *droit de roi*. Indeed his browbeating of those whose houses he visited to gift him their household treasures is redolent of the similarly brazen conduct colloquially (and possibly unfairly) attributed to Queen Mary during her stays in England's country houses.[59] However, by the 1950s, the frequent retelling (and undoubted elaboration) of anecdotes about Farouk's acquisitive tendencies as monarch needs to be set in the context of anxieties surrounding increased affluence, many of which coalesced around the apparently pathological behaviour of people who purloined items from stores, but who were neither career criminals nor suffering from serious financial deprivation. In the nineteenth century the phenomenon of kleptomania had been explained as a means to secure material goods that elevated or maintained social status, especially for women.[60] Clearly this motivation could not be attributed to Farouk, where explanations for his greedy procurement are more likely to lie in an arrested psychological development fostered by the contrast between the ease with which he could satisfy his material needs and the failure to attend to his emotional needs by his distant parents. However, the broader diagnosis of kleptomania offered by Victorian expert opinion had renewed pertinence in the 1950s, particularly its critique of consumerism and the exposure (through advertising and popular media) of the public to overstimulation and the encouragement of unrealistic desires and expectations. In 1951 Rowntree and Lavers reported that shoplifting had become rife in postwar Britain, with a West End dress shop having 5,000 garments stolen every year, a large London general store requiring the services of twelve full-time detectives and magistrates reporting that among those convicted of shoplifting in bookshops had been a dentist, a schoolmaster, a senior civil servant and a vicar.[61] As the decade progressed, a rise in shoplifting offences was attributed to the emergence of new retail environments (particularly self-service stores) which tempted the otherwise respectable to steal.[62] While this was obviously a very different context to Farouk's Egypt, the identification of the Egyptian monarch as a kleptomaniac does underline the way his excesses matched distinctly metropolitan preoccupations during the emergence of the affluent society.

In the descriptions of the royal collections offered by both British journalists and Egypt's new rulers, inanimate objects had served to embody and incarnate the absent person, in this case the now exiled Farouk.[63] By contrast, other discourses of excess and dissolution surrounding Farouk were intensely embodied. Farouk, who had been a slim and handsome teen at the start of his reign, became both fat and bald in the course of his twenties. His weight has been estimated at over 200 pounds by the mid-1940s and over 300 pounds a decade later.[64] Nationalist authors located this transformation in the aftermath of the Abdin incident of February 1942, the changing appearance of the king's body thereby serving as a register of Egypt's national humiliation under imperial tutelage.[65] Others attributed Farouk's ballooning figure to a possibly botched operation, carried out on the king after a road accident in November 1943. A *Picture Post* profile in 1955 insisted Farouk's 'unprepossessing fatness' was the result of a glandular condition, and others, noting the propensity to corpulence among earlier members of the Mehmet Ali dynasty, highlighted the king's genetic inheritance.[66] However, amidst such speculation, most contemporaries identified Farouk's expanding waistline with the unrestrained hedonism, to which he seemed to have abandoned himself in the last decade of his reign. References to Farouk's excessive weight were a key constituent in both press coverage and newspaper caricature.[67]

Farouk had an insatiable appetite for fine cuisine, 'his mania for food', in the words of one biographer, 'as eclectic as those for sex and collecting'.[68] Whether in his palaces or in Europe's grand hotels, Farouk devoured multi-course grand buffets, composed of salmon, calf, cold poultry, suckling lamb, pigeon, mushrooms swamped in cream sauce, beef tongue with port jelly, pheasant terrines with truffles, fruit charlotte, petits-fours and caviar. Such lavish eating by a royal personage would have passed without remark at the beginning of the century. Indeed Farouk's gargantuan meals were reminiscent of those regularly enjoyed by the Edwardian upper classes, not least King Edward VII himself.[69] Like 'Tum-Tum', Farouk enjoyed shooting as much as eating. At the start of his reign, he was commended by the British for his enjoyment of shooting-parties, which was perceived as a useful qualification for socializing with fellow royals and aristocrats, and ensured he might share at least some of his leisure time with Lampson and other members of the Cairo Residency.[70] At the shoot, Farouk's proclivity for excess was manifested in his tendency to boasting about the number of birds he had bagged. Inevitably, Lampson regarded such behaviour (especially since there was also evidence that the king frequently falsified his count) as both ungentlemanly and unsportsmanlike.[71] After the war, Farouk's commitment to shooting waned, but not his enthusiasm for eating. Not for nothing did a French confectionary company name a chocolate bar after the ex-monarch in 1957.[72]

In the colonial imagination, a propensity to corpulence and a supposed love of fat had regularly been cited as symptomatic of the chaotic, perverse and abject bodies of non-Europeans, a somatic indicator of the contrast between imperial self-discipline and oriental self-indulgence. Fatness was also associated with both savagery and lust.[73] The notion that it was no sin to be fat in the Arab world (and that it might be seen as a sign of virility) was a hoary stereotype which Western observers continued to repeat, and which (judging from a strong emphasis on reasserting their masculinity against their imperial rulers through sports and fitness regimes) had also been internalized by many young Egyptian effendi nationalists.[74] However, Farouk's failure to rein in either his appetite or his waistline was rarely conceived in terms of long-established tropes of imperial knowledge. Rather, representations of Farouk's physicality were more closely aligned with contemporary concerns about obesity serving as an indicator of the ill-discipline and materialism of mid-century affluence. With rising living standards in the 1950s, the aspiration to enjoy fine dining and a greater variety of foods was viewed positively. Nonetheless, discriminating taste could not be allowed to degenerate into voracious appetite. Gastronomy was acceptable, but gluttony was not.[75]

In his exile years, paparazzi photographers delighted in dramatizing both Farouk's love of food and its corporeal ramifications. He was snapped enjoying a meal in a curbside restaurant on the Via Veneto or exposing his flabby stomach while stripped down to his bathing trunks on beaches or at the side of swimming pools. Such photographs sensationalized the intersection of the visceral and the social, exposing the ambiguities of the age. Farouk's sebaceous body implied a world of plenty, a dramatic contrast to the emaciated and malnourished figures who had stalked the Depression years and the ravaged cadavers (alive and dead) found among the rubble of war-shattered Europe in 1945. However, excess fat also inferred that affluence had prioritized comfort over resilience, indulgence over obligation, materialism over morality.

That said, Farouk's bloated appearance conversely suggested that he was unable to satisfy some of the pressing prerequisites of the affluent society. Farouk's portly (and, critically, prematurely aged) appearance distanced him from the growing emphasis in 1950s culture on youthful sex appeal. He was certainly not without personal style, with an impeccable taste in tailored clothing, fashionable shoes and designer watches. His delicately striped shirts and dark-grey suits came from Carlo Palazzi, tailor to young Hollywood stars such as Marlon Brando, and an arbiter of style for young male pleasure seekers in both Western Europe and the United States.[76] It also should not be forgotten that at the time he was deposed, Farouk was still only thirty-two years old (only four years older than Brando, the role model of the nascent rock and roll generation). Farouk's womanizing and penchant for pin-up magazines, luxury cars or yachts and expensive wrist watches might superficially align him with the 1950s swinging bachelor (with his combination of conspicuous consumption and sexual licence) created by leisure-style entrepreneur Hugh Hefner.[77] However, while Farouk was undoubtedly a playboy, what he certainly was not was a Playboy. Not merely would his royal status have been impossible to reconcile with Hefner's meritocratic prescriptions, but his body all too clearly lacked the sleek and aerodynamic sophistication appropriate to the narcissistic, youthful masculinity of the 'jet age'. To add insult to injury, it was widely reported that Farouk's Ferrari, what should have been the ultimate Playboy accessory, required a wide bench due to the ex-king's inability to squeeze his bulky frame into the regular bucket seat.[78]

While Farouk's body was held up for scorn or pity, the bodies of the women associated with him were exhibited as a spectacle of desirability or allure. Images of Farouk's (erstwhile and real) girlfriends traded on a growing emphasis on sexuality and youth as key components of contemporary femininity. Some possessed the upscale glamour of the *haute couture*-clothed body of the model or socialite.[79] The pin-up bodies of the starlets who sought him out were presented less decorously, their low-cut dresses and curvaceous contours exhibited for the titillation of male newspaper and magazine readers.[80] In the popular imagining

**Figure 9** Farouk and playmates on the beach at Anzio, 4 August 1956 (Bettmann/Getty Images).

of Farouk, ballooning bellies were regularly affiliated with big breasts. Even Narriman's royal status did not prevent comparisons between her buxom figure and the bathycolpian charms of Hollywood star Jane Russell.[81] However, here too, Farouk's relation to the human body betrayed unease about the affluent society. The pneumatic charms of some of the less refined women associated with Farouk (particularly in his last years) uneasily bordered on the grotesque and outlandish, implying the more squalid component to 1950s plentitude.[82]

Farouk's ostentatious displays of high living inevitably contrasted with the self-abnegation required of ordinary Britons during wartime and the austerity years immediately after 1945. The Board of Trade was often grudging about granting export licences for household goods, notably silk ties, being sent to Farouk from England. In June 1944, a Foreign Office official complained about the decision to send £50 of pipes and cigar holders to the Egyptian monarch, seething that it was currently 'practically impossible' to buy a pipe in Britain and that he did not see why 'King Farouk should carry off a proportion of such pipes that are available'. He was overruled by one of his superiors, who insisted, 'A pipe is a good habit and H[is] M[ajesty] has not many such'.[83] In 1951 the Labour MP Irene Ward wrote to the Foreign Office to share the complaints of her constituents that, in straitened times, the British government had seen fit to present Farouk and Narriman with a solid gold tea and coffee service as their wedding present.[84] Farouk's all-too-conspicuous consumption certainly seemed to belong to a different world to the drabness and deferred gratification of British life in the late 1940s and early 1950s.

It is therefore critical to realize that narratives of Farouk's propensity to excess had a distinct affinity with popular interest in Britain's own super-rich in this period. While life was undoubtedly hard for many Britons after 1945, the dislocations of wartime and postwar recovery also created opportunities for some fortuitous individuals to make a great deal of money in a relatively short period of time. In the last years of the Labour government and during Churchill's peacetime administration, the press was captivated by the gaudy lives of a cluster of high-profile self-made millionaires who appeared to have no inhibitions about flaunting their newly made fortunes. As in other times and places, luxury became a critical site for exposing the difficulty of maintaining social identities and distinctions.[85] However, it was given a contingent inflection here by the decidedly plutocratic, no to say parvenu, background of these figures, and by the fact that the individualistic genres of aspiration and social mobility they represented failed to match either Conservative ideals of established social hierarchy or Labour visions of collectively secured egalitarianism. The possibility of a shared rubric of comprehension that encompassed both Farouk and British self-made millionaires such as George Dawson and Dudley Docker is bolstered by the fact that they all frequented the same luxury playgrounds, especially the Riviera.

Farouk shared a love for Cannes with George Dawson, the 'boy from Brixton', who 'likes jellied eels and chateau wines'. Dawson was a scrap-metal dealer who made a fortune from selling war surplus equipment, in some cases to some rather dubious customers. Weighing over 220 pounds, with a chubby baby face and a permanent red carnation in his button hole, he was regularly to be found in nightclubs, ordering crates of champagne for his companions, generously tipping hostesses from the wad of notes that bulged from his trouser pocket and very often getting involved in rowdy brawls. In his villa at Cannes he was more circumspect, deploying his lavish hospitality to secure influence among French businessmen and politicians, but Peter Wildeblood spotted him in the same Cannes hotel lobby as Farouk in 1951.[86]

In Monte Carlo, Farouk would have found it impossible to ignore the *Shermara*, the massive ocean-going yacht moored in the principality's marina which belonged to Sir Bernard Docker, chairman of Birmingham Small Armaments. Unlike Dawson, Docker was the member of an established and respectable Midlands business and legal dynasty. However, his marriage to former showgirl Norah Collins in 1949 initiated a decade-long self-promotional social whirl, which incorporated Lady Docker's luxury shopping sprees and garish jewels, ostentatious social events attended by Hollywood stars and the commissioning of a gold-plated Daimler for the 1951 Motor Show.[87] The Dockers' grand style did not extend to hosting the king of Egypt, and Norah later alleged that her husband had Farouk removed from his yacht when the latter attempted an impromptu visit.[88] However, the press frequently paired these conspicuous consumers, for instance when in 1951 readers of the *Daily Mail* who had just been provided with gossip about the Dockers spring sojourn in Cannes were on the front page specifically exhorted to turn to the next page 'for news of Farouk at Monte Carlo'.[89] The most dramatic (and fatal) intersection between British pleasure-seeking plutocrats and Farouk took place in the Cannes casino in September 1950. Myers Hyman, a Lancashire textile manufacturer, had been playing chemin-de-fer with Farouk, Hollywood magnate Jack Warner, Fiat director Gianni Agnelli and the Nawab of Palanpur. As three of the players retired, 'Lucky Mickie' Hyman eventually won a three-bet showdown with Farouk (a rare outcome), but then collapsed and died as he was reaching for the winning chips.[90]

Some might have believed that dropping dead while raking in his winnings at the casino table might have been an equally appropriate fate for Farouk. In fact, as has already been noted, it was to be another aspect of Farouk's high living – his passion for lavish dining – which may have triggered his premature demise. What is critical is that, however much stories about Farouk's propensity to excess underlined his singularity (which, in turn, appeared to be accounted for by both his social privilege and the idiosyncrasies of his personality), they also spoke to the preoccupations of British culture in the 1940s and 1950s. Farouk's pursuit of treasure and pleasure were traits that were certainly available for anyone who wished to refurbish the hackneyed stereotypes of the oriental potentate, to present the king as a latter-day version of the grotesque voluptuaries who had featured in the popular imaginary during the heyday of the British Empire. However, this proved not to be the use to which stories of Farouk's gluttony, cupidity and lechery was to be put.

Instead they served as a mirror on British society at a time when it was wrestling with the emergence of new structures of desire, some of which had been enhanced by the changing sexual standards of wartime, others fostered by the increased possibility of social mobility in the immediate postwar years and (most significant of all) some the product of the dramatic rise in living standards that took place in the mid-1950s. If there were obviously limited opportunities in Britain at this time to replicate the scale of Farouk's propensity for excess, there were plentiful observers who would have insisted that the culture of self-gratification he emblematized was no less apparent in changing metropolitan attitudes towards sexuality, consumption and materialism. In this environment, attempts to align Farouk with his wealthy dynastic peers in the Arab and Muslim worlds lacked genuine plausibility. Rather, he seemed more qualified to serve as an exaggerated version of the pleasures and perils that characterized Britain's emerging age of affluence. Affluence was, of course, not an exclusively British phenomenon, and was frequently linked by contemporaries with the rising economic, political and cultural power of the United States. What, then, was Farouk's status in American culture, and what might it be able to contribute to our understanding of the so-called 'Americanization' of postwar Britain?

6

# American Farouk, Fictional Farouk

In February 1953 a police raid on the Rancho Lido, an upscale bordello located near Miami airport, brought to a dramatic end the career of notorious Florida madam Ruth Barnes, better known as Madam Sherry. Madam Sherry had run a number of upscale brothels in the Miami area since the Prohibition era, and counted among her clientele the exiled heir to the Spanish throne, numerous jockeys, crime bosses and a nymphomaniac female socialite. Now she became a fugitive from justice, her whereabouts unknown. It came as something of a shock therefore when, in 1961, a New York publishing house released *Pleasure Was My Business*, what purported to be the luridly unexpurgated memoirs of Madam Sherry.[1] Sherry's foray into print had been achieved with the assistance of a ghostwriter, Robert Tralins, at the time the author of a rather desiccated manual on *How to Be a Power Closer in Selling*, but now about to launch on a decades-long career committed to sleazy and exploitative pulp fiction with titles as edifying as *Operation Boudoir*, *Invasion of the Nymphomaniacs* and *Topless Kitties*.[2] *Pleasure Was My Business* sold well in the United States, resulting in a paperback edition. This was despite, or perhaps because of, an obscenity trial in May 1962, which upheld a ban on the book that had been imposed in the state of Florida. The ban was ultimately reversed in June 1964, after what amounted to a landmark case in the reform of literary censorship legislation in the United States.[3]

However, it was not just those concerned about the corrupting influence of Madam Sherry's salacious revelations on the impressionable minds of the youth of the Sunshine State who had been affronted by the contents of *Pleasure Was My Business*. Sherry and Tralins had dedicated a whole chapter of the book to the four occasions in which she had entertained a client who, she asserted, 'deserves the place of honor in my Rancho Lido's hall of fame'. This client's first visit had been prefaced by a call from a man who had inspected her premises, reserved the establishment for the evening, requested 'three of your best girls for my master', before handing the stunned Sherry a thousand dollars in fifty-dollar bills. When the mystery client arrived, Sherry immediately recognized him: 'That huge bulk, those round dark glasses and that big hairy moustache couldn't be mistaken anywhere'. In the brothel's parlour, she introduced him to her 'girls': 'Ladies', I said, 'welcome his most gracious majesty, King Farouk'.

Sherry's account went on to detail the testimony of her employees in regard to Farouk's particular sexual preferences, before proclaiming her elevated status as 'the first and only American whorehouse madam to formally receive royalty on American soil'.[4] Somehow a copy of *Pleasure Was My Business* found its way to Italy, and Farouk responded by suing the book's publishers for libel, to the tune of $750,000. How serious this suit was is open to conjecture, since Farouk chose not to appear in person to testify at a court hearing in Florida in May 1963 and the judge simply dismissed the case. However, Tralins clearly believed the court's decision exonerated him, especially since he claimed to have offered definitive 'evidence' that Farouk had been in Miami in 1947. In fact, any close inspection would have quickly established the insubstantiality of Tralins' claims, which were little more than an unverified report that Farouk's yacht had been seen in dry dock in the Miami River and that Farouk had visited a former ambassador in Palm Beach around the same time.[5] So patently spurious were these claims that Tralins was probably lucky not to have been held in contempt. Whether as king of Egypt or as royal exile, Farouk had never set foot on American soil, and nor was he to do so in the remaining years of his life.

Farouk's bizarre entanglement in this story of a Baltimore-born pulp author, a Florida brothel proprietor and a high-profile obscenity trial that ultimately went all the way to the US Supreme Court provided an extravagantly inflated confirmation of two aspects of how Egypt's ruler was understood and represented in British culture. First, it underlined that Farouk was as immediately recognizable to the American as he was to the British public. Farouk featured in a variety of contexts within American popular culture. Newspapers and magazines shared the interest of their British equivalents in Farouk's adventures and excesses, and, while Farouk himself never visited the United States, a materially grounded transatlantic connection was forged when his sister married an American and moved to California. The African American press were interested in Farouk as a public figure who appeared to possess a positive valuation of black female beauty. Publicists saw Farouk as an international celebrity who could be exploited to further the careers of American actresses and socialites. As in Britain, Farouk was referenced in a range of cultural texts, encompassing film, sport, song lyrics and jazz scores. This shared familiarity on both sides of the Atlantic with Farouk challenges the conceit that the 'Americanization' of British culture after the Second World War was predicated on a turning away from an understanding of the world rooted in imperially derived associations. If 'Americanization' was a critical force in reshaping British metropolitan identity in the postwar decades, it is necessary to comprehend it as a genuinely transnational cultural formation, which incorporated referents which had originated not in the United States but in the contexts of the British Empire.

Second, the fact that Farouk's appearance in Sherry's memoirs, regardless of the precipitative dismissal of the ex-king's libel suit by the justices of the Eleventh Circuit, was patently a fabrication establishes *Pleasure Was My Business* as yet another (albeit one of the more outlandish) example of what might be categorized as 'Farouk apocrypha'. In both Britain and the United States, even stories about Farouk that had some foundation in truth were regularly embellished, especially when they bore the marks of interventions from agents and publicists. However, there were also stories, particularly those concerned with Farouk's debauchery, that were entirely fanciful, and sometimes calumnious. The fictional Farouk, moreover, was a presence not confined to the domains of privileged gossip or tabloid sensationalism. Novelists including Gore Vidal, Lawrence Durrell and Barbara Skelton were all attracted to the possibility of including Farouk in their writings, appearing either as himself or in the form of a character whose bearing and traits clearly matched those of Egypt's last monarch. Farouk's larger-than-life personality also attracted the attention of Hollywood. In 1955, the feature film *Abdullah the Great* not merely offered a thinly disguised portrayal of the recently deposed king but marked a point of intersection between the two imperatives of Americanization and fictionalization, with which this chapter is concerned.

# I

Farouk's first appearance on the cover of *Time*, the leading weekly news magazine in the United States, with its self-professed mission to 'tell news through people', came as early as August 1937. Inside this issue, Farouk was the subject of a largely sympathetic profile, which (as had been the case in the British media at this time) emphasized his youthful promise and popularity with ordinary Egyptians, although it also acknowledged that Lampson, 'a grand surviving figure in the Victorian tradition of Bearing the White Man's Burden', was the 'de facto ruler of Egypt'.[6] The approving tone of the American media was reinforced by his 1938 marriage to Farida, *Life* magazine commending Farouk's apparently democratic credentials that had been evident in the young king's decision to wed 'this pretty commoner'.[7] The sensitivities of Allied diplomacy ensured that a feature on the Abdin palace which appeared in *Life* in April 1944 was extremely favourable to Farouk. The king was praised for his 'unprecedented generosity' in opening his royal home to photographer John Phillips. The resulting photo essay conformed that 'very few people in the world live today with such undimmed splendor', but it also presented Farouk as a serious-minded young monarch who, while 'obviously a modern man', was personally devout and had eschewed the 'irreligious' outlook of Egypt's upper classes.[8]

In subsequent years, neither *Time* nor *Life* was to be as well disposed towards Farouk. When Farouk next appeared on the cover of *Time* in September 1951, it was to preface an article which credited the king for being 'intelligent and energetic', but condemned him for failing to provide the sustained leadership that would prevent Egypt succumbing to either Arab nationalism or, worse, Soviet infiltration. Farouk had become 'a glutton, a high-stakes gambler and a wolf', a 'huge, lusty man who puffs eight-inch cigars and gambles with machine-like energy', hence his nickname 'The Locomotive'.[9] An article in *Life* in April 1950 entitled 'The Problem King of Egypt' was sympathetic to the challenges Farouk faced when his room for manoeuvre was restricted by the ongoing British presence in Egypt. However, it condemned his imperious approach to his royal prerogatives, likening him to 'a pampered child'. Even if its political evaluation of Farouk attempted to be judiciously balanced, the article's unflattering physical description of the king – 'a porcine, thick-featured man with thinning hair and the pompous bearing of a bank president' – proved sufficient for *Life* to be banned in Egypt.[10]

The less favourable image of Farouk found in American mass media at the opening of the 1950s was undoubtedly informed by the new postwar international order. The Cold War and the growing awareness of the Middle East's oil resources had made the United States increasingly impatient with the failure of either Farouk or the British to ensure stability in Egypt. Indeed some leading figures in the CIA later claimed that the United States had covertly sought to destabilize Farouk's regime, but the evidence for this remains speculative, and the Americans appeared no less surprised by the Free Officers' coup in 1952 than the British. An additional factor that impacted on changing attitudes towards Farouk in the United States was the 1948–1949 Arab-Israeli war. Farouk's prominent role in the military effort by its Arab neighbours to crush the nascent state of Israel came at an inopportune time, coinciding with growing public and political support in the United States for a Jewish state.[11] Farouk's reputation in this regard was further tarnished when a record of the 'collaboration of King Farouk of Egypt with the Nazis and their ally, the Mufti' was submitted to the United Nations and several American foreign correspondents publicized the presence of former Nazis among the Egyptian king's military advisers.[12]

That said, American media coverage of Farouk worked harder than its British equivalents in locating Farouk's personal failings within the broader context of the emerging postcolonial world, relating the king's playboy lifestyle to a more general critique of the profound inequalities that scarred his kingdom, an emphasis that betrayed anxieties that unless the yawning gulf between pashas and peasants was bridged, Egypt might fall prey to communism. *Life* presented Farouk as the symptom, as much as the cause, of the fact that Egypt was a country 'in which social injustice is so palpable'.[13] More generally, any 'orientalist' element in US media coverage of Farouk reflected an emphasis on affiliation, rather than difference, and accorded with American preference for grounding postwar world power status in an ideology of global interdependence, rather than British-style territorial imperialism. As Christina Klein has argued, America's 'Cold War orientalism' sought to replace a 'national imaginary based on separation with a global imaginary based on connection'. Farouk's apparent appearance in a Florida bordello might be seen as a bizarre manifestation of American insistence that global expansion was based not on coercion but on economic and emotional exchange between Americans and the world at large.[14]

The broader political context generally yielded to detailed reports on Farouk's private cavortings, and (as in Britain) this emphasis inevitably became dominant after his fall from power in 1952. Most of the stories published by *Life* covered exactly the same ground as the British popular press: the extended bachelor vacation in Deauville, the shifting fortunes of his marriage to Narriman, his first days in exile on Capri and his pursuit of nightclub entertainers during his years in Rome.[15] However, the more copious resources (especially in regard to the quantity and quality of photographic illustration available to readers of glossy magazines in the United States) of American print culture ensured that stories about Farouk could be presented in even more amplified and exaggerated form than they were in Britain. For example, a *Life* feature on 'The Treasures Farouk Left Behind' reiterated the British press' preoccupation not merely with the opulent fittings of Farouk's palaces but with the tawdry kitsch he had indiscriminately collected. However, here, the full gaudy extravagance of Farouk's regime could be conveyed, by means of fifteen full colour photographs (many of them filling a complete page) of the ex-king's throne room, his ornate bedroom furnishings and the 'fantastic and revealing collection' of 'jewelry and junk'. There was even a double-page spread of some of the tamer examples of the nude paintings and statues to be found littering the floor of the Koubbeh palace's 'secret museum'.[16] This technicolour spectacle (and its juxtaposition with the headily aspirational and arrestingly seductive advertising of consumer goods which was such a notable feature of the magazine) dramatized the ability of American media to more effectively impart the relationship between Farouk's excesses and the extrovert materialism of the 1950s affluent society.

Interest in Farouk among the middle-class readership of glossy publications such as *Life* may also account for the decision of the *Ladies Home Journal*, the magazine of choice for discerning suburban homemakers, to publish the ghost-written autobiography of ex-Queen Narriman in February 1953. By this point, Narriman had already grown estranged from Farouk, but drawing on the overheated idioms of the Harlequin romance, she was still willing to share with her readers her fascination with her husband's shoulders and his 'powerful wrists covered with dark virile hair'. Ironically, Narriman's story appeared in the very same year that the *LHJ* introduced its famed 'Can This Marriage Be Saved?' column.[17] In Narriman's case the answer was a resounding no: within a month a *Life* feature disclosed that 'Narriman Calls It Quits'.[18] Some Americans did not have to experience Farouk vicariously through magazines and newspapers. The fact that Farouk never came to America did not preclude America coming to him. Some of the growing number of American tourists visiting Europe in the 1950s encountered Farouk in the hotels and casinos of Capri, Rome or the Riviera. Catching a glimpse (or snatching an unsanctioned photograph) of the ex-king probably provided a pleasurable interlude during extended vacations that, despite their emphasis on visiting the more edifying sights of European history and culture, were ultimately enjoyed by Americans with what a commentator disparagingly characterized as 'upper-middle-class incomes and lower-middle-brow tastes'.[19] At a less salubrious level, in February 1952 it was widely reported that New York 'café society call girl' Dianne Harris, who had 'scampered all over Europe' in search of wealthy clients, had sought a 'personal introduction' to Farouk.[20] American publicists also attempted to contrive encounters in European resorts between Farouk and coquettish ingénue actresses or socialites.

Conversely, while Farouk remained resolutely fixed on the other side of the Atlantic, fate determined that several figures who had once been close to him relocated to the United States. In Egypt, legendary belly dancer Samia Gamal's mesmerizing gyrations had won her the approval of Farouk, who bestowed on her the title of National Dancer of Egypt, and the monarch and his dancer were romantically linked in some reports. Gamal had certainly regularly been incorporated into the king's entourage and had been specially flown out from Egypt to entertain him during his notorious September 1950 jaunt in Deauville. Images of Gamal's 'vigorous and voluptuous' dancing at Deauville found their way into the American, as well as the British, press.[21] Gamal visited the United States and performed at the Latin Quarter club in New York. It was in a Paris nightclub, though, that she met the man who became her husband, the wealthy Texan, Sheppard King III. In interviews, King seemed infatuated with his new bride, but the marriage began in distinctly unpropitious circumstances, when the groom (who has already been married twice – to the same woman) found himself threatened with disinheritance by his mother. The press inevitably made play of Gamal's apparent shift of affections from the king of Egypt to an 'American King'.[22]

Even within superabundant 1950s and 1960s America, super-sized Texas, with its flair for the big and the showy, probably appeared to *Life* readers as a singularly appropriate destination for someone accustomed to the gaudy excesses of Farouk's court. In the year of Farouk's death, the world's first indoor multi-sport stadium opened in Houston. The Superdome, plastic-topped and air-conditioned, was the draw-dropping creation of Roy Hofheinz, a flamboyant Texas advertising salesman, whose propensity to garish extravagance was borne out by his lavishly appointed office suite in the stadium complex. Visitors were awed by Hofheinz's fifteen-foot-wide desk inlaid with black marble, flanked by two six-foot antique carved dogs from a Thai temple, in a room surrounded by illuminated walls made of Mexican onyx. The suite also incorporated a committee room with zebra-skinned chairs and a full-scale shooting gallery. Among the select cohort of guests who were given a preview of Hofheinz's exercise in tasteless fanfaronade was comedian Bob Hope, who quipped that the style of the Astrodome's stadium office might most aptly be described as 'early King Farouk'.[23]

The most significant materialization of a close intimate of Farouk on American soil was not his favourite belly dancer but his mother and one of his sisters. Queen Nazli had been sequestered in the royal palace by Farouk's father, King Fuad. On Fuad's death, Nazli took the opportunity to embrace a much more liberated life, eschewing the veil in favour of a colourful life of partying and scandalous romances. Lampson was perturbed by the potential political consequences of the Queen Mother's behaviour, but Farouk also came to feel his mother had betrayed him, not least when he discovered her long-term affair with Ahmed Mohammed Hassanein, a scholar-explorer who had been the king's mentor in his youth. In the late 1940s Nazli spent an increasing amount of time in the United States. She set up a base for her entourage and herself in San Francisco, where she conducted an indiscreet dalliance with Riad Ghali, an Egyptian Copt. In 1950, in a move which led to a decisive split between mother and son, Nazli married off Farouk's younger sister Fathia to Ghali. The wedding was attended by leading California socialites such as Virginia, the daughter of Governor Earl Warren, and millionaire oilman Edwin Pauley. The ménage of Nazli, Fathia and Ghali settled in Beverly Hills, while Farouk stripped his mother and sister of their royal titles and seized their assets in Egypt. Media coverage of Fathia's wedding juxtaposed its traditional Muslim and Egyptian elements (notably the prohibition on the groom kissing his bride) with its decidedly American inflections (the choice of the ballroom of the Fairmount Hotel in San Francisco as the venue for the ceremony, and of Honolulu for the honeymoon destination).[24]

More generally, as in Britain, Farouk served as a metonym for excess, particularly sexual licentiousness. In the 1960 film comedy *The Apartment*, the hapless C. C. Baxter (portrayed by Jack Lemmon) is mistaken for a womanizing lothario, leading another character to declare, 'I thought he was Ivy League, but it turns out he's King Farouk'.[25] Keen to confirm just how depraved were the routines of a group of chorus girls performing striptease shows for American servicemen on US air bases in Britain, a writer in *Billboard* magazine insisted he had witnessed 'some of the hottest sequences seen outside Cairo under the Farouk regime'.[26] Familiarity with Farouk seeped into the consciousness of the American heartland, although we do not necessarily know the contingencies of the affinities and associations that were being made. For example, it is not entirely clear why Chicago jazz master Harry Fields was nicknamed 'King Farouk' (there was virtually no physical resemblance).[27] Nor can we ascertain why a regular contender in a series of light heavyweight boxing bouts held at Chicago's MidWest Gym in the late 1950s adopted the pugilistic *nom de guerre* of 'King Farouk'.[28] Farouk also featured in American popular music. Jazz saxophonist (and protégé of Count Basie) Eddie 'Jockjaw' Davis released a medium blues track 'Farouk' in 1957.[29] In her song 'Monotonous', Eartha Kitt adopted the persona of a jaded sophisticate, a woman who, after a lifetime of being wooed by the rich and famous, now appears to find the whole business a crushing bore. Among her exotic suitors were both austere American poets and Egyptian playboy monarchs: 'T.S. Eliot writes books for me/King Farouk's on tenterhooks for me.'[30]

Both Eddie Davis and Eartha Kitt were African American, but their music also offered an opportunity for racial connection and synthesis that appealed to cosmopolitan white Americans. This begs the question of how far Farouk featured in the black American consciousness. A perusal of the African-American press reveals intermittent coverage of Farouk, as both a political figure and a celebrity, and suggests a definite level of interest in, and familiarity with, Egypt's king. To what extent, though, did an African-American subject position result in a different take on Farouk (especially in regard to comprehending his ethnic-racial identity, but also in terms of appreciating the colonial contexts to his life and reign) to that adopted in the American media as a whole? Those African-American activists who were keen to locate the struggle against injustice at home in the broader context of anti-colonial movements across the globe were eager to report on (and evaluate) the contemporary claims for esteem, freedom and racial equality being made by the non-white subjects of the rapidly disintegrating British Empire.[31] Moreover, as Melani McAllister has charted, in the early postwar decades, black American artists and writers looked not merely to sub-Saharan Africa but to the Middle East as a resource for the creation of black identity and heritage.[32]

However, rather than serving as an advantage, the fact that Farouk could be incorporated into both these tropes only assured that African-American commentary on Farouk shared the same inability to fix his identity which had vexed both politicians and public in Britain. An article in *Jet* (a popular African-American magazine) in October 1952 declared that Haile Selassie and Farouk (unflatteringly described as a 'stove-shaped kinglet') had been the 'last remaining' African monarchs, until the latter's demise earlier that year had left Ethiopia's ruler as the continent's sole independent sovereign.[33] *Chicago Defender* columnist Eric Waters condemned the American public for viewing Africa as 'a vast mysterious dark continent peopled by black, loincloth-wearing savages'. Their images of Africa fashioned by 'hearsay and Hollywood', Americans 'don't think of the great Egyptian playboy, deposed King Farouk, as an African'.[34] The inference of this remark was that Americans didn't regard Farouk as African because they didn't think he was black.[35] Unfortunately Waters did not offer any reflection on whether this notion was less likely to have been uncritically accepted by black, as opposed to white, Americans. It is certainly the case that, whether he was either African or black, or neither, Farouk was seen by progressive African-American political commentators as representing the decadent and corrupt regimes across the Middle East that were being swept away by an emerging 'social revolution' in the Arab world.[36]

That said, Farouk was credited with acts of philanthropic generosity which benefited the African-American community, for example his donation of a collection of rare Egyptian insects to the Biology Department of Kentucky State College, a historic black university in Frankfort, Kentucky.[37] The black press was also happy to commend Farouk for his appreciation of, and enthusiasm for, the artistic talent of African-American singers and musicians. There was genuine pride, when in early 1938, Willie Lewis' black swing orchestra had performed for 'Egypt's new young king'.[38] In the postwar years, Farouk's roving eye was invested with positive connotations in black American magazines such as *Jet*, since it seemed to encompass an appreciation not merely of flaxen-haired Scandinavian blondes and raven-haired Neapolitans but also of African-American women.[39] What appeared to be Farouk's positive valuation of the physical charms of black singers, dancers and actresses (while tainted both by sexual objectification and by insidious definitions of acceptable beauty that internalized racial hierarchies) gratified the stipulations of racial pride, particularly the insistence that black bodies were not inherently less desirable than those of whites. When *Jet* profiled Ada Bricktop Smith, the African-American cabaret singer and owner of a Rome nightclub, it claimed that 'her great love' was Farouk.[40] It also reported an incident in which Farouk and an unnamed Italian prince 'exchanged cold glances and hot words' in an Italian nightclub, as they competed for the attentions of curvaceous Jamaican dancer Tessa Prendergast.[41] African-American singer Pat Rainey's involvement with Farouk in 1955 reportedly left 'the ex-king in a lather and Rome in a dither'.[42] In 1954, Mable Love, a teacher at Fisk University, reportedly returned from a vacation in Rome with a diamond bracelet given to her by Farouk after she danced with him at Bricktop's night spot.[43] Further testimony to Farouk's amatory negrophilia came from the occasion in 1958 in which he tussled with the management of Rome's Open Gate Club, after he barged into the venue, 'escorting a Negro beauty on each arm'.[44] Where others merely saw lascivious and boorish behaviour, it is possible African-American audiences were encouraged to see Farouk as an (albeit unconscious, and certainly incognizant) accessory in the causes of both racial pride and progressive interracial relations.

Farouk was a consumer of, and not merely a presence within, American popular culture. Among the personal effects Farouk left in the Koubbeh Palace were thousands of American comic books, pulp novels and film fan magazines. There were also magic tricks ordered from a Michigan mail order firm and two life-size photographic portraits of Hollywood star Lana Turner.[45] Farouk actually employed a purchasing agent in the United States, Victor Hammer (brother of noted industrialist Armand), who owned a gallery on 57th Street in New York. Hammer later revealed that Farouk subscribed to every magazine published in the United States, the pages of which he would peruse in search of novelty gadgets, which he then ordered. Hammer claimed that Farouk had little interest in the plots of the American movies the king had screened in his private palace cinema, but took the opportunity to note any innovative contraption he saw in the film, before asking his agent to purchase it for him.[46] However, other anecdotes suggest Farouk's interest in American cinema was more substantial. In the late 1940s Farouk asked American foreign correspondent John Gunther, 'How do you think I would do in Hollywood?'. Somewhat taken aback, Gunther replied that he had no idea that the king was interested in a career in Tinseltown. 'Interested?', exclaimed Farouk, 'My dream girl, in the whole wide world, is Ginger Rogers'.[47]

What, then, is the significance of Farouk's presence in American culture for our understanding of his value as an index of changing configurations of identity and representation in Britain in the immediate postwar decades? There are obvious parallels and affinities in the media coverage of Farouk on both sides of the Atlantic, notably a shift from initial praise to subsequent denigration, and the deployment of Farouk as a byword for personal and materialistic overindulgence. However, what is more critical is that, while understandings of Farouk emerged from the context of the British Empire (and the aftermath of its dissolution), these understandings were disseminated not merely in Britain but in the United States, and were sometimes recirculated to British audiences via the medium of American popular culture. An appreciation of this fact not merely requires us to acknowledge American culture as a co-author of the scripts about Farouk which circulated in metropolitan Britain in the 1940s and 1950s. It also bolsters more recent interventions in the historiography of 'Americanization'. These have rejected older interpretations of the impact of US mass culture on Western Europe in the early Cold War era as an unambiguous act of cultural colonization or annexation. Rather 'Americanization' has been re-evaluated as the creation of a genuinely transnational culture, a product of myriad and complex global interactions that crossed national boundaries, but did not simply mirror the shifting balance of geopolitical power between the Old and New worlds.[48] Recognizing the existence of this elaborate circulatory model of cultural interconnection and exchange has important implications for how we think about the chronologies of British history. 'Americanization' of British culture in the 1950s might be considered a symptom of the end of empire, a succumbing to a form of cultural imperialism that was an inevitable consequence of Britain's own imperial demise, and the resultant inability to continue to shape the world in their own image. However, representations of Farouk suggest the existence of a more mutually constitutive Anglo-American global culture, one which, far from turning its back on the imperial world, continued to incorporate figures from the last days of the British Empire and the no less imperially minded understandings that were attached to them. At the very least, it should be acknowledged that the complex provenance of scripts featuring Farouk requires more attention to how the imperatives of 'Americanization' and the discourses of both late imperialism and imperial decommission need to be more effectively integrated if we are to achieve a more comprehensive and ambitious understanding of postwar British history.

## II

The ex-king's presence in the memoirs of a Florida madam not merely confirmed the American public's familiarity with Farouk. It was also yet another example of the propensity of stories about Farouk to regularly transgress the boundary between fact and fiction. On the rare occasions that Farouk granted an interview, he complained that many of the unfavourable stories published about him in the British and American press had absolutely no foundation in fact. He was particularly exercised by claims that, in blatant contradiction of his Muslim faith, he secretly consumed alcohol (an accusation that was generally repudiated in the recollections of those who knew Farouk intimately) or that he had divorced Farida because she failed to provide him with a male heir.[49] However, the telling of spurious stories about Farouk was not helped by the king's own apparent inability to disentangle truth from falsehood. In late 1952 and early 1953 the *Empire News* serialized Farouk's ghost-written memoirs. They offered a self-justificatory apologia for his failures as man and monarch, but also a tendency for boastful fabrication. Farouk gave a detailed description of rallying his guards to defend the besieged Ras-el-tin palace from the Free Officers, claimed he had threatened his mother and her lover Hassanein with a pistol, and even insisted that he once been on the brink of shooting Lampson in the stomach.[50] Stories *by* Farouk, no less than stories *about* Farouk, always had to be taken with a very large pinch of salt.

Farouk's peripatetic life (a consequence initially of his penchant for Europe's luxury playgrounds, and subsequently of the necessities of exile) created the possibility that Farouk might show up in unexpected places. In the days when air travel remained glamorous and exclusive, less privileged Britons were willing to pay sixpence for the vicarious pleasure of watching the arrival and departure of passengers at Heathrow airport. A feature on this phenomenon in *Punch* in 1955 recorded one of the patrons of this contemporary peepshow musing, 'Am I going crazy, Charlie, or is that Farouk over there?'[51] Charlie's companion was indeed mistaken, since Farouk never returned to British soil after his short visit in 1937. However, Farouk's transient existence in the early 1950s made such a scenario not entirely fanciful. Moreover, it also seemed possible that Farouk could be in several places at the same time. Farouk employed a number of doubles, in order to reduce the risk of assassination. One of them, Ahmed Hassan el Hagagy, possessed such a close physical resemblance to the king that he was openly insulted and unable to go out to restaurants in the months after Farouk's abdication.[52] There were also incidences of non-sanctioned impersonation which took the form of confidence tricksters who pretended to be the king in order to secure antiques at more favourable rates from antique dealers.[53]

More significantly, the culture of celebrity and, more specifically, the machinations of agents and publicists ensured the regular embellishment of tenuous or even entirely concocted stories about Farouk. Martine Carol, the 'wicked woman' of French cinema, was rumoured to have had an affair with Farouk, whom she met at a reception. The story, accompanied by Carol's furious denial, was repeated in an article authored by her husband, director Christian Jacque, in what was clearly an attempt to both defend the actress' moral reputation and to exploit what amounted to a distinctly insubstantial connection to Farouk in order to promote her career in Britain.[54] When Eva Bartok, a Hungarian actress trying (with limited success) to establish herself in British film, was photographed with Farouk, even *Picturegoer* (a largely deferential film fan magazine) concluded that this established beyond doubt that 'Eva Bartok is a classic example of press-agent stardom.'[55] Fabricating stories about Farouk and his supposed paramours did not necessarily secure aspiring young actresses and socialites popularity, but it certainly delivered publicity.

The way that unscrupulous agents deliberately sought to profit from Farouk's notoriety was disclosed in the candid recollections of Italian American publicist Guy Orlando. Orlando, who immodestly claimed to have 'helped hundreds of actors, artists, writers and industrialists and just plain people to fame and fortune', had long sought to add a reigning monarch ('Not a maharajah or an ex-king or a pretender – they're a dime a dozen') to his list of clients. In 1950 Orlando approached Farouk during his visit to Deauville, using his Italian inheritance (and linguistic proficiency) to enlist Pulli, Farouk's loyal retainer, as an intermediary. His initial proposal was that Farouk should be publicized as 'the gambling king'. 'In a world full of horse-players', Orlando later recalled, 'I figured this would make him popular'. Sympathy from non-gamblers could be secured by having Farouk donate all his winnings to charity. When Farouk quashed this proposition, Orlando quickly shifted his attention to another opportunity.[56]

Another visitor to Deauville at this time was Mimi Medart, the sixteen-year-old daughter of Blossom Medart, née Breneman, a silent-era Hollywood actress and Bill Medart, a St. Louis hamburger restaurateur. Orlando, an acquaintance of Blossom since the 1920s, had Midi stand by the doorway of a room which Farouk was departing after dinner, wearing the Egyptian national colours as a *fichu* on her evening gown. Such a blatant stratagem succeeded when the king stopped and engaged Mimi in conversation. Orlando folded Mimi's parents into his scheme, promising Blossom it would help Mimi 'get a chance in pictures' and Bill that it would sell more of his hamburgers. Knowing Farouk's itinerary in detail, Orlando made sure that when the king moved on to Biarritz and San Sebastian, the Medarts were already ensconced in hotels in these resorts. He was thereby able to feed the press with the story that Farouk, 'a lecherous Oriental potentate', was pursuing the 'lovely American maiden' around the playgrounds of Europe but that she had fortunately succeeded in eluding 'his hot little hands'. Mimi Medart was offered a film part. Bill Medart's restaurants in Missouri were swamped with customers (although this failed to prevent him jumping from a Paris hotel window a few months later), and Orlando had done well out of Farouk, albeit not as his agent. In late 1952 Orlando was able to use Farouk, whom he met again in Rome, to get publicity for a plastic label manufacturer from Pittsburgh, and in the following year contrived to challenge Farouk to a duel (after the ex-king finally discovered how Orlando had used him during the Medart affair, and publicly insulted the publicist). In his autobiography, Orlando dedicated a whole chapter to his adventures with Farouk, concluding that 'I don't quite know what I've have done without him'.[57]

### III

The desire to create fictional Farouks was not confined to sensationalist journalists and conniving publicists. Novelists were also attracted to the Egyptian king, and Farouk appeared in a number of works of literary fiction, either as himself or in the form of fictitious characters who bore some of his characteristic attributes. Farouk as a *habitue* of the Via Veneto makes a brief appearance in *Orphans of Gethsemane*, the one-thousand-page-long final instalment of Vardis Fisher's monumentally turgid twelve-volume mystical history of human civilization, *The Testament of Man*.⁵⁸ In Agatha Christie's short story (a medium that rarely did justice to her genius as a writer of crime fiction) 'The Adventure of the Christmas Pudding', Hercule Poirot is enlisted to help a young foreign potentate who resembles Farouk in his irresponsibility and luxurious lifestyle, and has become embroiled in scandal after losing a priceless family heirloom – a ruby necklace – to a woman he has an affair with.⁵⁹ However, there are three novelists – Gore Vidal, Lawrence Durrell and Barbara Skelton – who had more extended exposure to Farouk, by virtue of their presence in Egypt during the 1940s, and who used the Egyptian monarch to dramatize their own literary and personal preoccupations.

In 1948, the career of the precocious young American author Gore Vidal, not yet twenty-three years old, seemed to have hit an impasse. His third novel, *The City and the Pillar*, had alienated critics and lost him readers, largely because of its dispassionately presented view of male homosexuality. Vidal retreated to Cairo, to lick his wounds and to embark on *Search for the King*, the first novel in the genre that he later came to master, historical fiction.⁶⁰ As a regular visitor to the Auberge des Pyramides, Vidal often observed Farouk, 'like a mafia don, with his dark glasses', surrounded by his plain clothes bodyguards, 'on the prowl for large blond women'.⁶¹ *Search for the King* was published in 1950, and was not unfavourably received. However, Vidal still needed to find a way to make his writing pay, especially given his tendency to live well beyond his means. The answer was to author a number of deliberately unsophisticated pulp novels, which were then published under various pseudonyms in the early 1950s. Most of these were in the private eye and mystery novel genres. However, *Thieves Fall Out*, published in 1953, under the name of 'Cameron Kay', drew on Vidal's stay in Egypt.

The novel's hero, Pete Wells, is a cash-strapped American who is persuaded to smuggle a valuable ancient artefact out of Egypt. In the meantime, he falls prey to the sexual charms of a German refugee, Anna Mueller, who has a romantic history which connects her to the Egyptian monarch. Farouk himself appears in the novel, first spotted by Pete in the Auberge des Pyramides, 'a short fat man wearing dark glasses', looking more 'like a dentist than a king'. Pete is advised that those who pursue relationships with the king's mistresses are either expelled from Egypt or 'become eunuchs'. When he fails to pay heed, Pete narrowly avoids being castrated by a group of hired assailants who attack him at night outside Luxor. It eventually transpires that Anna's liaison with the king is a cover for her involvement in the revolutionary opposition to the regime. Pete and Anna succeed in using the distraction of the 1952 Cairo riots to secure a flight out of Egypt, with Anna anticipating the imminent demise of the monarchy: 'The Farouks never last long, even in countries like Egypt.'[62]

Inevitably, the decidedly overheated *Thieves Fall Out* lacks Vidal's renowned elegance and erudition, which is possibly why Vidal disowned it for the remainder of his life.[63] However, Vidal's time in Egypt inspired a more serious, not to say portentous, novel, *The Judgment of Paris*, which also featured Farouk as a character. *The Judgment of Paris* was a haphazardly executed *bildungsroman*, in which Philip Warren, an American, fresh out of law school, embarks on a journey of self-discovery that takes him to the high life of Paris, Rome and Cairo. Philip is introduced to Cairo by Philip de Cluny, who is eager to share with his guest gossip about the scandalous behaviour of Farouk, 'a plump young Albanian, a ribald successor to those austere Pharaohs who had reigned before him'. When Philip describes Farouk's desert palace, with its absence of trees or garden, as 'gloomy-looking', de Cluny counters:

> But the view! Think of it! Having the pyramids in front of you on a starlit night, with a beautiful woman beside you… how evocative to recall in the midst of an orgy that one owns the pyramids out there and all the desert around, to know one is king. What a lovely prospect for a young man! No wonder it's gone to his head.

Philip's response to this statement is initially to resort to the 'popular American view' that the rich and powerful were 'hopelessly miserable with no whims left to be granted' and their wealth 'invariably attended by guilt and shame'. However, almost immediately Philip concedes that 'the King of Egypt probably never suffered from much more than an occasional hangover or a moment's anguish at the little figure he had sacrificed to a robust appetite'.[64] In this passage, Vidal folds Farouk into his waspish critique of the demoralizing consequences of decadence and corruption. The moral vacuum that Farouk inhabits is underlined when Philip encounters Farouk at a reception, the king's physical appearance serving as a register of his fundamental shallowness: 'Philip immediately recognized the curiously stiff figure and immobile face, half hidden now by dark glasses that made him look, more than ever, like an interesting experiment in taxidermy.'[65]

Lawrence Durrell's stint as the foreign press officer in the British Embassy in wartime Cairo provided the raw material for *The Alexandria Quartet*, his enigmatic chronicle of the cosmopolitan world of the Egyptian elite, and their interaction with the British. Durrell was certainly too ready to trade in the stereotypes of orientalism (especially in regard to his Muslim and Coptic characters), but he also used the story of David Mountolive, the British ambassador, to expose the inner emptiness and ultimate futility of Britain's imperial project in Egypt. Mountolive was clearly a fictional character, an insecure and excessively introspective figure who was considerably younger than, and lacked the proconsular swagger of his real-life equivalent, Sir Miles Lampson.[66] However, it is another fictional character in the quartet that concerns us here. Memlik Pasha is the Egyptian interior minister, a man whom Durrell presents as only a marginally updated version of the feudal tyrant of the orientalist imaginary. Memlik is cruel, morbidly suspicious and venal.

In his informed reading of the political contexts to *The Alexandria Quartet*, Mike Diboll maintains that the real-life model for Memlik was Ismail Sidky Pasha, the authoritarian Egyptian prime minister between 1930 and 1935 (and, again, in 1946).[67] However, the specific details that Durrell includes in his portrait of Memlik clearly reference Farouk. Memlik shares Farouk's Albanian ancestry, and sports a sartorial style reminiscent of the king, notably an enthusiasm for 'pearl-grey spats'. Memlik's entourage includes an Italian barber, who (like Farouk's Italian servant, Pulli) acts as a procurer for his sovereign. The sycophantic attendants who surround Memlik flatter and entertain him by suggesting pleasures 'whose perversity might ignite a man who appeared to have worn away every mental appetite'. Memlik certainly was not intended to be a simulacrum of Farouk. Farouk simply isn't terrifying enough to be the inspiration for Memlik, and Durrell's novel also makes reference to Memlik's powerful influence over 'the old king'. However, the fact that Memlik possesses some of Farouk's immediately recognizable attributes would suggest that Durrell wanted to incorporate the king into his denunciation of the aristocratic pasha class, and their contribution to the continued political and social backwardness of Egypt. What Memlik certainly shared with Farouk was the fact that, as Durrell's narrator points out, 'Legends collect easily around such a personage because he belongs more to legend than to life'.[68]

The flashy charms of wartime Cairo were inevitably compellingly attractive for Barbara Skelton, the Foreign Office cipher clerk whose obituary characterized her as 'the most celebrated *femme fatale* of that generation which took its first pleasures between the air-raid and the all-clear'.[69] Growing up with a distinctly raffish inheritance (her father was an ex-army officer, her mother an Edwardian chorus girl), she had been the 'kept woman' of a London millionaire and a model for Schiaparelli, before being drafted into wartime government service. With her perfect figure, high cheekbones and green almond-shaped eyes, she attracted the attentions of a variety of literary and artistic figures, including Alan Ross, Michael Wishart, Peter Quennell and Anthony Steel. While in Cairo, she became Farouk's mistress, before the British Embassy, fearing a scandal, unceremoniously shipped her away to an alternative assignment. After the war she married the writer Cyril Connolly, but maintained a torrid and libidinous private life.[70] It was when her marriage was in its death throes, in 1956, that she published her first novel, *A Young Girl's Touch*. This provided a barely fictionalized account of her time in wartime Egypt, and, more specifically, her affair with Farouk. The heroine of this *roman a clef*, Melinda Paleface, is clearly Skelton herself, its setting – Jubaland – is Egypt; the Wompach club is Cairo's Gezira Sporting Club and the Auberge des Morts Farouk's private rest house and nightclub, the Auberge des Pyramides.[71]

Farouk appears as King Yoyo, who shares the real king's appetite for both treasure and young women. In one incident, Yoyo deliberately shares vulgar jokes at a banquet in order to embarrass and provoke a British diplomat and his wife, a scene that could easily have come from Lampson's diaries, with their constant readiness to record Farouk's uncouth behaviour and discourtesy towards the ambassador and his wife, Jacqueline.[72] Skelton provided some memorable descriptions of Yoyo, notably one of the king's routine on waking in the morning:

> He was expecting a large bunch of letters and the latest American magazines with pin-up covers which were soon brought to him on a tray with a rock-crystal goblet of fresh fruit juice. Dismissing the two armed guards who slept at the foot of his bed he lovingly turned each page, now and then moistening his forefinger with a broad wet tongue. After a cursory glance through the pile of begging letters that came to him from cranks all over the world, he stepped into a bubble bath prepared by a black masseur who, after scenting and soaping the hairy thighs, tickled him in his itchy spots with a gilt-handled back-scratcher shaped at the tip in the likeness of a female hand with pointed, ruby, enamel nails. Wrapped in a silk toga he seated himself before an amber glass while one Nubian tweaked his toes, another massaged his scalp with an aromatic hair grower, as the court barber slapped his balloon cheeks with a warm towel and tweaked his imperial moustaches with a pair of curling tongs.[73]

The similarities between the detailed descriptions of Yoyo and her reminiscences of Farouk in Skelton's subsequently published autobiography meant that *A Young Girl's Touch* was employed as a resource for journalists and popular biographers preoccupied with charting the more salacious aspects of Farouk's life and loves.[74] In particular, Yoyo's insistence on spanking Melinda (which leaves her with 'a forlorn feeling which was not unpleasant') has too regularly been presented as unqualified corroboration of Farouk's penchant for flagellation.[75]

It seems critical therefore to remember that *A Young Girl's Touch* is a novel, not an autobiography, and to comprehend the character of Yoyo/Farouk within that context. The blurb which accompanied the book on its release declared that its author was 'a buoyant satirist, a mistress of the picaresque, a fresh and original humourist who casts a vivid and haunting eye on the problem of men and women'.[76] Considered in this context, Melinda's relationship with Yoyo seems to be a foil to her complicated romantic entanglements with two British officers, Darcy and Roger. Yoyo is presented as immature and spoilt, his sexual advances preceded by chat-up lines that are corny and unoriginal. However, he possesses an affable and ingenuous honesty about his sexual needs. Melinda clearly finds Yoyo a refreshing contrast to her two army beaux, the boorish Darcy (who too readily takes her for granted) and Roger (who offers her security but whose 'efforts at love-making were to prove like those of a mechanical man who solemnly flicked away at a lighter that needed refilling').[77] While Melinda's love life is tangled and unsettled, her affair with Yoyo dramatizes her independence, and her willingness to embark on a life of sexual adventure and experiment on her own terms.

It was Barbara Skelton's misfortune to have her literary talents overshadowed by her reputation as muse and siren to prominent male literary bohemians. She was generally acknowledged to be the model for the man-eater Pamela Fitton in Anthony Powell's *Dance to the Music of Time*, and much was made of her high-profile divorce from Connolly, prompted by her adulterous affair with publisher George Weidenfeld.[78] One newspaper obituary evaluated her from an exclusively male perspective (and one that veered into open misogyny) claiming that, while at first sight, she was 'kittenish, amusingly troublesome, irresistibly attractive', it soon emerged 'what a challenging woman she was: selfish, sulky, socially unmanageable', prone to 'promiscuity and notorious rudeness'.[79] Perhaps Melinda's affair with Yoyo might be seen as a metaphor for the woman writer inhibited by the men whose company she kept, or at the very least an effort to restore agency and animation to the female object of male sexual objectification.[80]

## IV

A critical location where the forces of Americanization and fictionalization intersect is obviously the world of Hollywood. In January 1954 British film fan magazine *Picturegoer* reported that 'Hollywood producers are going to give us a cycle of stories about the kind of a king Farouk was'.[81] One project in the works was rumoured to have emanated from Errol Flynn and would feature Orson Welles in a role inspired by the former Egyptian monarch. Such a pairing did not seem especially propitious, given that both former Hollywood major players were in effective European exile at this point, Flynn compromised by lurid stories of heavy drinking, voyeurism and under-age sex, and Welles having appeared to have squandered his youthful promise by embarking on a series of self-aggrandizing film projects which confounded critics and lacked popular appeal.[82] On the other hand, Flynn's excesses and Welles' extravagances might have made them highly appropriate co-authors of a cinematic rendering of Farouk's larger-than-life adventures. While nothing came of this tantalizing collaboration, the other 'Farouk' project *Picturegoer* alluded to was already underway in the winter of 1953/4, and indeed it progressed all the way to a completed motion picture, albeit one that, while widely publicized in both Britain and America, never secured a cinema release.

The first details of the development of this film, whose working title was 'My Kingdom for a Woman', were revealed to readers of the *Daily Mirror* in November 1953. Donald Zec reported from Cairo that the Egyptian government was funding, in conjunction with an Egyptian Italian financier, an English-language film about a playboy monarch with 'an enthusiasm for life and women'. Those involved in the film's production insisted that it was to be the story of 'a non-existent man in a non-existent country' and that it was a mere coincidence that the leading character bore 'a remarkable resemblance to an ex-king whose fabulous story everyone knows'. Zec brushed aside such raillery, declaring that it was patently obvious that the film's central character 'clearly portrays' Egypt's former king.[83] More information about the film became available in the weeks that followed. The setting would be a fantasized Middle Eastern kingdom named Banderia, while the central character, named King Abdullah, would be played by Gregory Ratoff, a Russian émigré who had worked in Hollywood since the 1920s. Ratoff would also direct and produce the film. English actress Kay Kendall had been cast as an elegant *haute couture* model who is pursued by Abdullah. The *Daily Mirror* was quick to establish how this plot echoed the real-life story of Gabby Wegge, a Belgian model who, in March 1953, visited Farouk in Rome and was subject to intense speculation that she was his chosen replacement for his soon-to-be-divorced wife, Narriman. Wegge was summoned home to Antwerp by her outraged parents, but not before their daughter received the soubriquet of 'the model who said no to Farouk'.[84]

The *Daily Mirror* sent Donald Zec to the set of the film where he found Ratoff struggling with the problems of an ever-changing script and constant interference from the Egyptian authorities, who having allowed the film to be shot in Farouk's former palaces and on his yacht, now reserved the right to prohibit actors from wearing red fezzes and to alter the script to excise perceived insults to the Egyptian army. They also insisted that wardrobe assistants placed tinsel leaves on the navels of the film's cast of belly dancers.[85] In April 1954 it was the turn of *Picture Post* to visit the film on location. Ratoff continued to insist that the film was not based on Farouk (the decidedly flimsy validation for this denial being the fact that Ratoff's character sported a beard and did not wear Farouk's trademark rimless dark glasses), even though the film featured Farouk's former palaces and yachts, and 'possibly some of his ex-girlfriends'.[86] The persistence with this disingenuous conceit did not end with the film's completion. In November 1954 even Zec, who had secured an exclusive preview of the film, wrote of Ratoff's Abdullah that he 'reminds me of a character I once bumped in to in Rome – or was it Cannes? But I'm hanged if I can remember his name'.[87]

By the time of its completion the film was renamed *Abdullah the Great*. The film's plot was relatively straightforward. The debauched King Abdullah, dining at the Ibis Club, catches sight of Ronnie, a beautiful young woman who is visiting

**Figure 10** *Abdullah the Great*: Abdullah (Gregory Ratoff) and Aziz (Martina Berti) (Moviestore Collection/Alamy).

Banderia to display the latest collections of a noted Parisian atelier, George St. George. Ronnie spurns the king's advances, but falls in love with an idealistic young army officer, Ahmed Farid, who begs her not to judge Banderia by its monarch. To the consternation of his advisors, the king becomes increasingly obsessed with Ronnie, and has her followed to Monte Carlo, kidnapped and brought to his yacht. Again Ronnie recoils at his attentions and Abdullah is obliged to free her. Ahmed tries to assassinate the king. When he fails and is arrested, Ronnie offers herself to Abdullah in return for her lover's life, but the king refuses to bargain. He releases both Ronnie and Ahmed, and, with his palace surrounded by his mutinous troops, abdicates and goes into exile in Monte Carlo. Ratoff had promised that his film offered both 'belly-dancers and belly-laughs', and it certainly featured some moments of effective humour. When an unsteady and wheezing Abdullah collapses after chasing Ronnie around his yacht, she waspishly comments, 'You know you've got to decide right now – it's either women or starches – you just can't handle them both'.[88] Pre-release reviews praised the 'glittering settings' and 'sumptuous sets' of this 'opulent technicolor romantic melodrama' which was 'obviously inspired by comparatively recent headlines'.[89] The film's visual magnificence was also evident in Kay Kendall's (playing Ronnie) 'ravishing' gowns, and audiences were promised that they were unlikely to have previously seen 'a screen harem with such luscious inhabitants'.[90] Ratoff was credited for 'really getting under the skin of the dissolute, prodigal and pathetic king', although the supporting cast, notably Charlie Chaplin's son Sydney (who played Ahmed), was judged 'uneven'.[91]

*Abdullah the Great* may be dismissed at an inconsequential romp. However, it incorporates many of the complexities and ambiguities which surrounded the ways that the real Farouk was comprehended and represented. Most critically, it reinforces and reiterates the indeterminacy surrounding Farouk. If Farouk's racial and national identity seemed as uncertain as the geographical positioning of the kingdom he ruled, it possibly made more sense than it really should have done that, while Banderia is clearly an Arab state, its ruler is a Caucasian male with a heavy Russian accent.[92] Farouk's geographical mobility is matched by the way *Abdullah the Great* shifts between Banderia and Monte Carlo, and the prominent role of the king's yacht in the film's narrative.[93] The film luxuriates in overblown orientalism (featuring belly dancers and Ronnie telling Ahmed how Banderia reminds her of 'my first box of dates – you know, camels and palm trees and stuff') but also presents Abdullah/Farouk's comfort with the worlds of the night club and *haute couture*.[94] Abdullah's pursuit of Ronnie presents potential miscegenation as farce, not as the anxiety-inducing trope that it had become in the United States at the dawn of the Civil Rights era and Britain in a decade characterized by (predominantly young male) immigration from the West Indies.[95]

Just as Farouk became detached from exclusively imperially based understandings of the world, the British Empire (or indeed any European imperial power) is completely absent from *Abdullah the Great*. This is not to say that the film does not possess political connotations. Abdullah's pursuit of Ronnie is presented as yet another example of his inability to give sustained attention to the material deprivation and political repression of his people. Aziza (played by Italian actress Marina Berti), the belly dancer who remains loyal to her king to the end, reminds Abdullah of his youthful popularity among his ordinary subjects: 'You were their only hope in their misery and you betrayed them. You cast your lot in with their oppressors… with all the leeches who grew fat on their suffering, and you grew fat with them.' Such sentiments would obviously have been most congenial to Egypt's new military leaders, who, after all, had helped finance the film in the first place. (They were presumably even more delighted with Ahmed informing Ronnie that he cannot resign his commission because 'You see, the Army is the last hope of my people'.)[96] *Abdullah the Great* was as much a co-authored project with the Free Officers as were the narratives of Farouk's excess and depravity promoted in British newspaper coverage of the opening of the private suites of the king's former palaces.[97]

With its backcloth of luxuriously appointed palace rooms and extravagant dinners, the potentially demoralizing impact of conspicuous consumption that Farouk may have symbolized is equally apparent. One review concluded that the film 'achieves a certain dubious topicality in the obvious invitation to "identify" its central character', but that its plot 'with its polyglot accents, lavish settings and undulating dancing girls, belongs firmly in the Hollywood tradition'.[98] Given that Farouk transcended the boundaries between politics and celebrity, and featured in the popular culture of America, as well as Britain, the apparent dichotomy between the 'real' Farouk and a Hollywood fantasy seems less secure than this reviewer would clearly have liked it to be.

The fact that writers for the *Daily Mirror* and *Picture Post* could produce copy on *Abdullah the Great* that often never even referred to Farouk by name, at the very same time that it left readers in no doubt who they had in mind, underlines just how extensive and profound was the level of familiarity enjoyed by the Egyptian monarch among the British public. *Abdullah the Great* was, for reasons that remain obscure, never released. However, its indirect presence through feature articles on its production and reviews in the major film journals testifies to the extraordinary ubiquity of Farouk in British culture in the late 1940s and 1950s, with which this book opened. Moreover, as has been constantly reiterated throughout the previous chapters, ubiquity was also accompanied by a lack of fixity surrounding Farouk's status. This final chapter has illustrated this point in its most expanded form. In part, the journey Farouk had taken as he moved out of the designations of imperial high politics into the world beyond was a spatial one: from his gilded palaces and reception rooms, first to the nightclubs of Cairo, and then on to the casinos of Cannes, the holiday lidos of Capri and, finally, the curbside restaurant tables of the Via Veneto.

It also, though, became a discursive one as Farouk was comprehended not merely as a king and a national figurehead but as an ex-king and exile, a presence in cosmopolitan celebrity culture and a symbol of both established elite forms of conspicuous consumption and new forms of affluent leisure. Farouk appeared to possess clear affinities with broader changes in contemporary culture, while still calling to mind highly resonant affinities with the historical past. The geographical and discursive unfixing of Farouk culminated in him securing a place in the popular imaginary of the United States, a place (despite the views of Florida circuit judges) he never visited, and traversing the frontier between fact and fiction, between material reality and myth. In this manner, Farouk came to match the unfixed and mutable postwar world in which he was such a flamboyantly compelling presence.

# Conclusion: Two Funerals, 1965

For two days after his death, ex-King Farouk lay in a modest walnut coffin in a Rome mortuary, while the Italian authorities wrangled with officials from a number of Arab states over how to dispose of his body. Then, on 20 March 1965, a brief funeral ceremony was held at the mortuary chapel, attended by a motley assortment of mourners: Farouk's children, two of his most recent mistresses, the Prince and Princess of Hesse, and representatives from the Italian Foreign Office and the House of Savoy. As the motor hearse carrying the coffin departed the chapel, it was followed by a small crowd, composed of curiosity-seekers and the barmen and waiters who had attended to Farouk during his final years on the Via Veneto. Farouk's remains now found themselves in a temporary crypt in Rome's municipal cemetery. A week later, President Nasser, who had initially opposed the repatriation of the body of Egypt's former ruler, relented, and Farouk's coffin was discreetly flown to Cairo. Transported from the airport in a simple military truck, Farouk was interred at two in the morning at a relatively obscure location near the slums of the City of the Dead, in a ten-minute ceremony that was witnessed solely by his sisters and brothers-in-law.[1]

Farouk's last rites were characterized by a frugality and diffidence that were an obvious contrast to the flamboyance and spectacle with which he had been associated as a monarch. Moreover, the limited press attention to his death and burial suggested his status, not merely as an ex-king but as a celebrity and significant figure in popular culture, was already on the wane. The front page of the morning edition of the *Daily Mail* on 18 March 1965 did include the report 'Farouk Dies after Dinner', but it had to jostle for space with 'Milk Price Storm', which detailed the outrage among dairy farmers generated by the Wilson government's decision to limit the price paid for milk to producers.[2] In the days prior to Farouk's funeral, the same newspaper carried a brief feature on 'Seven Women Weep for Dead Playboy Ex-King Farouk' and a report on the reading of Farouk's will and testament in his former apartment in the Parioli.[3] The *Daily*

*Mirror*'s sole report on Farouk in the week of his death and funeral was relegated to page nine of an edition of the paper that was more preoccupied with the trial of the East End gangsters the Krays and the completion of the first somersault in space (by Russian cosmonaut Alexei Leonov).[4]

The limited press interest in Farouk's demise was in stark contrast to the media frenzy which accompanied the death and burial of another public figure in the first quarter of 1965. On 12 January, less than two months before Farouk's fatal night out at the Ile de France, Winston Churchill suffered the last of a series of strokes which had beset him for over a decade, and died almost two weeks later. His funeral, held on 30 January, could not have been more different to Farouk's. While the obsequies of the ex-king were decidedly unprepossessing, culminating in a clandestine burial more suited to a pauper or a convicted murderer than a former monarch, Churchill's funeral was extensively covered – and acclaimed – by the world's media. It was, furthermore, a meticulously choreographed grand spectacle, both stately (literally in this particular case, a rare honour for a non-royal personage) and dignified (by the presence, in St Pauls' Cathedral, of officials from 112 countries, including five kings, two queens, one emperor, a grand duke, fifteen presidents and fourteen prime ministers).[5]

This dramatic asymmetry which characterized the death and internment of Churchill and Farouk was hardly surprising. By 1965, Churchill had been elevated to the status of 'Man of the Century', esteemed as the saviour of his nation, if not the whole free world.[6] Noel Coward and his show business friends who gathered to watch the funeral on television were undoubtedly not the only ones who were 'in floods of proud tears' on that day of solemn pageantry.[7] Despite the fact that he was only forty-five when he died (literally half Churchill's age) Farouk – mortifyingly profligate, personally depraved and publicly despised – appeared to have been mourned by no one outside his family and ever-present Albanian bodyguards.

This is not to say that there were not definite intersections between, and commonalities in the lives of, the two men. When Farouk was two years old, his father had been elevated from the Sultanate to the status of Egypt's first monarch, Fuad I. Critical to this process was Churchill, then serving as colonial secretary, whose romantic and hierarchical instincts had encouraged him to create a series of new royal regimes in those parts of the Arab world where Britain held sway, not merely Egypt but also the recently acquired Mandates of Transjordan and Iraq.[8] Churchill and Farouk inevitably encountered each other during Churchill's wartime visits to Cairo to supervise grand strategy in the Middle East, and (in the summer of 1942) to take a personal hand in restoring the fortunes of the British Eighth Army, after it had suffered a series of humiliating reverses in the Western Desert. These meetings were cordial enough, but did little to mitigate the mutual suspicion which had developed between the king and the British, after the Abdin crisis and concerns about Farouk's pro-Axis sympathies. Churchill was in the opening months of his second (and final) term as prime minister when the crisis of both British and royal authority in Egypt reached its climacteric in the Cairo riots of January 1952, and the coup which removed Farouk from the throne, six months later.[9]

While Churchill would have found it impossible to match Farouk's opulent lifestyle and certainly did not share the king's apparently voracious appetite for food and sex, both men had no truck with puritanical self-abnegation. Churchill's flagrant lifestyle entailed endless cases of champagne and boxes of cigars, silk underclothes, vacations in the Bahamas, yachting in the Mediterranean, shoots in Normandy, overdrafts at the bank and unpaid bills at the shirtmakers. Although he did not play for the same heady stakes as Farouk did, Churchill was no stranger to the tables of the casinos of Monte Carlo and Biarritz.[10] However, the worlds of luxury and privilege that both of these two flamboyant personalities felt was theirs by right had more in common with the insouciant elitism of pre-1914 High Society than it did with the 'affluent society' which was already in full swing by the time they died in 1965. While Farouk was considerably younger than Churchill, both men lacked the youthful meritocracy of an era in which improved material conditions had become linked to burgeoning opportunities for the recalibrating of social esteem.

However, such superficial affinities cannot even begin to obscure the very different public profiles (and reputations) of Farouk and Churchill in the years following their deaths. Once, one of the most recognizable figures in the world, by the end of the century, Farouk had drifted into near obscurity. His strongmen successors in Egypt – first Nasser, and then Sadat – had abolished the monarchy and bulldozed the Khedive Ismail's *belle epoque* Cairo that had served as a sumptuous backcloth to Farouk's public and private lives.[11] While some bemoaned the dramatic shift from hedonism to puritanism that accompanied the new republican dispensation, most Egyptians were happy to erase from their national memory a figure identified with both European subjugation and the humiliating failure to thwart the creation of a viable Israeli state.

However, the gradual unravelling of the Mubarak regime in the opening years of the twenty-first century created the opportunity for increased interest in, and even a measure of revaluation of, Farouk in the country he had once ruled. For several decades, exiled or disregarded Egyptian royals and aristocrats had undertaken the somewhat thankless task of trying to recuperate Farouk's reputation, presenting him as a victim of both cynical British and American realpolitik and a disrespectful foreign news media.[12] An impressive line-up of former princesses and pashas provided much of the testimony gathered by Hollywood journalist William Stadiem in his largely sympathetic 1991 biography of Farouk.[13] However, in the early 2000s, Farouk seemed to have been rediscovered by the wider Egyptian population. In 2007, *Al-Malek Farouk*, a thirty-episode drama about Farouk's loves and lives, was broadcast on Egyptian television.[14] It was favourably received, although there were complaints about its status as an essentially Arab, as opposed to Egyptian, enterprise (produced as it was in Saudi Arabia, with many of the leading actors from Syria) and the fact that it had failed to secure the opportunity to film on location in the King's remaining residences.[15] In the last decade, Farouk has increasingly featured in Arab-language social media forums. A Facebook account dedicated to Farouk by Amr Abu Seif in 2011 (which sidestepped controversial political issues in favour of an emphasis on the cultural and artistic effervescence over which Farouk presided in the 1940s) at one point was reputed to have had five million followers.[16] At a more local level, the online travel forum TripAdvisor reveals that 'King Farouk' has been adopted as the alias of at least one professional tour guide in Egypt.[17]

Outside of Egypt, references to Farouk at the close of the twentieth and the dawn of the twenty-first centuries have been sporadic and indiscriminate. In 1979, *The Fat Show*, a play by artist and writer Ken Lee performed at Watford Palace Theatre, envisioned an imaginary meeting between Hermann Goering, Errol Flynn, Bernard Docker and King Farouk.[18] When, in 1987, Roddy Doyle was unable to find a publisher for his novel of unemployment and soul music among the youth of north Dublin, *The Commitments*, he founded his own publishing company: King Farouk Press. In 1991, Farouk appeared in Len Deighton's Second World War spy thriller *City of Gold*.[19] In the previous year, 'The Yellow Palace', a short story by American author Barry Gifford (best known for his screenplay of the David Lynch film *Wild at Heart*), featured a libidinous Egyptian king viewed from the perspective of his manservant.[20] In Warren Adler's *Mother Nile* (2016), the American-born son of an Irish father and Egyptian mother goes in search of his long lost half-sister, conceived during his mother's affair with King Farouk.[21]

Three years later, the protagonist of Nobel Prize winner Patrick Modiano's confection of autobiography and invention, *Family Record*, recalls a chance boyhood friendship with the exiled Farouk.[22] In 2018 science-fiction writer

John Whitbourn offered a bizarrely fantasized counterfactual history, in which Farouk is not merely the twentieth century's most notorious erotic adventurer but proves to be its greatest statesman.[23] Also in 2018, online magazine *The Rake* (which purported to be 'the modern voice of classic elegance') featured as one of its 'Icons', the 'King of Bling: Farouk of Egypt'.[24] However, Farouk's most offbeat posthumous appearance has to be in the lyrics to Bruce Springsteen's 1987 ballad 'Ain't Got You'. By cryptically declaring that he had more good luck 'than old King Farouk', the American singer and songwriter left his bewildered fans to speculate not merely about the meaning of this reference but about who King Farouk even was.[25]

Indeed all these dispersed and fragmented citations of Farouk are little more than flotsam and jetsam when compared to the extraordinary reach and pervasiveness that has continued to characterize the official and popular afterlives of Winston Churchill. Unfortunately such disproportionality, while entirely understandable, is symptomatic of a broader deficiency in our approach, both academic and popular, to the history and memory of the British Empire. Remembering Churchill while forgetting Farouk reflects a narrowing – temporal, spatial and conceptual – of how we understand the operation (and discursive possibilities) of empire. Churchill's funeral has often been presented as a critical moment in modern British history, an occasion which demonstrated an increased investment in the myth of an 'island nation' standing alone during its 'finest hour' in 1940. In the process, the imperial dimension to Churchill's life was largely erased, with references to the wider world confined to Churchill's personal and diplomatic affinities with the United States. The funeral certainly contrasted with the central role that had been played by the Empire-Commonwealth in the coronation of Elizabeth II twelve years previously, underlining the rapid diminishing of Britain's colonial possessions (and British imperial prestige more generally) in the years immediately following the Suez debacle.[26]

However, if Churchill's funeral displayed few traces of the late colonial present, popular memory and memorialization in subsequent decades ensured a definite association between Churchill and Britain's imperial past. Within seven years of his death, the film *Young Winston* enthusiastically re-created Churchill's formative years as a cavalry officer in India, his participation in the Battle of Omdurman and his adventures as a war correspondent during the Boer War.[27] If Churchill's imperial story was less prominent in the decades that immediately followed his death, by the second decade of the twenty-first century, the association between Churchill and empire had become much more salient, if also more controversial and divisive. Indeed Churchill appears to have become a lightning rod in the post-Brexit 'culture wars', singled out for either exoneration or indictment by, respectively, apologists for empire and critics of Britain's continued failure to acknowledge the contribution of its imperial past to racial inequality in the present.[28] By contrast, Farouk has played no role whatsoever in this war of words, not least because the complex truths he reveals about imperial identities are difficult to accommodate into a debate which has been characterized – on both sides – by an unappealing mix of affronted indignation and reductionist platitudes.[29]

The notion of empire that Churchill has come to embody is immediately discernible, temporally affiliated to Britain's imperial meridian in the period between the 1880s and the 1920s. Its reference points are the reign of Queen Victoria (whom Churchill had served as a cavalry subaltern on the Northwest Frontier and in Kitchener's Sudan expeditionary force, and who was still monarch when Churchill was first elected to parliament), the South African War, the pride and prestige of the Edwardian navy (which Churchill oversaw as First Lord of the Admiralty) and punitive assaults on Iraqi civilians (encouraged by Churchill as colonial secretary in the early 1920s). Of course, Churchill's engagement with empire continued throughout his long public career, and indeed encompassed such notorious incidents in late imperial history as the apparent failure to avert the Bengal famine of 1943–1944. However, by the 1930s Churchill was already something of an anachronism, even among his fellow imperialists, most obviously in his uncompromising attitudes towards demands for even limited measures of self-government in India. As prime minister, in both the 1940s and 1950s, he was unable to reverse the diminution in British power which made empire increasingly less tenable. Contrary to his famous boast, Churchill *did* ultimately preside over the dissolution of the British Empire.[30] In spite of this, popular myth and memory have chosen to associate him with imperial hubris rather than with its nemesis. Both Churchill's boosters and detractors are guilty of seriously underestimating the instability and contestation which disrupted the imperial project, even its heyday. The British Empire, as it is comprehended in recent debates over Churchill's reputation, possesses a self-confident supremacy, clarity and coherence that, while it serves the purposes of both imperial nostalgia and postcolonial reproach, fails to recognize a historical reality that is much more convoluted and insecure. As Antoinette Burton, in a powerful critique of 'the ability of hegemons to rule unchallenged', has insisted, uncertainty was 'the standard experience, rather than the exception' in the British Empire.[31]

## Conclusion: Two Funerals, 1965

This intrinsic 'turbulence of empire' may have been overlooked by historians of the late-nineteenth- and early-twentieth-century imperial high tide, but the inherent insecurity of the imperial project had become only too palpable by the era of Farouk. Egypt's last king reflected the instabilities and complexities that marked late imperialism and the dawn of the postcolonial world. Farouk was born in 1920, the year usually credited with being the point at which the British Empire attained its largest extent (its unsurpassed reach facilitated by the addition – under the dubious rubric of trusteeship – of former German and Ottoman colonies after the First World War). However, the previous year had seen serious nationalist agitation in three critical locations: Ireland and India, but also Egypt. When added to the economic cost of the First World War and the strains of imperial overreach, there was already substantial evidence that the long-term viability of the empire was far from certain. Farouk's life spanned the period in which that latent fragility progressed to outright dissolution. Egypt had long had a particular and peculiar status within the empire, but Farouk's position, after 1936, as a monarch of a nominally independent nation but one subject to comprehensive British supervision (embodied in Lampson's presumptive performance as an old-style imperial proconsul) reflected the contrary and conflicting tropes of late imperialism. Farouk confronted (but was also an element within) an imperial system in which continued British ascendancy was juxtaposed with an increased emphasis on paternalist development, and with – unsteady and inconsistent – moves towards colonial autonomy.

The product of a different generation, Farouk reflected, much more than Churchill, how the unstable components of late empire became entangled with other cultural formations, some of them novel, others less so. Most significantly in this regard, Farouk became a celebrity. Popular interest in Farouk went well beyond his status as a public figure, extending into his private life and preoccupying itself, not with his political prospects but with his personal proclivities. Farouk, it should not be forgotten, had a not insignificant role in the emergence of one of the totemic figures in the evolution of postwar celebrity culture: the paparazzi photographer. By contrast, Churchill was undoubtedly a media personality, but the public were granted little access to his private and affective lives. Churchill's personality was always projected in relation to his roles as politician and statesman, and never independently of these. Press coverage of Churchill lacked the elements of expose and 'human interest' that distinguished celebrity journalism. Popular understandings of Farouk may have lacked the elements of identification and affinity which are often considered vital components of modern celebrity culture, but he was nevertheless a fully mediated celebrity in the way Churchill was not.[32] Indeed, the contrast between Churchill and Farouk might be a useful exemplar of Daniel Boorstin's famous adage: 'The hero was a big man; the celebrity a big name.'[33]

Churchill had been an ardent admirer of the tradition and ceremony embodied in royalty ('Monarchical No.1', in his own words) and the recipient of a state funeral, an honour largely reserved for senior figures in the royal family.[34] However, Farouk actually *was* a king, and one committed to upholding the privileges, presumptions and prerogatives that were a monarch's due. The fates of royal dynasties and empires had long been intertwined, and Farouk's violent transition from monarch to ex-royal exile might be seen as symptomatic of the waning of both institutions in the twentieth century. That Farouk's story was far from unique was confirmed by the neat symmetry of the former Egyptian king dying in Italy, eight years after the ostracized Victor Emmanuel III of Italy had succumbed to a fatal pulmonary oedema while in exile (and living as Farouk's guest) in Alexandria. The presence of so many ex-kings in the postwar era was not merely a consequence of the creation of Communist regimes in Eastern Europe. It was also a corollary of the compelling process of imperial decomposition which had begun with the collapse of Europe's contiguous dynastic empires at the close of the First World War, and which, once it extended to the European overseas empires, had – by the 1950s – come to imperil the mandate monarchies of the Middle East.

Of course the British monarchy managed to avoid the fate of other royal houses in the twentieth century. At one level Farouk's story would seem to merely confirm the singularity of the experience of the House of Windsor, the latter characterized as it was by popularity and survival, rather than disgrace and exile. However, the intrusion and lack of deference that marked the coverage of Farouk in the postwar British press was, in time, to become the fate of the British royal family as well. Indeed, the period coinciding with Farouk's reign saw the British monarchy become increasingly susceptible to being framed within the tropes of celebrity culture. The apparent equivalence between British royals and Hollywood stars had been only too evident in media images of Edward, Prince of Wales, in the late 1920s and early 1930s. Coverage of Edward's abdication, in the year as Farouk's accession, indicated that the press remained circumspect in handling stories about royal private lives. The outlook of the press changed during the 1940s, and reporting of both the engagement of Princess Elizabeth and Prince Philip in 1947 and the Princess Margaret-Peter Townsend affair in 1953–1955 suggested journalists and editors had become significantly less complaisant than they had been before the war.

However, media obtrusion into the intimate lives of the Windsors really only accelerated after the late 1960s (ironically initiated by the imprudent decision to participate in the 1969 fly-on-the-wall documentary *Royal Family*), before culminating in the exposure of a succession of royal marriage crises in the 1990s.[35] As a foreigner, Farouk's royal status (despite intermittent, ineffective and often half-hearted interventions from the Foreign Office) failed to offer him much protection from a prurient British popular press. However, the impudent, and frequently salacious, media coverage which resulted was both a throwback to a rambunctious pre-Victorian past and an augury of what the House of Windsor itself would be subjected to before the century was out.

As an exile, Farouk's life after 1952 betokened a sense of dislocation that was clearly a postcolonial, rather than a colonial, condition. Imperially derived understandings of the world were merging into new forms of cultural knowledge, which were not merely predicated on new forms of relationship between metropole and colony but also incorporated locations (notably America and continental Europe) that lay beyond the recognized spaces of empire. If Farouk was unfixed, so were the worlds he inhabited.

Such lack of fixity was as much temporal as it was spatial. By the time Farouk died, a new liberalized sexual culture was clearly emerging in the Anglo-American world, although academic history (as opposed to popular memory) has been sceptical about how far, when exactly or in what ways this might have amounted to the creation of a 'permissive society'.[36] Within three months of Farouk's death, a mass market paperback account 'of the scandalous life and loves of the notorious playboy king' had appeared, authored by Rome-based American reporter Michael Stern. Its title (*Farouk Uncensored*), a blend of sexual frankness and sensationalist focus on Farouk's supposed perversions and 'bizarre lusts', matched the temper of the times, even if it was often doing little more than repeating for public consumption stories which had been privately circulated in the sexually charged environment of wartime Cairo.[37]

Indeed, for most of his life, Farouk's colourful exploits had been comprehended through popular mythologization of historical reference points – the debauchery of Ancient Rome, the marital misfortunes of Henry VIII, the upper-class hedonism of the Naughty Nineties – that had little to do with the new sexual culture which had emerged by the early 1960s. Sometimes spatial and temporal indeterminacy operated in tandem. Farouk's fall was part of the reordering of world geopolitics, notably the creation of the concept of the modern 'Middle East', which accompanied the eclipse of European empires and the onset of the Cold War. However, this did not prevent Britons from identifying him with much more venerable geographical constructions, notably a 'two-shore' Mediterranean, even if this was increasingly mediated through the more contemporary prism of postwar mass tourism.

Farouk's indeterminacy has been manifest throughout this book. Acknowledging and investigating this lack of fixity has provided an opportunity to develop a more discerning interpretation of British culture in the era of late imperialism and early post-imperialism. Farouk may be largely forgotten, and even the most die-hard nostalgist cannot deny that the British Empire as a political and economic entity has long gone. Nevertheless, many of the key components of Farouk's public personality – monarchy, celebrity, personal and material excess – remain a preoccupation in both the mass media and wider society. While empire in a formal sense may have passed from the pages of history, many of the cultural formations which had become attached to it in its final decades have been able to reposition themselves in a variety of new, ostensibly post-imperial, contexts. It should not be assumed that this process of cultural reconstitution marks a clear and decisive break with the imperial past. Recent claims made by Meghan, Duchess of Sussex, that she was subjected to racist abuse by both the press and members of the royal family disclose the complex ways in which monarchy, celebrity and the (in this case, decidedly uncongenial) legacies of empire can intersect.[38]

Despite his dramatic fall from both grace and favour, the life of King Farouk has usually been envisaged not as tragedy but as farce. For most of his reign, the British were disinclined to take Farouk seriously. Despite constant anxieties about Egypt's critical strategic status, British officials constantly belittled its monarch, bemoaning his immaturity and apparent lack of application to his royal duties. The British press came to present him as a preposterously bloated buffoon, while comedians and cartoonists found rich material in his fondness for shapely women and high living. However, the prevalence of Farouk was testimony to the multiple and intricate ways in which empire was intermeshed with British culture more broadly. While Farouk was never entirely free from the pernicious stereotypes of orientalism, what is striking is the affinity he appeared to possess with British metropolitan (and particularly, plebeian) culture: encompassing everything from stamp collecting and end-of-the-pier shows to package holidays and a day at the races. If Farouk was a mirror to British society, then that society was not significantly more prepossessing than the debauched profligate leering at them in the looking glass.

Britain, no less than Farouk, was wrestling with the violent displacements that accompanied the end of empire. Farouk's extravagant lifestyle appeared to be a warning of the moral costs of materialism in the emerging affluent society. Farouk's status as both a king and, subsequent, ex-king drew attention to Britain's continued captivation with a hereditary monarchy, even if it unintentionally disclosed that British attitudes to their own royal rulers were characterized more by resigned approval than active enthusiasm. The historical allusions that Farouk summoned up – to some of the more colourful of Britain's former sovereigns or to the carefree diversions of the *belle epoque* – seemed all too typical of an increasingly defensive culture that sought solace in nostalgia, rather than confront the discomforting realities of imperial and national decline. The fact that a key player in Britain's imperial politics could so easily be transformed into an itinerant celebrity was testimony to how far Britain was being refashioned by disconcerting cultural shifts that many balefully identified with the relentless advance of Americanization. However grotesque many of the representations were of Farouk in Britain, confronting him should not have been a matter of repulsion, ridicule or repudiation, but rather one of self-recognition. In this sense at least, for all the mockery and derision he endured, Faruq al-Awwal of Egypt may well have succeeded in having the last laugh.

# Notes

## Introduction

1. With the exception of Chapter 1 (which provides a materially grounded and unmediated life of the king in a predominantly Egyptian context), this book will use 'Farouk' as opposed to the alternative 'Faruq', since the former was the established rendering of the king's name in both official and nonofficial sources in the English medium between the 1930s and 1960s.
2. Todd Shepard, *The Invention of Decolonization: The Algerian War and the Remaking of France* (Ithaca: Cornell University Press, 2006).
3. There is no recent biography of Farouk in English. Farouk was the subject of a cluster of biographies in the years immediately after his death. Most of these works focused on the more salacious and outrageous aspects of his life, although some did seek to explain, and not merely condemn, Farouk's public and private failings, albeit by recourse to murky conspiracy theories involving the British Foreign Office, Israel and the CIA. See Michael Stern, *Farouk Uncensored* (New York: Bantam Books, 1965); Hugh McLeave, *The Last Pharaoh: Farouk of Egypt, 1920–1965* (New York: McCall Publishing, 1970); Barrie St Clair McBride, *Farouk of Egypt* (London: A.S. Barnes, 1968); William Stadiem, *Too Rich: The High Life and Tragic Death of King Farouk* (New York: Carroll and Graf, 1991). Adel Sabit, Farouk's former liaison officer, provided a spirited defence of the King in his memoir-biography *A King Betrayed: The Ill-Fated Reign of Farouk of Egypt* (London: Quartet Books, 1989).
4. Frank Mort, *Capital Affairs: London and the Making of the Permissive Society* (New Haven, CT: Yale University Press, 2010).
5. Notable exceptions are Priya Satia, *Spies in Arabia: The Great War and the Cultural Foundations of Britain's Covert Empire in the Middle East* (New York: Oxford University Press, 2008); James Whidden, *Egypt: British Colony, Imperial Capital* (Manchester: Manchester University Press, 2017). One might also concede Egypt's importance in scholarship *theorizing* (as opposed to *historicizing*) how empire operated, notably Timothy Mitchell, *Colonising Egypt* (Berkeley: University of California Press, 1989), which introduced the notion of the 'actively self-colonizing colonized' into the field of postcolonial studies. Authors of popular history have demonstrated more interest in the cultural aspects of the British presence in the region than their academic equivalents, for example Derek Hopwood, *Sexual Encounters in the Middle East* (Reading: Garnet Publishing, 1999). Critical studies

of Egypt's role in diplomacy and imperial politics are surveyed in Peter Sluggett, 'Formal and Informal Empire in the Middle East', in *The Oxford History of the British Empire, Vol. V: Historiography*, ed. Robin Winks (Oxford: Oxford University Press, 1999), 416–36. Important individual works include William Roger Louis, *The British Empire in the Middle East* (Oxford: Oxford University Press, 1984); John Darwin, 'An Undeclared Empire: The British in the Middle East, 1918–39', *Journal of Imperial and Commonwealth History* 27, no.2 (1999): 159–76, and the various writings of Michael T. Thornhill, culminating in his *Road to Suez: The Battle of the Canal Zone* (Cheltenham: History Press, 2016). For a rare attempt to explore the social history of British administrators in Egypt, albeit for a slightly earlier period, see Lanver Mak, *The British in Egypt: Community, Crime and Crises, 1882–1922* (London: I.B. Tauris, 2017).

6   This formulation is taken from Suzanne Zantop, *Colonial Fantasies: Conquest, Family and Nation in Precolonial* Germany, *1770–1870* (Durham, NC: Duke University Press, 1997), 7.

7   For a demand that historians 'weigh the importance of empire in the making of British culture alongside and against other formations that may have similar claims to be foundational', see Richard Price, 'One Big Thing: Britain, Its Empire and Their Imperial Culture', *Journal of British Studies* 45, no.3 (2006): 611.

8   Antoinette Burton, *The Postcolonial Careers of Santha Rama Rau* (Durham, NC: Duke University Press, 2006).

9   Ann Laura Stoler, 'On Degrees of Imperial Sovereignty', *Public Culture* 18, no.1 (2006): 125–46, especially 127–8 and 137–8. The notion that cultures cannot be unproblematically tied to fixed terrains has been a critical component of developments in historical geography in the last two decades. See *Displacement, Diaspora and Geographies of Identity*, ed. Shadar Lavie and Ted Swedenburg (Durham, NC: Duke University Press, 1996), especially 2–16; Charles W. J. Withers, 'Place and the "Spatial Turn" in Geography and in History', *Journal of the History of Ideas* 70, no.4 (2009): 637–58.

10  For a compelling example of how histories of Europe and histories of empire can be more imaginatively interlinked, in this case by focusing on a highly specific, but nevertheless globalized, location, see Jan Ruger, *Heligoland: Britain, Germany and the Struggle for the North Sea* (Oxford: Oxford University Press, 2017).

11  Significantly the pioneering work on late colonial violence, Caroline Elkins, *Britain's Gulag: The Brutal End of Empire in Kenya* (London: Jonathan Cape, 2005) came, not from a historian of Britain or its empire, but from an Africanist. See also Christopher Bayly and Tim Harper, *Forgotten Wars: The End of Britain's Asian Empire* (London: Allen Lane, 2004); Benjamin Grob-Fitzgibbon, *Imperial Endgame: Britain's Dirty Wars and the End of Empire* (Houndmills: Palgrave Macmillan, 2011).

12 *British Culture and the End of Empire*, ed. Stuart Ward (Manchester: Manchester University Press, 2001), Wendy Webster, *Englishness and Empire, 1939–1965* (Oxford: Oxford University Press, 2005). For those who remained skeptical about the domestic impact of decolonization, Joanna Lewis, see 'Daddy Wouldn't Buy Me a Mau Mau: The British Popular Press and the Demoralization of Empire', in *Mau Mau and Nationhood: Arms, Authority and Narration*, ed. E. S. Atieno Odhiambo and John Lonsdale (Athens, GA: University of Georgia Press, 2003), 227–50 or Stephen Howe, 'When (if Ever) Did Empire End? "Internal Decolonisation" in British Culture since the 1950s' in *The British Empire in the 1950s: Retreat or Revival?*, ed. Martin Lynn (Houndmills: Palgrave Macmillan, 2006), 214–37.

13 Jordanna Bailkin, *The Afterlife of Empire* (Berkeley, CA: University of California Press, 2012). The drawn-out nature of British decolonization is a key motif in two recent studies of the relationship of charitable, educational and financial institutions to the end of empire, namely Sarah Stockwell, *The British End of the End of Empire* (Cambridge: Cambridge University Press, 2018); Anna Bocking-Welch, *British Civil Society at the End of Empire* (Manchester: Manchester University Press, 2019).

14 There is still nothing in the field of postwar British history to match the innovative methodology and sophistication of Kristin Ross, *Fast Cars, Clean Bodies: Decolonization and the Reordering of French Culture* (Cambridge, MA: MIT Press, 1996).

15 A plea made initially as long ago as Bill Schwarz, 'The Only White Man in There: The Re-Racialisation of England, 1956–1968', *Race and Class* 38 (1996): 65–78. For a subsequent reiteration, see Bill Schwarz, *Memories of Empire Volume 1: The White Man's World* (Oxford: Oxford University Press, 2012). For a work that exemplifies the rewards of writing histories that integrate race in the metropole and the politics of imperial decline (and how these two, in turn, intersect with the memory of the Second World War), see Camilla Schofield, *Enoch Powell and the Making of Postcolonial Britain* (Cambridge: Cambridge University Press, 2013).

16 Bailkin, *Afterlife of Empire*, 2, 6. Possibly, indeterminacy at the end of empire was more marked in the Mediterranean and Middle East, since decolonization here was not accompanied by the elaborately choreographed (if decidedly disingenuous) ceremonies that marked the transfer of power to independent nations in Asia and sub-Saharan Africa. See Robert Holland, *Blue-Water Empire: The British in the Mediterranean since 1800* (London: Allen Lane, 2012), 34.

17 The title of *Celebrity Colonialism: Fame, Power and Representation in Colonial and Postcolonial Cultures*, ed. Robert Clarke (Newcastle upon Tyne: Cambridge Scholars Publishing, 2009) suggests it might provide some counsel on how to transcend the previously separated categories of empire and celebrity, but the essays in this collection are rarely historicized and are overwhelmingly focused on the contemporary world.

18 A notion first popularized by *Moments of Modernity: Reconstructing Britain, 1945–1964*, ed. Becky Conekin, Frank Mort and Chris Waters (London: Rivers Oram, 1999). By contrast, Lynda Nead's study of visual culture, journalism and fiction in the decade after 1945, *Tiger in the Smoke: Art and Culture in Postwar Britain* (New Haven: Yale University Press, 2017) suggests the culture of reconstruction failed to shrug off the past, and that the 'postwar modern' was therefore never fully realized. A more convoluted (and not altogether convincing) critique has been provided by the contributors to *The New Elizabethan Age: Culture, Society and National Identity after World War Two*, ed. Irene Morra and Scott Anthony (London: Bloomsbury, 2016), who argue that many figures in the postwar arts scene turned to the received example of the sixteenth-century Elizabethans as a means of articulating an emphatically anti-Victorian modernity.

19 An obvious inspiration here is Carolyn Steedman's classic *Landscape for a Good Woman: A Story of Two Women* (London: Virago, 1986), which exposed the disconcerting presence of personal longings which cannot be easily accommodated within the dominant political and social narratives of postwar British history.

20 This phrase is from Edith Sheffer, *Burned Bridge: How East and West Germans Made the Iron Curtain* (Oxford: Oxford University Press, 2014), 7. Sheffer takes her cue from influential general surveys such as Tony Judt, *Postwar: A History of Europe since 1945* (London: William Heinemann, 2005); Mark Mazower, *Dark Continent: Europe's Twentieth Century* (London: Allen Lane, 1998); *Histories of the Aftermath: The Legacies of the Second World War in Europe*, ed. Frank Biess and Robert Moeller (New York: Berghahn, 2010), all of which highlighted the myriad vulnerabilities that marked the postwar era.

21 Jo Guldi and David Armitage, *The History Manifesto* (Cambridge: Cambridge University Press, 2014).

22 Most of these works have been in the field of US foreign relations, notably those authored by Frank Costigliola. See, for example, his *Roosevelt's Lost Alliances: How Personal Politics Helped Start the Cold War* (Princeton, NJ: Princeton University Press, 2012). For two recent interventions concerned with the emotional dimension to British foreign policy, see Deborah Cohen, 'The Geopolitical Is Personal: India, Britain and American Foreign Correspondents in the 1930s and 1940s', *Twentieth Century British History* 29, no.3 (2018): 388–410; Martin Francis, 'Wounded Pride and Petty Jealousies: Private Lives and Public Diplomacy in Second World War Cairo', in *War: An Emotional History*, ed. Claire Langhamer, Lucy Noakes and Claudia Siebrecht (Oxford: Oxford University Press, 2020), 98–115.

23 A powerful appeal for historians to seek out 'connectivity… between events and across scales' in order to knit 'all kinds of disparate places and events together' is provided by Antoinette Burton, *A Primer for Teaching World History: Ten Design Principles* (Durham, NC: Duke University Press, 2012), 32, 41.

24  Notable among studies which reveal how transnational relations in the 1940s and 1950s were not confined to the realms of diplomacy and politics, but were shaped at every level of society, often within specific cultures of gender, race and sexuality, is Mary Louise Roberts, *What Soldiers Do: Sex and the American GI in World War Two France* (Chicago: Chicago University Press, 2013).
25  David Nasaw, 'Historians and Biography', *American Historical Review* 114, no.3 (2009): 576.
26  Jo Burr Margadant, *The New Biography: Performing Femininity in Nineteenth-Century France* (Berkeley, CA: University of California Press, 2000), 7.
27  For example, Kali Israel, *Names and Stories: Emilia Dilke and Victorian Culture* (New York: Oxford University Press, 1998).
28  Matt Houlbrook, *Prince of Tricksters: The Incredible True Story of Netley Lucas, Gentleman Crook* (Chicago: University of Chicago Press, 2016).
29  This approach is obviously inspired by Antoinette Burton's entreaty to seek out the history of those people in the past who were refugees (deliberate or otherwise) from both 'national history and its disciplinary regimes', 'Who Needs the Nation? Interrogating British History', *Journal of Historical Sociology* 10, no.3 (1997): 238.

# Chapter 1

1  Most of the information in this chapter is derived from Michael T. Thornhill, 'Farouk [Faruq] (1920–1965)', *Oxford Dictionary of National Biography*, 2004. Available online: https://doi.org/10.1093/ref:odnb/64939 (accessed 18 June 2021); Philip Mansel, 'The Fall of the Throne of Egypt', in his *Sultans in Splendour: The Last Years of the Ottoman World* (London: Andre Deutsch, 1988), 162–85 and the major Farouk biographies, namely McLeave, *The Last Pharaoh*, McBride, *Farouk of Egypt*, Stadiem, *Too Rich* and Sabit, *A King Betrayed*. Discussion of the context of Egyptian domestic politics draws on *Re-Envisioning Egypt, 1919–1952*, ed. Arthur Goldschmidt (Cairo: American University in Cairo Press, 2005); Selma Botman, *Egypt from Independence to Revolution, 1919–52* (Syracuse, NY: Syracuse University Press, 1991).
2  For official concern over Mrs Naylor's memoirs, see The National Archive, Kew [hereafter TNA] Foreign Office [hereafter FO] 141/649 Letter from David Kelly (Minister, Egypt) to Ronald Campbell (Egyptian Department, Foreign Office), 14 August 1937.
3  TNA FO 141/644 Miles Lampson to Anthony Eden, 25 February 1937.
4  While still married to Farouk, Narriman produced a brief memoir, in which she confirmed that Farouk had approached her in Naguib's shop, but that her initial visit had been to look for a gift for her father, not to accompany her fiancé in search

of a ring. Her Royal Highness Princess Narriman ('as told to Klaus Bloemer'), 'My True Self', *Ladies' Home Journal*, February 1953, 126–7.

5   TNA Prime Minister's Office Records [hereafter PREM] 11/1118 Letter from Dick Langridge (Rome Embassy) to D. F. de Zulueta, 24 September 1956, enclosing letter (in French) from Farouk on 'la situation desastreuse de l'Egypt' addressed to Eden.

## Chapter 2

1   'Egyptian Team Refuses Their Swimming Prizes', *Daily Mail*, 17 August 1951, 1; 'The Swimmers' Protest', *Daily Mail*, 20 August 1951, 1.
2   Thornhill, *Road to Suez*, Martin Kolinsky, *Britain's War in the Middle East: Strategy and Diplomacy, 1936-42* (Houndmills: Macmillan, 1999); Charles Tripp, 'Egypt, 1945–1952: The Uses of Disorder', in *Demise of the British Empire in the Middle East*, ed. M. J. Cohen and Martin Kolinsky (London: Routledge, 1998), 112–41; Louis, *British Empire in the Middle East*, Peter Hahn, *The United States, Great Britain and Egypt, 1945–1956* (Chapel Hill: UNC Press, 1991).
3   TNA FO 371/90228 Memorandum by Roger Allen to Sir Ralph Stevenson on Complaints by Egyptian Ambassador about British Press Coverage of King Farouk, 26 July 1951; Head of Chancery British Embassy, Alexandria to African Department, Foreign Office, 11 August 1951; FO 371/97064 Foreign Office Correspondence on Cartoons featuring Farouk in the *Daily Express* (December 1951–February 1952); the quotation is from FO 371/90228 Handwritten note by William Strang, 16 November [1951].
4   TNA FO 371/90228 Herbert Morrison to Lord Beaverbrook, 6 September 1951; Beaverbrook to Morrison, 12 September 1951. Morrison appears to have persisted, drafting a second letter to Beaverbrook, but there is no evidence this was sent, FO 371/90228 Draft Letter from Morrison to Beaverbrook, n.d. [September/October 1951].
5   Adrian Bingham, *Family Newspapers? Sex, Private Life and the British Popular Press, 1918-1978* (Oxford: Oxford University Press, 2009), especially 229–61; Adrian Bingham and Martin Conboy, *Tabloid Century: The Popular Press in Britain, 1896 to the Present* (Oxford: Peter Lang, 2015).
6   Daniel Boorstin, *The Image, or What Happened to the American Dream* (London: Weidenfeld and Nicolson, 1961), 57.
7   P. David Marshall, *Celebrity and Power: Fame in Contemporary Culture* (Minneapolis: University of Minnesota Press, 1997); Graeme Turner, *Understanding Celebrity* (London: Sage Publications, 2004).
8   Chris Rojek, *Celebrity* (London: Reaktion Books, 2001), 17–29. A similar criticism could be made of the celebrity taxonomies of Hero, Star and Quasar promoted by

James Monaco, 'Celebration', in *Celebrity: The Media as Image Makers*, ed. James Monaco (New York: Dell, 1978), 3–14.

9    For instance, there have been several scholarly studies of nineteenth-century celebrities, notably Hugh Cunningham, *Grace Darling: Victorian Heroine* (London: Continuum, 2007); Simon Morgan, 'From Warehouse Clerk to Corn Law Celebrity: The Making of a National Hero', in *Rethinking Nineteenth Century Liberalism: Richard Cobden Bicentenary Essays*, ed. Anthony Howe and Simon Morgan (London: Routledge, 2006), 39–55; Lucy Riall, *Garibaldi: Invention of a Hero* (New Haven: Yale University Press, 2008). For a useful discussion, Simon Morgan, 'Celebrity: Academic "Pseudo-Event" or a Useful Concept for Historians?' *Cultural and Social History* 8, no.1 (2011): 95–114.

10   Ronald Robinson and John Gallagher, *Africa and the Victorians: The Official Mind of Imperialism* (London: Macmillan, 1961); Thomas G. Otte, *The Foreign Office Mind: The Making of British Foreign Policy, 1865–1914* (Cambridge: Cambridge University Press, 2011).

11   Anthony Kirk-Greene, *Britain's Imperial Administrators, 1858–1966* (Houndmills: Macmillan, 2000), 49, 64–71.

12   Contemporary elucidations of the British diplomatic ideal include Harold Nicolson, *Diplomacy: A Basic Guide to the Conduct of Contemporary Foreign Affairs* (London: Thornton Butterworth, 1939); Lord Strang, *The Foreign Office* (London: Allen & Unwin, 1955). The 'official mind' was also overwhelmingly masculine, as women were not admitted to the diplomatic service before 1946, and, even then, marriage bars persisted. See Helen McCarthy, 'Petticoat Diplomacy: The Admission of Women to the British Foreign Service, c.1910–1946', *Twentieth Century British History* 20, no.3 (2009): 85–321.

13   For Lampson, *The Killearn Diaries, 1934–1946*, ed. Trefor Evans (London: Sidgwick & Jackson, 1972), xii–xv. For Campbell, 'Obituary: Sir Ronald Campbell', *The Times*, 23 April 1983. For Stevenson, 'Sir Ralph Claremont Skrine Stevenson (1895–1977)', *Who Was Who Vol.7 1971–1980* (London: A & C Black, 1990). For Eden, see David Dutton, *Anthony Eden: A Life and Reputation* (London: Arnold, 1997), 20–55. In the context of the culture of Foreign Office parochialism, it is only fair to note that Eden attained a double first in Persian and Arabic.

14   Frank Heinlein, *British Government Policy and Decolonisation, 1945–1963: Scrutinizing the Official Mind* (London: Routledge, 2002).

15   Michael T. Thornhill, 'Informal Empire, Independent Egypt and the Accession of King Farouk', *Journal of Imperial and Commonwealth History* 38, no.2 (2010): 279–302; *Politics and Diplomacy in Egypt: The Diaries of Sir Miles Lampson, 1935–1937*, ed. Malcom Yapp (Oxford: Oxford University Press, 1997).

16   James Whidden, *Monarchy and Modernity in Egypt: Politics, Islam and Neo-Colonialism between the Wars* (London: I.B. Tauris, 2013).

17 Whidden, *Egypt: British Colony, Imperial Capital*.
18 Laila Morsy, 'Farouk in British Policy', *Middle Eastern Studies* 20, no.4 (1984): 193–212.
19 TNA FO 141/772 Sir Miles Lampson to Anthony Eden, 19 May 1936.
20 TNA FO 141/772 Minute by David Kelly, 27 June 1936; Letter of Recommendation for Edward Ford from Claude Elliott (Master of Eton), 18 June 1936; FO 141/644 'Report on HM King Farouk's Tour of Upper Egypt' by Edward Ford, with accompanying note from Sir Miles Lampson to Sir Lancelot Oliphant, 15 February 1937.
21 Farouk was particularly concerned about the King's Italian aide, Antonio Pulli. See for example, Middle Eastern Centre, St Antony's College, Oxford, Lampson Diaries [hereafter LD] 18 November 1942. For Italian influence within Farouk's court, see Nir Arielli, *Fascist Italy and the Middle East, 1933–1940* (London: Palgrave Macmillan, 2010), 160. On Irene Guinle, Stadiem, *Too Rich*, 54–69.
22 FO 141/644 Miles Lampson to Anthony Eden, 25 February 1937.
23 For example, LD 1 November 1938.
24 FO 1421/481 Report by Lampson of meeting with Mohammed Hassanein Pasha, 15 September 1937.
25 As articulated by Leo Amery, 'Empire and Commonwealth' [1943] in his *The Framework of the Future* (London: Oxford University Press, 1944), 4–5. See also Suke Wolton, *Lord Hailey, the Colonial Office and the Politics of Race and Empire in the Second World War* (Houndmills: Macmillan, 2000).
26 For example, LD 26 October 1938, 3 January 1944, 21 April 1944.
27 William B. Cohen, 'The Colonized as Child: British and French Colonial Rule', *African Historical Studies* 3, no.2 (1970): 427–31.
28 Henry Maitland Wilson, *Eight Years Overseas, 1939–1947* (London: Hutchinson, 1950), 159.
29 Sholto Douglas, *Years of Command* (London: Collins, 1966), 197–202.
30 Lampson's resentment is obvious from both his diaries and the hand-written note he sent to the foreign secretary, in which he attempted to discredit Douglas by disclosing details of Douglas' 'roving eye' and his affair in Cairo with the actress Connie Carpenter, LD 18 August 1943, 13 January 1944, TNA FO 954/5C Lampson to Eden, 5 August 1943.
31 Michael T. Thornhill, 'Britain and the Collapse of Egypt's Constitutional Order, 1950–52', *Diplomacy and Statecraft* 13, no.1 (2002): 121–52.
32 A sample of pertinent introductory works here would need to include Thomas Scheffler, 'Fertile Crescent, Orient, Middle East: The Changing Mental Maps of Southwest Asia', *European Review of History* 10, no.2 (2003): 253–72; Roderic H. Davison, 'Where Is the Middle East?' *Foreign Affairs* 38, no.4 (1960): 665–75; James Renton, 'Changing Languages of Empire and the Orient: Britain and the

Invention of the Middle East, 1917–1918', *Historical Journal* 50, no.3 (2007): 645–67; Zachary Lockman, *Contending Visions of the Middle East: The History and Politics of Orientalism* (Cambridge: Cambridge University Press, 2009); Nile Green, 'Spacetime and the Muslim Journey West: Industrial Communications in the Making of the "Muslim World"', *American Historical Review* 118, no.2 (2013): 401–29. Additional confusion was created by the fact that the Foreign Office's Egyptian Department was also responsible for Italian North Africa, Somaliland and Abyssinia, David Kelly, *The Ruling Few* (London: Hollis & Carter, 1952), 263–4.

33  Mohammed Naguib, *Egypt's Destiny: A Personal Statement* (New York: Doubleday, 1955), 127–8.

34  Matthew H. Ellis, 'Repackaging the Egyptian Monarchy: Faruq in the Public Spotlight, 1936–1939', *History Compass* 7, no.1 (2009): 181–213.

35  Julian Amery, *Sons of the Eagle: A Study in Guerrilla Warfare* (London: Macmillan, 1948); Anthony Quayle, *Eight Hours from England* (London: Heinemann, 1945); Roderick Bailey, *The Wildest Province: SOE in the Land of the Eagle* (London: Jonathan Cape, 2008); David Smiley, *Albanian Assignment* (London: Chatto and Windus, 1984).

36  For example, 'Our Desert Attack', *Picture Post*, 28 December 1940, 26. See also Bernd J. Fischer, *Albania at War, 1939–1945* (West Lafayette, IN: C. Hurst, 1999), 92–3.

37  *Time*, 9 August 1937.

38  Trevor Mostyn, *Egypt's Belle Epoque: Cairo and the Age of the Hedonists* (London: Quartet, 1989).

39  Freya Stark, *The Arab Island: The Middle East, 1939–1943* (New York: Alfred Knopf, 1945), 82.

40  'Prime Provenance: The King Farouk Bedroom Suite', *Artfix*, 27 October 2010. Available online: http://www.artfixdaily.com/blogs/post/9242-prime-provenance-the-king-farouk-bedroom-suite (accessed 12 December 2018); 'The Louis Farouk Tradition', *Financial Times*, 16 December 2009.

41  Will Hanley, *Identifying with Nationality: Europeans, Ottomans and Egyptians in Alexandria* (New York: Columbia University Press, 2017).

42  Stadiem, *Too Rich,* 184–5, 246–7.

43  I am grateful to Professor Vanessa Schwartz for a fruitful conversation about Farouk, Jews and the notion of the 'cultural peripatetic'.

44  'The Firebrand of Jerusalem', *Picture Post*, 6 July 1946.

45  The Nation Associates, *The Record of Collaboration of King Farouk of Egypt with the Nazis, and Their Ally, the Mufti: Memorandum Submitted to the United Nations* (New York: Nation Associates, 1948). A copy of this published memorandum was scrutinized within the Foreign Office, TNA FO 371/69271. The British were also conducting their own investigation, using records seized in Germany after 1945,

TNA GFM 33/594/1446 'Summaries of Documents Found in the Captured Records of the German Foreign Ministry Relating to Farouk and His Wartime Contacts with the Axis' n.d. For Schmitt, Sabit, *A King Betrayed*, 3-4.

46  Kathryn Tidrick, *Heart Beguiling Araby: The English Romance with Arabia* (London: I.B. Tauris, 1990), 193-219. For the resilience of British lionization of the Desert Arab, see John Bagot Glubb (Glubb Pasha), *The Story of the Arab Legion* (London: Hodder and Stoughton, 1948); Stewart Symes, *Tour of Duty* (London: Collins, 1946), 159.

47  Farouk's yacht *Mahroussa*, according to information passed on from Lloyd's Register of Shipping to the Foreign Office, was the fourth largest in the world. TNA FO 371/46043 Egyptian Department, Untitled Note, 20 November 1945. For a sophisticated argument for taking the Levant seriously as a unit of historical analysis, see Desanka Schwara, 'Discovering the Levant: A Heterogeneous Structure as a Homogeneous Historical Region', *European Review of History* 10, no.2 (2003): 233-51.

48  *Time*, 10 September 1951.

49  For the Egyptian dimension, Elliott Colla, *Conflicted Antiquities: Egyptology, Egyptomania, Egyptian Modernity* (Durham, NC: Duke University Press, 2008). For responses in metropolitan Britain, see Allegra Fryxell, 'Tutankhamen. Egyptomania and Temporal Enchantment in Interwar Britain', *Twentieth Century British History* 28, no.4 (2017): 516-42. These films included: *Caesar and Cleopatra* (1945), [Film] Dir. Gabriel Pascal UK/USA: Eagle-Lion; *The Egyptian* (1954), [Film] Dir. Michael Curtiz, USA: Twentieth-Century Fox; *Land of the Pharaohs* (1955), [Film] Dir. Howard Hawks USA: Warner Brothers; *The Ten Commandments* (1956), [Film] Dir. Cecil B. deMille USA: Cecil B. deMille Productions.

50  TNA FO 141/644 'Report on HM King Farouk's Tour', 12. Ford may have been a trifle unfair here, given the king's later interest in Pharaonic archaeology as a means to enhance the prestige of his regime. See Donald M. Reid, *Contesting Antiquity in Egypt: Archaeologies, Museums and the Struggle for Identities from World War One to Nasser* (Cairo: American University in Cairo Press, 2015). For the Pyramides' Rest House, see Mahmoud El-Gawhary, *Ex-Royal Palaces of Egypt* (Cairo: Dar Al-Maaref, 1954), 111-18.

51  Sefton Delmer, 'New Kind of King in an Ancient Land', *Daily Express*, 25 November 1938.

52  Eve M. Troutt Powell, *A Different Shade of Colonialism: Egypt, Great Britain and the Mastery of the Sudan* (Berkeley, CA: University of California Press, 2003). Broader reflections on Egypt's attitudes towards its black Nubian and Sudanese neighbours are provided by: Alon Tam, 'Blackface in Egypt: The Theatre and Film of Ali al-Kassar', *British Journal of Middle Eastern Studies* 48, no.4 (2021): 733-52; Eve Troutt Powell, 'Brothers along the Nile: Egyptian Concepts of Race and Ethnicity,

1895–1910', in *The Nile: Histories, Cultures, Myths*, ed. Haggai Erlich and Israel Gershoni (London: Lynne Reiner Publishers, 2000), 171–81.

53 For consideration of indeterminacy in regard to skin colour in the colonial context, see Radhika Mohanram, *Imperial White: Race, Diaspora and the British Empire* (Minneapolis: University of Minnesota Press, 2007), 173–7.

54 British Cartoon Archive, University of Kent JL 4624 Cartoon by Joseph Lee 'In Lightest Africa', *Evening News*, 15 October 1951.

55 TNA FO 141/1303 Sir Philip Mitchell (Governor of Kenya) to Andrew Cohen (Colonial Office Assistant Undersecretary for African Affairs), 3 November 1948; Ronald Campbell to Sir Philip Mitchell, 23 November 1948. On how the possibility of 'racial passing' might reveal the 'permeable border' between black and white, see Allyson Hobbs, *A Chosen Exile: A History of Racial Passing in American Life* (Cambridge, MA: Harvard University Press, 2014). In the postwar British context, Lynda Nead, 'Red Taffeta Under Tweed: The Color of Post-War Clothes', *Fashion Theory* 21, no.4 (2017): 365–89.

56 For Rubirosa, Shawn Levy, *The Last Playboy: The High Life of Porfiro Rubirosa* (New York: Harper, 2005).

57 Edward William Lane, *Manners and Customs of Modern Egyptians* (London: Charles Knight, 1836).

58 Andrew Hammond, 'British Literary Responses to the Suez Crisis', *Literature & History* 22, no.2 (2013): 53–72. The quotation from Durrell is from Gordon Bowker, *Through the Dark Labyrinth: A Biography of Lawrence Durrell* (London: St Martin's Press, 1997), 435.

59 Critical interventions in what has become a burgeoning field would include: Paul Gilroy, *'There Ain't No Black in the Union Jack': The Cultural Politics of Race and Nation* (London: Routledge, 2002); Chris Waters, '"Dark Strangers" in our Midst: Discourses of Race and Nation in Britain, 1947–1963', *Journal of British Studies* 36, no.2 (1997): 207–238; Kathleen Paul, *Whitewashing Britain: Race and Citizenship in the Postwar Era* (Ithaca, NY: Cornell University Press, 1997); Kennetta Hammond Perry, *London Is the Place for Me: Black Britons, Citizenship and the Politics of Race* (New York: Oxford University Press, 2015); Schofield, *Enoch Powell and the Making of Postcolonial Britain*.

60 Schwarz, 'The Only White Man in There'; Webster, *Empire and Englishness*.

61 Quoted in Keith Kyle, *Suez* (London: Weidenfeld and Nicolson, 1992), 19.

62 Satia, *Spies in Arabia*.

63 For the continued significance of orientalism in the ideologies of late imperialism, see Ali Behdad, *Belated Travelers: Orientalism in the Age of Colonial Dissolution* (Durham, NC: Duke University Press, 1994).

64 TNA FO 141/481 Minute by Lampson, 11 November 1937.

65 TNA FO 141/644 Lampson to Oliphant, 15 February 1937.

66 'Why Egypt Supports Our Cause', *Picture Post*, 12 September 1942, 5–7.

67 Kelly, *Ruling Few*, 238.
68 For example. 'The Two Farouks', *Picture Post*, 15 December 1951, 20–1.
69 'Troubles of King Farouk', *Picture Post*, 10 June 1950, 14. Condemnation of the 'oriental tyranny' of the Mehmet Ali dynasty was long established in British writings about Egypt. See for example the condemnations of the royal house's innate cruelty and avarice in Emmeline Lott, *Harem Life in Egypt and Constantinople* (London: Richard Bentley, 1867), 138–45.
70 Laurence Grafftey-Smith, *Bright Levant* (London: John Murray, 1970), 235–6.
71 Anna Clark, *Scandal: The Sexual Politics of the British Constitution* (Princeton, NJ: Princeton University Press, 2004), 86.
72 'William Hickey Lifts the Yashmak on the Farouk Romance', *Daily Express*, 10 February 1950, 3.
73 As made clear by studies of 'belly dance' such as Anthony Shay and Barbara Sellers-Young, *Belly Dance: Orientalism, Transnationalism and Harem Fantasy* (Costa Mesa, CA: Mazda Publishers, 2005) and Stavros Karayanni, *Dancing, Fear and Desire: Race, Sexuality and Imperial Politics in Middle Eastern Dance* (Waterloo: Wilfrid Laurier University Press, 2004).
74 'Farouk Drives in Alone', *Daily Express*, 18 August 1950, 1.
75 'She Dances Bride of the Nile for Her King', *Daily Mirror*, 18 August 1950, 1.
76 Such works have taken issue with what they see as the simplistic conception, in Edward Said's account of Orientalism, that texts about the Orient are almost 'self-enclosed'. For example, Asli Cirkaman, *From the 'Terror of the World' to the 'Sick Man of Europe': European Images of Ottoman Empire and Society from the Sixteenth Century to the Nineteenth* (New York: Peter Lang, 2005), 1–32.
77 These notions of selective 'self-orientalizing' are borrowed from Julia Philips Cohen, 'Oriental by Design: Ottoman Jews, Imperial Style, and the Performance of Heritage', *American Historical Review* 119, no.2 (2014): 364–98.
78 For the relationship of the House of Fuad to the emergence of a modern 'developmental state' under British tutelage, see Whidden, *Monarchy and Modernity in Egypt*.
79 Delmer, 'New Kind of King', 10.
80 Ellis, 'Repackaging the Egyptian Monarchy', 189–91.
81 'Farouk and Bride Run Away', *Daily Express*, 25 January 1938, 7; 'A King Learns to Fly', *Daily Express*, 5 October 1938, 9. For the notion of 'glamourized technology', see Bernhard Rieger, 'Fast Couples: Technology, Gender and Modernity in Britain and Germany during the Nineteen-Thirties', *Historical Research* 76, no.193 (2003): 364–88.
82 'Farouk's Bride Says I Want Paris Gowns', *Daily Express*, 10 September 1937, 3; 'Royal Bride Has Emeralds', *Daily Express*, 16 January 1938, 7; 'The Bride Will Not Be There', *Daily Express*, 19 January 1938, 8.
83 'Farouk's Bride Breaks Custom But Keeps Veil', *Daily Express*, 13 September 1937, 9.

84  Delmer, 'New Kind of King'.
85  'Troubles of King Farouk', 15–16. What the British press failed to acknowledge was that Farouk's behaviour also went against a growing emphasis in Egyptian nationalist discourse on domesticity and the 'family man' (even if these prescriptions were sometimes accompanied by a considerable degree of ambivalence), Lisa Pollard, 'From Husbands and Housewives to Suckers and Whores: Marital-Political Anxieties in the "House of Egypt", 1919–48', *Gender and History* 21, no.3 (2009): 647–69.
86  'Ex-King Farouk Says I Am Looking for a Job', *Picture Post*, 21 May 1955, 57.
87  Eileen Bigland, *Journey to Egypt* (London: Jarrolds, 1948), 187–8.
88  Lord Strang, *Home and Abroad* (London: Andre Deutsch, 1956), 253.
89  'Profile – King Farouk', *The Observer*, 3 February 1952, 2.
90  Laila Morsy, 'Britain's Wartime Policy in Egypt, 1940–1942', *Middle Eastern Studies* 25, no.1 (1989): 64–94. Lampson's desire to control Farouk was not merely evident in the heavy-handed show of force at Abdin but in the ambassador's subsequent preoccupation with maintaining control over the narrative of what actually took place in February 1942. See Francis, 'Wounded Pride and Petty Jealousies', 110–111.
91  TNA FO 371/53387 Ronald Campbell to Foreign Office, 27 August 1946.
92  'Troubles of King Farouk', 16.
93  Jean Cocteau, *Past Tense: Diaries, Volume Two*, trans. Richard Howard (New York: Harcourt Brace Jovanovich, 1988), 92 (entry for 18 April 1953). For the hotel vestibule as a metaphor for both the unfixed and the impersonality of modern life, see Siegfried Kracauer, 'The Hotel Lobby' (1963), reprinted in *The City Cultures Reader*, ed. Malcolm Miles, Tim Hall and Iain Borden, 2nd edn (London: Routledge, 2003). For an eloquent literary rendering of the notion of hotel lobbies as 'waiting rooms', heavy with sickly sweet odours of 'anxiety, of instability, of exile… the lingering scent of Nansen Passports', see Patrick Modiano, *Villa Triste* [1975], trans. John Cullen (London: Daunt Books, 2016), 137.
94  This phrase comes from Rob Nixon, 'Refugees and Homecomings', in *Travellers Tales: Narratives of Home and Displacement*, ed. George Robertson (London: Routledge, 1994), 115.
95  'Goodbye, on the Isle of Capri', *Picture Post*, 23 August 1952, 16.
96  Leo Braudy, *The Frenzy of Renown: Fame and Its History* (New York: Oxford University Press, 1986).
97  Morgan, 'Celebrity'.
98  For newspapers, Bingham, *Family Newspapers*. For magazines (particularly the significance of illustrated magazines such as *Picture Post* in the emergence of celebrity culture), Fred Inglis, *A Short History of Celebrity* (Princeton, NJ: Princeton University Press, 2010), 13. For Pathe see https://www.britishpathe.com/

99. For example. 'He's Starting Parties Again', *Daily Express*, 30 July 1952, 1.
100. This phrase is from Martin Conboy, *The Press and Popular Culture* (London: SAGE, 2002), 61. For important interventions which explore an emerging 'equivalence' between celebrity culture and the domain of formal politics and statecraft, see Laura Nym Mayhall, 'The Prince of Wales versus Clark Gable: Anglophone Celebrity and Citizenship between the Wars', *Cultural and Social History* 4, no.4 (2007): 529–43; Laura Beers, 'A Model MP? Ellen Wilkinson, Gender, Politics and Celebrity Culture in Interwar Britain', *Cultural and Social History* 10, no.2 (2013): 231–50; Edward Owens, 'All the World Loves a Lover: Mass Media and the 1934 Royal Wedding of Prince George and Princess Marina', *English Historical Review* 133, no.562 (2018): 597–633.
101. TNA FO 371/87690 Memorandum from British Embassy in Athens, December 1950.
102. 'A King's Holiday – with Much Publicity!' *Daily Mirror*, 18 August 1950, 2.
103. TNA FO 371/90228 Memorandum by Ralph Stevenson, 23 May 1951; FO 371/1449 Minute by Ralph Stevenson on 'King Farouk's Movements and Other Matters', 23 May 1951.
104. 'Sparkling Eyes Upset Three Nations', *Daily Express*, 7 February 1950, 4.
105. TNA FO 954/5B 'Record of Conversation between Her Excellency Queen Farida, Her Excellency Lady Lampson and Lady Moira Lyttelton, 25 February 1942', Lampson to Eden, 26 February 1942. See Francis, 'Wounded Pride and Petty Jealousies', 113–14.
106. TNA FO 371/90228 Ralph Stevenson to William Strang, 30 May 1951. This self-confessed 'chatty letter' was initially sent to George VI's private secretary, to pass on to the king, Stevenson to Sir Alan Lascelles, 19 May 1951. For sensationalist media coverage of Farouk's divorce and remarriage, see 'Marriage Tangle in the Middle East', *Daily Mail*, 20 November 1948; 'The Girl King Farouk Has Fallen For', *Daily Mail*, 29 December 1949; 'Farouk's Rival Says "I Still Love Her"', *Daily Mirror*, 13 January 1950; 'Farouk Sends His Rival Packing', *Daily Express*, 19 December 1949; 'Farouk: I Wed Next Year', *Daily Express*, 19 August 1950.
107. TNA FO 371/90228 John W. Russell (British Embassy, Rome) to J. H. Wardle-Smith (British Embassy, Cairo), 1 June 1951, 3 July 1951, 25 July 1951.
108. For example, TNA FO 371/7363 Ronald Campbell to Sir William Strang, 7 December 1949 and 21 December 1949.
109. TNA FO 141/1303 Memorandum on 'Who Will Be the New Queen of Egypt?' n.d.[1949].
110. TNA FO 371/97066 John W. Russell to British Middle East Office, Cairo, 10 December 1952.

111 A convincing argument for seeing gossip not as a communication confined to intimate groups in private spaces but as 'a political instrument that had crucial public effects', is offered by Nicola Parsons, *Reading Gossip in Early Eighteenth Century England* (Houndmills: Palgrave Macmillan, 2009), 8.

# Chapter 3

1. *Daily Express*, 31 October 1951, 7.
2. Sarah Bradford, *George VI* (London: Fontana, 1991), 598–602.
3. Lord Delfont, *Curtain's Up! The Story of the Royal Variety Performance* (London: Robson Books, 1989), 91–4.
4. TNA FO 371/90228 Ralph Stevenson to William Strang, 12 November 1951, Strang to Stevenson, 26 November 1952.
5. TNA FO 371/97064 Memorandum from Sir John Bowker, 1 February 1952, annotated by Eden.
6. John Johnston, *The Lord Chamberlain's Blue Pencil* (London: Hodder and Stoughton, 1990), 103, 110, 146–55.
7. Harry Hopkins, *The New Look: A Social History of the Forties and Fifties in Britain* (London: Secker and Warburg, 1963), 108–9.
8. Oliver Double, *Britain Had Talent: A History of Variety Theatre* (Houndmills: Palgrave Macmillan, 2012), 51–68.
9. John Osborne, *The Entertainer* (London: Faber & Faber, 1957).
10. Hopkins, *New Look*, 107–8; David Kynaston, *Family Britain, 1951–57* (London: Bloomsbury, 2009), 205–8.
11. For example, Richard Findlater, 'Spotlight on the Theatre', *Liliput* 256 (October 1958), 12–17; Harold Davidson, 'Belief in Live Entertainment', *Stage and Television Today*, 14 January 1960, 5.
12. Hoggart's essential argument was most famously encapsulated in his discussion of 'juke box boys' in northern milk bars, Richard Hoggart, *The Uses of Literacy* (Harmondsworth: Penguin, 1957), 247–50.
13. A representative sample of contributions to this debate might include: Dominic Strinati, 'The Taste of America: Americanization and Popular Culture in Britain', in *Come on Down? Popular Media Culture in Postwar Britain*, ed. Dominic Strinati and Stephen Wagg (London: Routledge, 1992); Neil Campbell, 'Landscapes of Americanisation in Britain: Learning from the 1950s', in *Issues in Americanisation and Culture*, ed. Neil Campbell, Jude Davies and George McKay (Edinburgh: Edinburgh University Press, 2004); Adrian Horn, *Juke Box Britain: Americanization and Youth Culture, 1945–60* (Manchester: Manchester University Press, 2009).
14. 'King Farouk Drops Out of the Cabaret', *Daily Mail*, 8 November 1951, 3.

15 Peter Bailey, 'White Collars, Gray Lives? The Lower Middle Class Revisited', *Journal of British Studies* 38, no.2 (1999): 289.
16 Leslie Smith, *Modern British Farce* (Houndmills: Macmillan, 1989), 65–6.
17 Rebecca N. Mitchell, 'The Victorian Fancy Dress Ball, 1870–1900', *Fashion Theory* 21, no.3 (2017): 291–315; Anthea Jarvis, 'There Was a Young Man from Bengal: The Vogue for Fancy Dress, 1830–1950', *Costume* 16 (1982): 33–46.
18 Pathe newsreel, 'Football with the Lid Off', n.d. [1952]. Available online: https://www.britishpathe.com/video/selected-originals-special-football-with-the-lid/query/football+with+the+lid+off (accessed 21 September 2021).
19 Newspaper Clipping n.d. to be found on personal webpage of Tim White, http://www.whitehouse2002.co.uk/cuttings1.html (accessed 21 June 2021).
20 British Cartoon Archive, University of Kent [hereafter BCA] LSE 4399 'Hide-and-Seek in Egypt', *Daily Herald*, 15 April 1952; LSE 4433 'Middle East Olympics', *Daily Herald*, 24 July 1952.
21 BCA LSE 7959 'The Gambler's Grab', *Daily Herald*, 11 October 1951.
22 TNA FO 371/90228 'Press Cutting: Giles Cartoon', *Sunday Express*, 2 September 1951.
23 Idem. Untitled Foreign Office Memorandum, 15 September 1951; Press Cuttings: 'Giles Is Censored by the Army', *Sunday Express*, 16 September 1951; Untitled column from *Daily Worker*, 19 September 1951.
24 Notably BCA CG/1/4/1/3/11/29, 'Don't Mind Us – We're the Canal Users' Association', *Sunday Express*, 25 November 1956. In this cartoon by Giles, Farouk, apparently unnoticed, floats past a group of British soldiers observing salvage operations at Port Said in the aftermath of the Suez crisis.
25 John Jensen, 'Giles, Ronald [Carl] (1916–1995)', *Oxford Dictionary of National Biography*, 2004. Available online: https://doi.org/10.1093/ref:odnb/60110 (accessed 21 June 2021).
26 BCA CG/1/4/1/3/7/61 Giles cartoon, *Daily Express*, 13 April 1956, 16 April 1953; Uncaptioned Giles cartoon, *Daily Express*, 19 April 1956, 1.
27 BCA JL 5526 Joseph Lee, 'Valentine Hopes', *Evening News*, 13 February 1955.
28 BCA JL 5244 Joseph Lee original artwork 'Increased Travel Allowance', n.d. [1953].
29 BCA JL 4421, 'Would-Be King Farouk', *Evening News*, 25 August 1950.
30 BCA JL 4852, 'Abdication of Farouk', *Evening News*, 29 July 1952.
31 TNA FO 371/97064 Memorandum from Sir James Bowker (Assistant Under-Secretary, Foreign Office: Middle East and North Africa), 1 February 1952.
32 *Variety*, 28 October 1953, 55.
33 Mass-Observation Archive [hereafter MOA] File Report 3026 'The British Sense of Humour', August 1948, 11.
34 MOA Topic Collection 16-3-F 'Music Hall Report: Caprice Parisien, Brixton Empire', 22 January 1940.

35 John M. East, *Max Miller: The Cheeky Chappie* (London: W.H. Allen, 1977); Simon Featherstone, 'The Mill Girl and the Cheeky Chappie: British Popular Comedy and Mass Culture in the Thirties', *Critical Survey* 15, no.2 (2003): 3–22.
36 Featherstone, 'Mill Girl'; Jeffrey Richards, 'Gracie Fields: Consensus Personified', in *The Age of the Dream Palace: Cinema and Society in Britain, 1930–1939* (London: Routledge, 1984), 169–90.
37 'Gracie: It's All Yours, Luv', *Daily Express,* 2 August 1952, 1; David Bret, *Gracie Fields: The Authorized Biography* (London: Robson Books, 1995), 143–4.
38 BCA LSE 4438 David Low, 'Silly Season Topics', *Daily Herald,* 5 August 1952.
39 BCA CG/1/1/2/204 'Giles Cartoon', *Sunday Express,* 10 August 1952.
40 Dennis Hackett, 'Getting to Grips with Glamour', *Picturegoer*, 18 December 1954, 10–11; Joan Rhodes, *Coming on Strong* (Darlington: Serendipity, 2007), 83–6.
41 John Mullen, 'Anti-Black Racism in British Popular Music (1880–1920)', *French Journal of British Studies* 17, no.2 (2012): 61–80.
42 John K. Walton, *The British Seaside: Holidays and Resorts in the Twentieth Century* (Manchester: Manchester University Press, 2000), 3–8, 18–20; Tony Bennett, 'Hegemony, Ideology, Pleasure, Blackpool', in *Popular Culture and Social Relations*, ed. Tony Bennett, Colin Mercer and Janet Woollacott (Milton Keynes: Open University Press, 1986).
43 George Orwell, 'The Art of Donald McGill', *Horizon* 4, no.21 (September 1941).
44 Emma Purce, 'Scales of Normality: Displays of Extreme Weight and Weight Loss in Blackpool, 1920–1940', *Cultural and Social History* 14, no.5 (2017): 669–89.
45 John K. Walton, *Blackpool* (Edinburgh: Carnegie Publishing, 1998).
46 Jeff Nuttall, *King Twist: A Portrait of Frank Randle* (London: Routledge, 2007); Andy Medhurst, *A National Joke: Popular Comedy and English Cultural Identities* (London: Routledge, 2007), 72–7.
47 'Frank Randle Accused', *Liverpool Echo,* 3 September 1952, 7; Philip Martin Williams, *Wired to the Moon: A Life of Frank Randle* (Ashton-under-Lyne: History on Your Doorstep, 2006), 116.
48 For a contemporary, if predictably outraged, report on the extent of commercialized gambling, see B. Seebohm Rowntree and G. R. Lavers, *English Life and Leisure* (London: Longmans, 1951), 122–158. Historians have been much less censorious. See, for example, Ross McKibbin, 'Working-Class Gambling, 1880–1939', in his *Ideologies of Class: Social Relations in Britain, 1880–1950* (Oxford: Oxford University Press, 1990), 101–38; Mark Clapson, *A Bit of a Flutter: Popular Gambling in England, c.1820–1961* (Manchester: Manchester University Press, 1992).
49 Peter Bailey, 'Champagne Charlie and the Music-Hall Swell Song', in his *Popular Culture and Performance in the Victorian City* (Cambridge: Cambridge University Press, 1998), 101–27. The continued purchase of such performances of upper-class

dissipation is testified to in the release in 1949 of a screen biography of the legendary *lion comique* George Leybourne, *Champagne Charlie* (1944), [Film] Dir. Alberto Cavalcanti UK: Ealing Studios.

50  Mike Huggins, *Horseracing and the British, 1919–1939* (Manchester: Manchester University Press, 2003), 201–11. There is a chapter on the Arabian racehorse in an edited collection for which the young Farouk provided a foreword, *Sport in Egypt*, ed. J. Wentworth Day (London: Country Life, 1938).
51  Braudy, *Frenzy of Renown*, 556.
52  For the Conservative Party's strategy before 1914 to present itself as the defender of the Englishman's rights to his private pleasures, Jon Lawrence, 'Class and Gender in the Making of Urban Toryism, 1880–1914', *English Historical Review* 108, no.428 (1993): 629–52. For the more ambivalent approach adopted after female enfranchisement in 1918, see Martin Francis, 'Set the People Free? Conservatives and the State, 1920–1960', in *The Conservatives and British Society, 1880–1990*, ed. Martin Francis and Ina Zweiniger-Bargielowska (Cardiff: University of Wales Press, 1996).
53  Adrian Bingham, *Gender, Modernity and the Popular Press in Interwar Britain* (Oxford: Oxford University Press, 2004).
54  For some representative interventions in this voluminous literature, see Selina Todd, *Young Women, Work and Family in England, 1918–1950* (Oxford: Oxford University Press, 2005); Marcus Collins, *Modern Love: An Intimate History of Men and Women in Twentieth-Century Britain* (London: Atlantic, 2003); Claire Langhamer, *The English in Love: The Intimate Story of an Emotional Revolution* (Oxford: Oxford University Press, 2013); Laura King, *Family Men: Fatherhood and Masculinity in Britain, 1914–1960* (Oxford: Oxford University Press, 2015).
55  Martin Francis, 'The Domestication of the Male? Recent Research on Nineteenth- and Twentieth Century British Masculinity', *Historical Journal* 45, no.3 (2002): 637–52.
56  Richard Vinen, *A Generation in Uniform, 1945–1963* (London: Penguin, 2015); Tom Hickman, *The Call Up: A History of National Service* (London: Headline, 2005).
57  Les Cleveland, 'Soldiers' Songs: the Folklore of the Powerless', *New York Folklore* 11, no.1 (1985): 81–3.
58  Information supplied by Professor Peter Bailey via email 25 May 2011.
59  Geoffrey Gorer, *Exploring English Character* (New York: Criterion, 1955), 75–6.
60  'When Husbands Go Away', *Picture Post*, 16 May 1953, 40–1.
61  Gorer, *English Character*, 144.
62  Laraine Porter, 'Tarts, Tampons and Tyrants: Women and Representation in British Comedy', in *Because I Tell a Joke or Two: Comedy, Politics and Social Difference*, ed. Stephen Wragg (London: Routledge, 2004), 65–93, especially 84–7.
63  'Why Narriman Walked Out on Me', *Daily Mirror*, 14 May 1953, 1; 'Farouk Breaks with Narriman', *Yorkshire Post*, 13 March 1953, 1.

64  BCA CG/1/4/1/3/7/55 Giles cartoon 'Mother's Day', *Sunday Express,* 15 March 1953.
65  Ross McKibbin, 'Work and Hobbies in Britain, 1880–1950' in his *Ideologies of Class,* 139–66.
66  'Rare Stamps at Birmingham Auction for Dollar Bidders', *Birmingham Daily Post,* 4 June 1954.
67  A. J. Cruse, *Cigarette Card Collecting* (London: Vawser and Wiles, 1951), 3–4, 63.
68  TNA FO 371/108580 P.B. Lucas, MP to Selwyn Lloyd, 27 April 1954.
69  'The Odd Things Folks Collect', *Daily Mail,* 15 December 1951, 2; 'Farouk, Their Patron, Has Not Paid Up', *Daily Mail,* 27 October 1952, 5.
70  TNA FO 371/80575 Report by F. Gillen, Chief Inspector, Metropolitan Police, 2 February 1950; Covering memorandum, n.d., addressed to Robert Dunbar, Treaty Department, Foreign Office.
71  For an important critique of an excessive preoccupation with notions of exoticism in our understandings of how colonialism was represented in metropolitan imaginaries, see Jennifer E. Sessions, *By Sword and Plow: France and the Conquest of Algeria* (Ithaca: Cornell University Press, 2011), 13–14.
72  David Cannadine, 'The Context, Performance and Meaning of Ritual: The British Monarchy and the "Invention of Tradition", c.1820–1977', in *The Invention of Tradition,* ed. Eric Hobsbawm and Terence Ranger (Cambridge: Cambridge University Press, 1983), 101–64.
73  A useful survey of this literature is Andrzej Olechnowicz, 'Historians and the Modern British Monarchy', in *The Monarchy and the British Nation, 1780 to the Present,* ed. Andrzej Olechnowicz (Cambridge: Cambridge University Press, 2007), 6–44.
74  Ben Roberts, 'The Complex Holiday Calendar of 1902: Responses to the Coronation of Edward VII and the Growth of Edwardian Event Fatigue', *Twentieth Century British History* 28, no.4 (2017): 489–515; Vernon Bogdanor, *The Monarchy and the Constitution* (Oxford: Oxford University Press, 1995).
75  Frank Prochaska, *Royal Bounty: The Making of a Welfare Monarchy* (New Haven: Yale University Press, 1995); Edward Owens, *The Family Firm: Monarchy, Mass Media and the British Public, 1932-1953* (London: University of London Press, 2019); Jeffrey Richards, 'The Monarchy and Film, 1900–2006', in *The Monarchy and the British Nation,* 258–79.
76  Philip Williamson, 'The Monarchy and Public Values, 1900–1953', in *The Monarchy and the British Nation,* 223–57; Frank Mort, 'Love in a Cold Climate: Letters, Public Opinion and Monarchy in the 1936 Abdication Crisis', *Twentieth Century British History* 25, no.1 (2014): 30–62.
77  Andrzej Olechnowicz, 'A Jealous Hatred: Royal Popularity and Social Inequality' in *The Monarchy and the British Nation,* 280–314.

78 Williamson, 'Monarchy and Public Values'; Ross McKibbin, *Classes and Cultures: England, 1918-1951* (Oxford: Oxford University Press, 1998), 3-15; Andrzej Olechnowicz, 'Britain's "Quasi-Magical" Monarchy in the Mid-Twentieth Century', in *Classes, Cultures and Politics*, ed. Clare V. Griffiths, James J. Nott and William Whyte (Oxford: Oxford University Press, 2011), 70-84.

79 For a rare comparative perspective, see Alexis Schwarzenbach, 'Royal Photographs: Emotions for the People', *Contemporary European History* 13, no.3 (2004): 255-80.

80 Owens, 'All the World Loves a Lover', 633. For the Windsors' continued responsibility for their continental cousins during the Second World War, see Bradford, *George VI*, 488-94.

81 Ellis, 'Repackaging the Egyptian Monarchy'.

82 'King Farouk's Romance Began in Britain', *Daily Express*, 24 August 1937, 9; Owens, 'All the World Loves a Lover', especially 608-9 and 613-14.

83 LD 10 October 1938.

84 TNA FO 141/644 'Report on HM King Farouk's Tour', 17.

85 TNA FO 371/20884 Minute by Ronald Campbell, 8 July 1937.

86 TNA FO 141/481 Lampson to Eden, 17 November 1937; Foreign Office minute, 11 November 1937.

87 David Cannadine, *Ornamentalism: How the British Saw Their Empire* (London: Penguin, 2002), 98, 113-14.

88 Owens, *Family Firm*, 305-10.

89 MOA Topic Collection14-I-L 'Famous Persons' 'King George VI: Death: Haslemere Waiting Room, 12 February 1952', 2. For reaction to George VI's death, Ina Zweiniger-Bargielowska, 'Royal Death and Living Memorials: The Funerals and Commemoration of George V and George VI, 1936-1952', *Historical Research* 89, no.243 (2016): 158-75.

90 Mayhall, 'Prince of Wales versus Clark Gable'; Owens, 'All the World Loves a Lover',

91 Ryan Linkof, '"The Photographic Attack on His Royal Highness": The Prince of Wales, Wallis Simpson and the Prehistory of the Paparazzi', *Photography and Culture* 4, no.3 (2011): 277-92.

92 Bingham, *Family Newspapers*, 239-50.

93 'King Hears Woman's Plea – and Pays' and 'Lakeside Where the Duke Will Spend His Honeymoon', *Daily Express*, 2 June 1937, 3.

94 For example 'Princess Fawzia Weds Today', *Daily Mail*, 15 March 1939, 14.

95 'Farouk, Farida and Fawzia', *Daily Mail*, 20 November 1948, 2; 'The Shah and the Girl', *Daily Mail*, 14 December 1949, 1.

96 Appropriately, Carol's biographers included one of Britain's most successful romantic novelists, Barbara Cartland, *The Scandalous Life of King Carol* (London: Frederick Muller, 1957).

97 John Buchan, *The House of the Four Winds* (London: Hodder and Stoughton, 1935); Ivor Novello and Christopher Hassall, *Glamorous Night: A Romantic Play with Music* (London: Samuel French, [1935] 1939). The play is discussed in Nicholas Daly, 'Modernism. Operetta and Ruritania: Ivor Novello's *Glamorous Night*', in *Popular Modernism and Its Legacies*, ed. Scott Ortolano (New York: Bloomsbury, 2017).

98 *King's Rhapsody, Written and Directed by Ivor Novello* (London: Palace Theatre, 1949).

99 Terence Rattigan, *The Sleeping Prince: An Occasional Fairy Tale* (London: Hamish Hamilton, 1954).

100 'Profile – King Farouk', *Observer*, 3 February 1952, 2.

101 To take a few examples: the succession of historical romances authored by Georgette Heyer, beginning with *Regency Buck* (London: William Heinemann, 1935); the novel by Lady Eleanor Smith, *The Man in Grey* (London: Hutchinson, 1941) adapted into the 1943 film of the same name (directed by George Arliss); popular biographies such as Doris Leslie, *The Great Corinthian: A Portrait of the Prince Regent* (London: Eyre and Spottiswoode, 1952).

102 *Cardboard Cavalier* (1949), [Film] Dir. Walter Forde UK: Two Cities.

103 *Nell Gwynn* (1934), [Film] Dir. Herbert Wilcox UK: Herbert Wilcox Productions. This was an unusually raunchy outing for both Wilcox and Neagle. See Sue Harper, *Picturing the Past: The Rise and Fall of the British Costume Film* (London: BFI Publishing, 1994), 50–2.

104 Kathleen Winsor, *Forever Amber* (London: Macmillan, 1944); *Forever Amber* (1947), [Film] Dir. Otto Preminger USA: Twentieth-Century Fox; 'Obituary: Kathleen Winsor', *The Guardian*, 4 June 2003.

105 *The Private Life of Henry VIII* (1933), [Film] Dir. Alexander Korda UK: London Films; *Young Bess* (1953), [Film] Dir. George Sidney USA: Metro-Goldwyn-Mayer; *The Sword and the Rose* (1953), [Film] Dir. Ken Annakin UK/USA: Walt Disney Productions. For interpretations of these films, see James Chapman. 'Merrie England: *The Private Life of Henry VIII* (1933)', in his *Past and Present: National Identity and the British Historical Film* (London: I.B. Tauris, 2005), 13–44; Thomas S. Freeman, 'A Tyrant for All Seasons: Henry VIII on Film', in *Tudors and Stuarts on Film*, ed. Susan Doran and Thomas S. Freeman (London: Palgrave Macmillan, 2009), 30–45.

106 R. P. Weston and Bert Lee, 'With Her Head Tucked under Her Arm', performed by Stanley Holloway. Available online: https://www.youtube.com/watch?v=jrxWFuvjsfY (accessed 25 June 2021).

107 Mary Rowlatt, *A Family in Egypt* (London: Robert Hale, 1956), 136.

108 Chapman Pincher, 'Henry VIII, King Farouk, and a Myth about a Son and Heir', *Daily Express*, 29 August 1950, 4.

109  Mort, 'Love in a Cold Climate'.
110  Hugo Vickers, *Cecil Beaton* (London: Weidenfeld and Nicolson, 1985), 268; *Henry 'Chips' Channon: The Diaries, 1938–43*, ed. Simon Heffer (London: Hutchinson, 2021), 846.
111  For the brief effervescence, and subsequent deflation, of the 'new Elizabethan age', Ben Pimlott, *The Queen: A Biography of Elizabeth II* (London: HarperCollins, 1997), 193–288.
112  Geoffrey Bocca, *Kings without Thrones: European Monarchy in the Twentieth Century* (New York: Dial Press, 1959), 311.

# Chapter 4

1  'Farouk in Exile', *Daily Express*, 30 July 1952, 1; 'Farouk Gets to Capri – by Tourist Boat', *Daily Mail*, 30 July 1952, 1.
2  Caren Kaplan, *Questions of Travel: Postmodern Discourses of Displacement* (Durham, NC: Duke University Press, 1996), 27–8.
3  Bocca, *Kings without Thrones*, 16–17.
4  'Duke of Windsor Visits Farouk', *Daily Mail*, 9 September 1950, 1.
5  Bocca, *Kings without Thrones*, 20.
6  Ibid., 102–81, 231–6.
7  Ibid., 221–227; 'Ex-Queen Slashes Her Wrists', *Daily Mirror*, 23 October 1953, 1.
8  King Peter II of Yugoslavia, *A King's Heritage* (New York: G.P. Putnam, 1954); Alexandra, Queen of Yugoslavia, *For Love of a King* (New York: Doubleday, 1956). Significantly, among the revelations promised to readers in promotional materials for Peter's memoirs were stories about the Yugoslav monarch's encounters with Farouk during his wartime exile. Advertisement for 'The Most Dramatic Royal Life Story of All', *Picture Post*, 13 March 1954, 48.
9  'Royalty on the Rocks', *Daily Mirror*, 4 July 1953, 5.
10  'Ex-King Farouk Says I Am Looking for a Job', *Picture Post*, 21 May 1955, 41–3, 57.
11  'Papa Farouk Plays Cupid', *Picture Post*, 4 March 1957, 7–9.
12  Bocca, *Kings without Thrones*, 19.
13  Jacques Vernant, *The Refugee in the Postwar World* (London: George Allen sand Unwin, 1953), 3.
14  Alexandra, *For Love of a King*, 182.
15  Bocca, *Kings without Thrones*, 238.
16  For DPs, Gerard Daniel Cohen, *In War's Wake: Europe's Displaced Persons in the Postwar Order* (New York: Oxford University Press, 2012). The specific British story is investigated by Jordanna Bailkin, *Unsettled: Refugee Camps and the Making of Multicultural Britain* (Oxford: Oxford University Press, 2018).

17  For example, Perry, *London Is the Place for Me*, 48–88.
18  Ngugi wa Thiong'o, *Homecoming: Essays on African and Caribbean Literature, Culture and Politics* (New York: Lawrence Hill, 1972); Imre Szeman, *Zones of Instability: Literature, Postcolonialism and the Nation* (Baltimore: Johns Hopkins University Press, 2003); Rosemary M. George, *The Politics of Home: Postcolonial Relocations and Twentieth-Century Fiction* (Berkeley, CA: University of California Press, 1999); Sandra Paquet, *Caribbean Autobiography: Cultural Identity and Self-Representation* (Madison: University of Wisconsin Press, 2002).
19  Phyllis Lassner, *Colonial Strangers: Women Writing the End of the British Empire* (New Brunswick, NJ: Rutgers University Press, 2004), especially 11, 21.
20  Robert C. Williams, 'European Political Emigrations: A Lost Subject', *Comparative Studies in Society and History* 12, no.2 (1970): 140–8, quote on 140.
21  Peter Fritzsche, 'Specters of History: On Nostalgia, Exile and Modernity', *American Historical Review* 106, no.5 (2001): 1587–1618; *The French Emigres in Europe and the Struggle against Revolution, 1789–1814*, ed. Kirsty Carpenter and Philip Mansel (Houndmills: Palgrave, 1999).
22  'The Four Little Farouks', *Picture Post*, 20 November 1954, 21–3.
23  Ferdinand Tuohy, 'Rulers in Exile – And How They Live', *Daily Mail*, 8 June 1936, 12; 'The Late Emperor Napoleon', *Illustrated London News* 62, no.1743 (25 January 1873); 'Napoleon III at Chislehurst', *Notes and Queries* Series 22 10, no.242 (15 August 1914): 135; John Van Der Kiste and Coryne Hall, *Once a Grand Duchess: Xenia, Sister of Nicholas II* (Stroud: Sutton, 2002), 148–241; 'The Negus May Settle in England', *Daily Mail*, 25 June 1936, 11.
24  George Lamming, *The Pleasures of Exile* (Ann Arbor: University of Michigan Press, [1960]1992), especially 229. For a commentary, see Celeste Wheat, 'Examining Colonialism and Exile in George Lamming's *In the Castle of My Skin* (1953), *The Emigrants* (1954) and *The Pleasures of Exile* (1960)', *Journal of Colonialism and Colonial History* 10, no.3 (2009). https://muse.jhu.edu/article/368533N1.
25  For a critique (directed largely at novelist Salman Rushdie) of the failure to recognize that the opportunity for a select number of displaced former colonial subjects to 'indulge in the postcolonial privileges of the borderzone' is not one that has been made available to the vast majority of non-European immigrants: *Displacement, Diaspora and Geographies of Identity*, ed. Shadar Lavie and Ted Swedenburg (Durham, NC: Duke University Press, 1996), 16.
26  One of the few attempts to address the psychic consequences of this sense of loss and regret is Paul Gilroy, *Postcolonial Melancholia* (New York: Columbia University Press, 2005). The complexity of how some individuals in Britain grappled with what one notorious figure identified as 'post-imperial neurosis' is evident in Schofield, *Enoch Powell and the Making of Postcolonial Britain*, especially 144–207. For the possibility that an apparent preoccupation with re-staging the end of empire

on film and stage ironically reflects an inability to acknowledge the trauma of decolonization, see Antoinette Burton, 'India Inc.? Nostalgia, Memory and the Empire of Things', in *British Culture and the End of Empire*, 217–32.

27 Stephen Gundle, *Glamour: A History* (Oxford: Oxford University Press, 2008), 199–230.
28 'The Hour of Marriage', *Picture Post*, 28 April 1957, 19–24.
29 Nicolas Stoskopf, 'Deauville: History of an Enterprise', *Histoire Urbaine* 41, no.3 (2014): 23–44; Peter Thorold, *The British in France: Visitors and Residents since the Revolution* (London: Continuum, 2008), 199–200.
30 'Farouk Drives in Alone', *Daily Express*, 18 August 1950, 1; 'Farouk: I Wed Next Year', *Daily Express*, 19 August 1950, 1; 'A King's Holiday – With Much Publicity', *Daily Mirror*, 18 August 1950, 2.
31 'Nine Taste Farouk's Food at the Gala', *Daily Express*, 21 August 1950, 5.
32 Robert Muller, 'Deauville: Millionaire's Playground', *Picture Post*, 8 September 1956, 38–41.
33 David Cannadine, 'Fantasy: Ian Fleming and the Realities of Escapism', in his *In Churchill's Shadow: Confronting the Past in Modern Britain* (Oxford: Oxford University Press, 2003), 279–311.
34 Ian Fleming, *Casino Royale* (London: Penguin, [1953] 2004), 29, 31.
35 Gundle, *Glamour*, 107–108; Stanley Weintraub, *Edward the Caresser: The Playboy Prince Who Became Edward VII* (New York: The Free Press, 2001), 270–360.
36 Sabine Baring-Gould, *A Book of the Riviera* (London: Methuen, 1909), 244–5.
37 E. Phillips Oppenheim, *Mr. Grex of Monte Carlo* (London: Methuen, [1915] 1925), 7.
38 Geoffrey Bocca, *Bikini Beach: The Wicked Riviera, as It Was and Is* (New York: McGraw Hill, 1962), 146–51.
39 'Farouk Demands a Suite', *Daily Mirror*, 6 April 1953, 6.
40 Bocca, *Bikini Beach*, 156–7.
41 Stanley Jackson, *Inside Monte Carlo* (New York: Stein and Day, 1975), 183–96.
42 Fred Gilbert, *The Man That Broke the Bank at Monte Carlo* (London: Francis Day and Hunter, 1891); The song featured in *Say It with Flowers* (1934) [Film] Dir. John Baxter UK: Twickenham Studios (where it was performed by the now 82 year old Coborn himself) and *Lawrence of Arabia* (1962), [Film] Dir. David Lean UK: Horizon Pictures. For Wells, Robin Quinn, *The Man Who Broke the Bank at Monte Carlo* (Stroud: The History Press, 2016).
43 Gundle, *Glamour*, 225–6; Edward Quinn, *Stars, Stars, Stars: Off The Screen* (Zurich: Scalo, 1997), 7–8.
44 For the Cannes film festival, Vanessa R. Schwarz, *It's So French! Hollywood, Paris, and the Making of Cosmopolitan Film Culture* (Chicago: University of Chicago Press, 2007), 56–99. For Farouk and the Palm Beach, see Jackson, *Inside Monte Carlo*, 196.

45  Diane Berger, *Riviera Style* (London: Scriptum Editions, 1999), 140–6.
46  Stephen Gundle, *Death and the Dolce Vita: The Dark Side of Rome in the 1950s* (Edinburgh: Canongate, 2011), 155, 272–305, 313–15; Melton S. Davis, *All Rome Trembled* (New York: G.P. Putnam, 1957), 162.
47  'Roses for a Blonde – From Your King', *Daily Mirror*, 16 March 1953, 16; Noel Barber, 'It Seems All Roads Still Lead to Rome', *Daily Mail*, 14 November 1953, 4.
48  Gundle, *Death and the Dolce Vita*, 283–4; Peter Howe, *Paparazzi* (New York: Artisan Books, 2005), 56–63; Diego Mormorio, *Tazio Secchiaroli: Greatest of the Paparazzi*, trans. Alexandra Bonfante-Warren (New York: Harry Abrams, 1999), 25–8; Giovanna Bertelli, *Dolce Italia: The Beautiful Life of Italy in the Fifties and Sixties* (New York: Rizzoli, 2005), 141–2.
49  *La Dolce Vita* (1960), [Film] Dir. Frederico Fellini Italy: Riama Films. For evidence of widespread interest in the film, reaching beyond the established devotees of continental cinema: 'Bed and Circuses', *Daily Mail*, 7 December 1960, 3; 'Too Tired for Orgies', *Daily Mail*, 9 December 1960, 10; 'Sweet Life!' *Daily Mirror*, 9 December 1960, 21.
50  For example, 'She Dreamed of Stardom', *Picture Post*, 21 May 1955, 31–2.
51  'Will This Girl's Diary Shock a Nation?', *Daily Mirror*, 19 February 1954, 7; 'Wilma Riddle – It Was Murder', *Daily Mirror*, 4 August 1954, 3; 'Girdle Clue in Drug Case', *Daily Mirror*, 2 February 1957, 4; 'Ex-Minister's Son Held in Drug Scandal', *Daily Mail*, 22 September 1954, 1; 'Red Lawyer Accused in Sex Scandal', *Daily Mail*, 17 November 1954, 3; 'The Riddle of the Roman Sands Is Nearly Solved', *Picture Post*, 9 October 1954, 32–3; 'Montesi Judges Go Down to the Beach', *Picture Post*, 27 April 1957, 16–17.
52  Gundle, *Death and the Dolce Vita*; Karen Pinkus, *The Montesi Scandal: The Death of Wilma Montesi and the Birth of the Paparazzi in Fellini's Rome* (Chicago: Chicago University Press, 2003); Wayland Young, *The Montesi Scandal* (London: Faber & Faber, 1957). Young (a Labour politician as well a journalist) was adamant that the affair demonstrated the fundamental differences between Latin politics and culture and the Anglo-Saxon world. There is, therefore, an undoubted irony in the fact that, six years later, he was to be the author of *The Profumo Affair: Aspects of Conservatism* (Harmondsworth: Penguin, 1963).
53  Fernand Braudel, *La Mediterranee et Le Monde Mediterraneen a L'Epoque de Philippe II* (Paris: Armand Colin, 1949); Fernand Braudel, 'Personal Testimony', *Journal of Modern History* 44, no.4 (1972): 448–67, especially 450–3.
54  As conceded by, among others, former champion of the 'pivotal' geopolitical significance of the Mediterranean, geographer William Gordon East, 'The Mediterranean: Pivot of Peace and War', *Foreign Affairs* 31, no.4 (1953): 619–33.
55  Simon Ball, *The Bitter Sea: The Brutal World War Two Fight for the Mediterranean* (London: HarperCollins, 2009); *Official Campaign History: The Mediterranean and the Middle East* 6 vols. ed. I. S. O. Playfair (London: HMSO, 1954–1987).

56 The memoirs of the Eighth Army's most famous commander neatly encapsulated this military itinerary, Bernard Montgomery, *From Alamein to the River Sangro* (London: Hutchinson, 1950).
57 Edward Hungerford, 'Durrell's Mediterranean Paradise', *Studies in the Literary Imagination* 24, no.1 (1991): 57–69; Elizabeth David, *A Book of Mediterranean Food* (London: John Lehmann, 1950); Artemis Cooper, *Writing at the Kitchen Table: The Authorized Biography of Elizabeth David* (New York: HarperCollins, 1999), 139–54.
58 Robert Holland, *The Warm South: How the Mediterranean Shaped the British Imagination* (New Haven: Yale University Press, 2018).
59 John Pemble, *The Mediterranean Passion: Victorians and Edwardians in the South* (Oxford: Oxford University Press, 1987), especially 8.
60 Luigi Barzini, *The Italians* (New York: Atheneum, 1964), 45.
61 Edward Bulwer-Lytton, *The Last Days of Pompeii* (London: Richard Bentley, 1834); Robert Graves, *I, Claudius* (London: Arthur Barker, 1934). For a survey, see Sandra Joshel, *Imperial Projections: Ancient Rome in Modern Popular Culture* (Baltimore: Johns Hopkins University Press, 2001).
62 Melani McAlister, *Epic Encounters: Culture, Media, and US Interests in the Middle East since 1945* (Berkeley: University of California Press, 2005), 43–83; Maria Wyke, *Projecting the Past: Ancient Rome, Cinema and History* (New York: Routledge, 1997).
63 Stadiem, *Too Rich*, 334.
64 Norman Lewis, *Naples '44* (New York: Pantheon Books, 1978), 111.
65 As detailed in two travelogues roughly contemporary with Farouk's time on Capri, Sydney Clark, *All The Best in Italy* (New York: Dodd, Mead and Company, 1953), 218; S. P. B. Mais and Gillian Mais, *Italian Holiday* (London: Alvin Redman, 1954), 29–30.
66 Kenneth Allsop, 'Fifty Years of Classical Scandal', *Picture Post*, 1 September 1951, 20–21.
67 Stadiem, *Too Rich*, 326.
68 Berger, *Riviera Style*, 140–7.
69 *The Golden Madonna* (1949). [Film] Dir. Luigi Carpentieri UK/Italy: Pendennis Productions; *That Dangerous Age* (1949), [Film] Dir. Gregory Ratoff UK: London Film Productions. For a feature on the making of the latter, see 'Beauty and the Director', *Picture Post*, 4 December 1948, 23. The broader context of both films is discussed in Steve Chibnall, 'Rome, Open for British Production: The Lost World of "Britalian" Films, 1946–1954', *Historical Journal of Film, Radio and Television* 33, no.2 (2013): 234–69.
70 Robin Maugham, *Escape from the Shadows: An Autobiography* (New York: McGraw-Hill, 1973), 188–90. For northern European homosexuals' attraction to

Italy and Greece, see Robert Aldrich, *The Seduction of the Mediterranean: Writing, Art and Homosexual Fantasy* (London: Routledge, 1993). On the repressive climate for homosexuals in Britain in the immediate postwar period, see Patrick Higgins, *Heterosexual Dictatorship: Male Homosexuality in Postwar Britain* (London: Fourth Estate, 1996).

71. *Contempt (Le Mepris)* (1963), [Film] Dir. Jean-Luc Godard France/Italy: Rome Paris Films); *Darling* (1965), [Film] Dir. John Schlesinger UK: Joseph Janni Productions. For the way *Darling* presents Capri as a place of licence and moral degradation, see Moya Luckett, 'Travel and Mobility: Femininity and National Identity in Swinging London Films' in *British Cinema, Past and Present*, ed. Justine Ashby and Andrew Higson (London: Routledge, 2000), 233–45, especially 235.
72. Hopkins, *New Look*, 461–3, Peter J. Lyth, 'From Privilege to Popularity: The Growth of Leisure Air Travel since 1945', *Journal of Transport History* 15, no.2 (1994): 101–15.
73. *Picture Post*, 7 February 1952, 5.
74. Ibid., 7 August 1954, 40.
75. Ibid., 6 February 1954, 42; 2 May 1953, 44.
76. *Daily Mirror*, 4 February 1952, 4.
77. 'We Hitch-Hiked to the Sun', *Picture Post*, 31 July 1954, 14–16.
78. Bocca, *Bikini Beach*, 25–7.
79. Peter Wildeblood, 'Riviera Sun Melts the British Reserve', *Daily Mail*, 20 August 1951, 2.
80. 'Trippers Turn Back Farouk's Yacht', *Daily Express*, 14 June 1951, 1.
81. Nicholas Blake, *The Widow's Cruise* (New York: Harper and Brothers, 1959), 22.
82. Mais, *Italian Holiday*, 10, 24, 42–3.
83. 'It's Like Brighton – Almost', *Daily Express*, 2 August 1952, 1.
84. 'Eve Perrick's Column', *Daily Express*, 2 August 1952, 3
85. Gordon Cooper, *A Fortnight around the Bay of Naples* (London: Percival Marshall, 1955), 52, 56.
86. 'King Farouk Confiscates Briton's Film', *Daily Mail*, 14 June 1951, 1; 'Man in Room 118 Upset Narriman', *Daily Mail*, 10 August 1951, 3.
87. Earl Wilson. 'My Secret Life with a Camera', *Photography* 34 (June 1954): 106–9.
88. 'Goodbye, on the Isle of Capri', *Picture Post*, 23 August 1952, 14–17, quotation and image 14.
89. Ibid., 17.
90. Ennio Flaiano, *The Via Veneto Papers*, trans. John Satriano (Marlboro, VT: Marlboro Press, 1992), 4–5.
91. McBride, *Farouk of Egypt*, 221; McLeave, *The Last Pharaoh*, 293–4.

## Chapter 5

1. 'The Doors Swung Open on Farouk's Palace Secrets', *Daily Mirror*, 25 August 1952, 1.
2. 'Farouk Had Secret Hoard in Palace', *Daily Mail*, 25 August 1952, 1.
3. El-Gawhary, *Ex-Royal Palaces of Egypt*.
4. This estimate comes from Stadiem, *Too Rich*, 35, who placed Farouk in the 'Getty league' of personal wealth.
5. 'Farouk's Bride Says I Want Paris Gowns', *Daily Express*, 10 September 1937, 3; 'Farida Happy but Tired', *Daily Express*, 20 January 1938, 3; 'Egypt Queen in Glass Coach', *Daily Mail*, 21 January 1938, 11–12. Pathe newsreel, 'The Egyptian Royal Wedding', 24 January 1938. Available online: https://www.britishpathe.com/video/king-farouk-of-egypt-is-married (accessed 5 July 2021).
6. 'Even Her Shoes Were Diamond-Studded', *Daily Mail*, 7 May 1951, 1. Pathe newsreel, 'Egypt Fetes Royal Wedding', 14 May 1951. Available online: https://www.britishpathe.com/video/egypt-fetes-royal-wedding (accessed 5 July 2021).
7. The press contented itself with merely announcing that Farouk had driven his bride to his country estate forty miles north of Cairo. 'Farouk and Bride Run away', *Daily Express*, 25 January 1938, 7.
8. 'King Farouk's Honeymoon Begins', *Daily Mail*, 4 June 1951, 3; Pathe newsreel, 'News in Flashes: Sicily', 5 July 1951. Available online: https://www.britishpathe.com/video/sicily-part-of-news-in-flashes (accessed 5 July 1951).
9. 'Egypt' [September 1942] in *Keith Douglas: The Complete Poems*, ed. Desmond Graham (London: Faber & Faber, 2000), 93.
10. Olechnowicz, 'A Jealous Hatred', 280.
11. Avi Shlaim, *Lion of Jordan: The Life of King Hussein in War and Peace* (New York: Alfred A. Knopf, 2008), 59–60, 181–5.
12. Hussein Bin Talal, *Uneasy Lies the Head: An Autobiography by King Hussein of Jordan* (London: Heinemann, 1962), 38.
13. For example 'Full of Western Promiscuity', *Daily Mirror*, 25 August 1976, 3; Linda Blandford, *Oil Sheikhs: Inside the Supercharged World of the Petrodollar* (Littlehampton: Star Books, 1976).
14. Ralph Izzard, 'Not All the Oil in the Middle East Is in Persia', *Daily Mail*, 22 June 1951, 2.
15. James Cameron, 'The Sand King Gets Britons in His Beard', *Daily Mirror*, 14 March 1952, 2; 'The King Who Slept by His Sword', *Daily Mirror*, 10 November 1953, 7.
16. Noel Monks, 'Arabian Nights Palaces Sprout in the Desert', *Daily Mail*, 23 April 1953, 4.
17. 'Venus Banned', *Daily Mail*, 17 May 1952, 1.

18 Cannadine, *Ornamentalism*, 41–57; John Lord, *The Maharajahs* (New York: Random House, 1971); Barbara Ramusack, *The Princes of India in the Twilight of Empire* (Columbus, OH: Ohio University Press, 1978).
19 'The Man Who Missed the Derby', *Picture Post*, 31 May 1952, 33–6.
20 Stanley Jackson, *The Aga Khan: Prince, Prophet and Sportsman* (London: Odhams, 1952); Qayyum A. Malick, *His Royal Highness Prince Aga Khan: Guide, Philosopher and Friend of the World of Islam* (Karachi: Ismailia Association, 1954).
21 Pathe newsreels 'Tanganyika: Aga Khan Weighed in Diamonds', 26 August 1946 and 'Aga Khan's Platinum Jubilee', 11 February 1954. Available online: https://www.britishpathe.com/video/VLVA464WWIS8WBXWZG4JJYV3ZIWHX-LIFE/query/Aga+Khan; https://www.britishpathe.com/video/aga-khans-platinum-jubilee-1 (both accessed 17 September 2021).
22 'There's Bubbly and Fun for the Aga Khan', *Daily Mail*, 22 April 1955, 5.
23 Indeed the Foreign Office clearly hoped the Aga Khan's visits to Cairo might offer an opportunity to improve Farouk's outlook and behaviour. For example, TNA 371/1449 Sir Ralph Stevenson to Sir John Bowker, 12 May 1951.
24 Sultan Muhammed Shah and Aga Khan III, *World Enough and Time* (New York: Simon and Schuster, 1954), 89–92, 301–304.
25 Leonard Slater, *Aly: A Biography* (London: W.H. Allen, 1966).
26 LD 1 May 1943.
27 Mary S. Lovell, *The Riviera Set, 1920–1960: The Golden Years of Glamour and Excess* (London: Abacus, 2017), 250–92.
28 'Nine Taste Farouk's Food at the Gala', *Daily Express,* 21 August 1950, 5.
29 Philip Hoare, *Noel Coward: A Biography* (New York: Simon and Schuster, 1996), 408–17.
30 Quoted in Noel Coward, *The Lyrics of Noel Coward* (London: Methuen, 2002), 265.
31 Elsa Maxwell, *RSVP* (New York: Little Brown and Co., 1954), 284–90; Idem, *The Celebrity Circus* (London: W.H. Allen, 1964), 47.
32 Catherine De La Roche, 'Those Two Volcanos', *Picture Post*, 4 March 1950, 37.
33 *The Sheik* (1921), [Film] Dir. George Melford USA: Famous Players-Lasky. For a seminal interpretation of both the film and the novel (by E. M. Hull) on which it was based, see Billie Melman, *Women and the Popular Imagination in the 1920s* (Basingstoke: Palgrave Macmillan, 1988), 89–104. Former courtesan Marguerite Alibert was charged in 1923 with the murder of her husband, Egyptian aristocrat Ali Kamel Fahmy Bey. She was acquitted after claiming that Fahmy displayed the sexual tastes and 'amoral sadism' of a depraved 'oriental husband'. See Lucy Bland, 'Mme Fahmy's Vindication: Orientalism, Miscegenation Fears and Female Fantasy', in her *Modern Women on Trial: Sexual Transgression in the Age of the Flapper* (Manchester: Manchester University Press, 2017).
34 Seretse Khama, king of the Bechuanaland Protectorate, was forced into exile in 1951 after he married a white British woman. See Susan Williams, *Colour Bar: The*

*Triumph of Seretse Khama and His Nation* (London: Allen Lane, 2006). For metropolitan concerns about sexual relationships between West Indian migrants and white British women (and the progeny of these mixed-race unions), see Elizabeth Buettner, "'Would You Let Your Daughter Marry a Negro?" Race and Sex in 1950s Britain', in *Gender, Labour, War and Empire: Essays on Modern Britain*, ed. Philippa Levine and Susan R. Grayzel (Houndmills: Palgrave Macmillan, 2009), 219–37.

35 Yasmin Khan, 'Sex in an Imperial War Zone: Transnational Encounters in Second World War India', *History Workshop Journal* 73, no.1 (2012): 240–58.
36 The temper of wartime Cairo is atmospherically recovered in Artemis Cooper, *Cairo in the War, 1939–1945* (London: Penguin, 1993).
37 LD 2 November 1942, 27 November 1942, 17 February 1943, 4 January 1944; TNA FO 954/5 Lampson to Eden, 28 October 1942.
38 LD 15 July 1942.
39 LD 25 August 1943.
40 LD 16 April 1941, 21 March 1942, 24 March 1942, 21 May 1942. See also Lord Birkenhead, *Walter Monckton* (London: Weidenfeld and Nicolson, 1969), 200–1.
41 Francis, 'Wounded Pride and Petty Jealousies', 106–9.
42 LD 5 November 1942; FO 954/5 TNA Lampson to Eden, 5 November 1942.
43 Stadiem, *Too Rich*, 9, 212–14, 255. LD 18 November 1942.
44 Cooper, *Cairo in the War*, 113–19.
45 Stadiem, *Too Rich*, 255–6, TNA FO 954/45 Lampson to Eden, 14 August 1944.
46 Elizabeth P. McIntosh, *Sisterhood of Spies: The Women of the OSS* (Annapolis, MD: Naval Institute Press, 1996), 171–2.
47 Nina Nelson, *Shepheard's Hotel* (London: Barrie and Rockliff, 1960), 170–2.
48 Barbara Skelton, *Tears before Bedtime* (London: Hamish Hamilton, 1987), 63–5. A similarly sympathetic account of Farouk as affectionate and solicitous was provided by Patricia Wilder, one of Farouk's lovers in the 1950s, Stadiem, *Too Rich*, 50–2.
49 Bingham, *Family Newspapers*, 43–50, 73–88, 104–17, 164–70, 201–18. For the changing sexual climate of the postwar years, see Claire Langhamer, 'Adultery in Postwar England', *History Workshop Journal* 62, no.1 (2006): 86–115; Deborah Cohen, *Family Secrets: Shame and Privacy in Modern Britain* (Oxford: Oxford University Press, 2013).
50 Wolf Mankowitz, 'Farouk's Trinkets' *Punch*, 20 May 1953, 606.
51 Jenny Nicholson, 'The Great Farouk Sale', *Picture Post*, 13 March 1954, 29–31 (image appears on 31).
52 Quoted in McBride, *Farouk of Egypt*, 211.
53 Rashed El-Barawy, *The Military Coup in Egypt: An Analytic Study* (Cairo: Renaissance Bookshop, 1952), 186.
54 El-Gawhary, *Ex-Royal Palaces*, 87.

55  TNA FO 371/108568 Press cutting 'Missing Plate Traced after Fifty Years', *Birmingham Daily Post*, 13 February 1954.
56  Stadiem, *Too Rich*, 65–6, 78–9, 254–5.
57  McBride, *Farouk of Egypt*, 159.
58  TNA FO 371/24622 Cairo Embassy Report, 9 January 1940; FO 371/24623 Cairo Embassy Report, 9 April 1940; FO 371/27446 Cairo Embassy Report, 18 January 1941. See also Cooper, *Cairo in the War*, 239.
59  Felicity James, 'Was Queen Mary Merely a Passionate Art Collector – Or a Kleptomaniac?', *Daily Telegraph*, 8 September 2019. Available online: https://www.telegraph.co.uk/films/2019/09/08/queen-mary-merely-passionate-art-collector-kleptomaniac/ (accessed 7 July 2021).
60  Patricia O' Brien, 'The Kleptomania Diagnosis: Bourgeois Women and Theft in Late Nineteenth Century France', *Journal of Social History* 17, no.1 (1983): 65–77; Susan Abelson, *When Ladies Go A-Thieving: Middle-Class Shoplifters in the Victorian Department Store* (Oxford: Oxford University Press, 1989); Tammy Whitlock, 'Gender, Medicine, and Consumer Culture in Victorian England: Creating the Kleptomaniac', *Albion* 31, no.3 (1999): 413–37.
61  Rowntree and Lavers, *English Life and Leisure*, 234–5.
62  Dawn Nell, 'Helping Yourself: Self-Service Grocery, Retailing and Shoplifting in Britain, c.1950–75', *Cultural and Social History* 8, no.3 (2011): 371–91.
63  For the notion that objects and places can embody the absent person, see Leora Auslander, 'Beyond Words', *American Historical Review* 110, no.4 (2005): 1015–45, especially 1019–20; James Hoskins, *Biographical Object: How Things Tell the Stories of People's Lives* (New York: Routledge, 1998).
64  Stadiem, *Too Rich*, 230.
65  Anwar Sadat, *Revolt on the Nile* (London: Allan Wingate, 1957), 14–16, 45.
66  'Farouk: I Am Looking for a Job', 57.
67  For example, 'Farouk Told by Spanish Duchess That Is "Too Fat"', *Daily Express*, 13 September 1950, 3. For cartoons, see the 'Emmwood' cartoon 'You've Got a Fat Lot of Room to Talk, Pop', in which Farouk is chided by a brassy female companion, *Daily Mail,* 26 February 1957, 6.
68  Stadiem, *Too Rich*, 214.
69  David Cannadine, 'Food', in *The Pleasures of the Past* (New York: Norton, 1991), 230–6.
70  'The King of Egypt's Duck Shoot', in *Sport in Egypt*, ed. J. Wentworth Day (London: Country Life Ltd., 1938), 89–90.
71  LD 15 December 1942, 6 February 1944 (in the latter entry, Lampson claims Farouk 'had a friend in the butts shooting for him').
72  'What They Are Saying about…', *Picture Post,* 7 January 1957, 34.
73  Christopher E. Forth, 'Fat, Desire and Disgust in the Colonial Imagination', *History Workshop Journal* 73 (2012): 211–39.

74 McLeave, *Last Pharaoh*, 151. For effendi fitness regimes as a challenge to the emasculating impact of imperial rule, see Wilson Chacko Jacob, *Working Out Egypt: Effendi Masculinity and Subject Formation in Colonial Modernity, 1870–1940* (Durham, NC: Duke University Press, 2011).

75 Avner Offer, 'Body Weight and Self Control', in his *The Challenge of Affluence* (Oxford: Oxford University Press, 2007), 138–70; Peter N. Stearns, *Fat History: Bodies and Beauty in the Modern West* (New York: NYU Press, 1997).

76 Stadiem, *Too Rich*, 46.

77 Bill Osgerby, *Playboys in Paradise: Masculinity, Youth and Leisure-Style in Modern America* (Oxford: Berg, 2001); Becky Conekin, 'Fashioning the Playboy: Messages of Style and Masculinity in the Pages of *Playboy* Magazine, 1953–1963', *Fashion Theory* 4, no.4 (2000): 447–66.

78 Ken Gross, 'The Last Pharaoh and His Ferrari', *Automobile Quarterly* 27, no.2 (1989): 149–59.

79 For instance, the 'elegant and well-dressed' Scottish fashion model Grace Andrews seen in Farouk's company in Cannes, 'A Coffee for Miss Andrews', *Daily Mail*, 13 August 1951, 5.

80 For example, the revue dancer Christiane Dury, spotted with Farouk the night Narriman left him. 'Picture Gallery', *Daily Mail*, 24 March 1953, 10. For the increasing presence of titillating images of female legs and cleavage in the press in the late 1940s and early 1950s, see Bingham, *Family Newspapers*, 203, 213–18.

81 As reported in 'Egypt's New Queen Has Figure Just Like Jane Russell's' *San Bernadino Sun*, 28 July 1951, 4.

82 A similar claim could be made for the voyeuristic media preoccupation in this same period with the forty-inch bosom of Lancashire model Norma Sykes, known as 'Sabrina', 'Sabrina: A Cult Takes to Culture', *Picture Post*, 25 February 1956, 18–19.

83 TNA FO 371/41393 Memorandum by Ronald Scrivener, 19 June 1944.

84 TNA FO 371/90228 Irene Ward to Kenneth Younger, 24 May 1951.

85 See, for example, Warren G. Breckman, 'Disciplining Consumption: The Debate about Luxury in Wilhelmine Germany, 1890–1914', *Journal of Social History* 24, no.3 (1991): 485–505.

86 Keith Waterhouse, 'A Whiff of Cod in Berkeley Square', *Daily Mirror*, 8 October 1953, 7; 'Dawson Goes to Zurich', *Daily Mail*, 29 November 1950, 1; Wildeblood, 'Riviera Sun Melts the British Reserve', 2.

87 Lady Docker, *Norah: The Autobiography* (London: W.H. Allen, 1969); Mort, *Capital Affairs*, 69–71.

88 Bernard Conolly, 'Who Sent a King Packing?' *Daily Mail*, 24 October 1969, 14.

89 'Monte Carlo Sends Roses to Lady Docker', *Daily Mail*, 6 April 1953, 1.

90 'Lucky Mickie Beats Farouk – And Dies', *Daily Mail*, 21 September 1950, 3.

## Chapter 6

1. S. Robert Tralins and Ruth Barnes (Madam Sherry), *Pleasure Was My Business* (New York: Lyle Stuart, 1961).
2. A selection of Tralins' pulp portfolio is available online: https://www.pulpinternational.com/pulp/keyword/Bob+Tralins.html (accessed 8 July 2021).
3. 'Writer Sues on Book Ban', *Miami Herald*, 22 March 1961, 34; Jean Wardlow, 'Remember Madame Sherry's Ghost?', *Miami Herald Sunday Magazine*, 15 November 1964, 15.
4. Tralins and Barnes, *Pleasure*, 199–204.
5. 'Farouk's $400,000 Libel Suit against That Miami Call House Madam', *Vice Squad*, July 1962, 2–3; Stadiem, *Too Rich*, 349.
6. 'Egypt: Boy Scout into Field Marshal', *Time*, 9 August 1937.
7. 'King of Egypt Marries His Prettiest Subject', *Life*, 14 February 1938, 50.
8. 'The King of Egypt's Palace', *Life*, 10 April 1944, 85–93.
9. 'Egypt: The Locomotive', *Time*, 10 September 1951.
10. 'The Problem King of Egypt', *Life*, 10 April 1950, 102–3, 110.
11. Hahn, *United States, Great Britain and Egypt*; Thornhill, 'Britain and the Collapse of Egypt's Institutional Order'.
12. Nation Associates, *Record of Collaboration of King Farouk*.
13. 'Problem King of Egypt', 103.
14. Christina Klein, *Cold War Orientalism: Asia in the Middlebrow Imagination, 1945–1961* (Berkeley, CA: University of California Press, 2003), especially 15–17.
15. 'Egypt's New Charmer Dances for Vacationing Farouk', *Life*, 4 September 1950, 28; 'Farouk's New Queen', *Life*, 21 May 1952, 24; 'Simple Life for a King', *Life*, 11 August 1952, 24; 'When in Rome', *Life*, 13 April 1953, 129–130.
16. 'Treasures Farouk Left behind', *Life*, 24 November 1952, 88–95.
17. Her Royal Highness Princess Narriman ('as told to Klaus Bloemer'), 'My True Self', *Ladies' Home Journal*, February 1953, 40–1, 126–9; March 1953, 54–5, 167–72.
18. 'Narriman Calls It Quits', *Life*, 23 March 1953, 42.
19. Harvey Levenstein, *We'll Always Have Paris: American Tourists in France since 1930* (Chicago: University of Chicago Press, 2004), 157, 183–4.
20. 'How Call Girls Made Their Dates', *Daily Mail*, 16 February 1953, 3.
21. 'Egypt's New Charmer', 28.
22. 'Egypt's National Dancer Gets American King', *Life*, 22 October 1951, 46; 'Nightclubs: Mazda Motion', *Life*, 24 March 1952, 45.
23. J. Michael Kennedy, 'Seven Floors Decorated in "Early Farouk": Hofheinz's Gaudy Suite in Astrodome Being Razed', *Los Angeles Times*, 18 March 1988. Available online: https://www.latimes.com/archives/la-xpm-1988-03-18-mn-1682-story.html (accessed 13 July 2021).

24. 'King Farouk's Wrath Fails to Change Plans for Sister's Wedding', *New York Daily News*, 21 May 1950, 39. The story was also carried in the British press, 'Princess Fathia Is Now Plain Mrs. G', *Daily Mirror*, 17 May 1950, 1.
25. *The Apartment* (1960), [Film] Dir. Billy Wilder USA: Mirisch Company.
26. 'VAR Scores Strip Act for US Airman', *Billboard*, 16 January 1954, 12.
27. 'Zig and Zag with Ziggy Johnson', *Chicago Defender* (National Edition), 5 September 1959, 19.
28. 'Bowdry to Head MidWest Slate', *Chicago Defender* (Daily Edition) 27 April 1959, 22.
29. *Count Basie Presents the Eddie Davis Trio* (Roulette SR-52007, 1958), Track 7 'Farouk'.
30. Robert Muller, 'Lyrics quoted in the Stars Turn Sepia', *Picture Post*, 9 April 1955, 33; John L. Williams, *America's Mistress: Eartha Kitt, Her Life and Times* (London: Quercus, 2014).
31. Penny M. Von Eschen, *Race against Empire: Black Americans and Anticolonialism, 1937–1957* (Ithaca, NY: Cornell University Press, 1997).
32. McAllister, *Epic Encounters*, 86–7.
33. 'Africa's Last King', *Jet*, 2 October 1952, 16.
34. Enoc P. Waters, 'Adventures in Race Relations', *Chicago Defender* (National Edition), 23 February 1957, 10.
35. On the controversies over whether (both ancient and modern) Egypt can be acknowledged as a (black or otherwise) African culture, see Aaron Kamugisha, 'Finally in Africa? Egypt, from Diop to Celenko', *Race & Class* 45, no.1 (2003): 31–60.
36. Robert G. Spivak, 'Watch on the Potomac', *Chicago Defender* (Daily Edition), 28 May 1958, 4.
37. 'King of Egypt Is Kentucky College Benefactor', *Jet*, 24 April 1952, 13.
38. 'Willie Lewis' Ork Swing for Egypt's New Young King', *Chicago Defender* (National Edition), 26 February 1938, 18.
39. Farouk's mistresses in his exile years included Swedish novelist Birgitta Stenberg and the former Miss Naples Irma Capece Minutolo, Stadiem, *Too Rich*, 30–5, 336–40.
40. 'Gerri Major's Society World', *Jet*, 8 July 1954, 41.
41. 'Mr. and Mrs.', *Jet*, 29 October 1953, 16.
42. 'People, Places and Things', *Chicago Defender* (National Edition), 5 November 1955, 8. Rainey, like Farouk, was an exile in Rome, one of a number of Black artists who had abandoned careers in an America thwarted by racism for a new life in Europe.
43. 'New York Beat', *Jet*, 7 October 1954, 63.
44. 'Ex-King Farouk, Negro Beauties Upset Club', *Jet*, 15 May 1958, 16.
45. 'Lyons Den', *Chicago Defender* (Daily Edition), 20 August 1958, 5.
46. Ibid., 10 September 1958, 5.
47. Ibid., 21 April 1958, 5.

48 Victoria De Grazia, *Irresistible Empire: America's Advance through Twentieth-Century Europe* (Cambridge, MA: Harvard University Press, 2005); Schwartz, *It's So French*, especially 5–11; Chris Waters, 'Beyond "Americanization": Rethinking Anglo-American Cultural Exchange between the Wars', *Cultural and Social History* 4, no.4 (2007): 451–9.

49 'Ex-King Farouk Says I Am Looking for a Job', 57.

50 McLeave, *Last Pharaoh*, 278. The ghost-writer was Norman Price, Stadiem, *Too Rich*, 326.

51 H. F. Ellis, 'Afternoon Diversion for Non-Fliers', *Punch*, 7 September 1955, 268.

52 'Tribulations of Farouk's Double', *Daily Mail*, 7 January 1953, 3.

53 McBride, *Farouk of Egypt*, 212.

54 Christian Jacque, 'How to Make Martine Mad', *Picturegoer*, 6 August 1955, 10–11.

55 Paul Ridgway, 'A Rocket for Bartok', *Picturegoer*, 12 December 1953, 7.

56 Guido Orlando, *Confessions of a Scoundrel* (Philadelphia: John C. Winston, 1954), 209–10. For Orlando's career, 'Obituary: Legendary Publicist Guido Orlando,' *Los Angeles Times*, 26 May 1988. Available online: https://www.latimes.com/archives/la-xpm-1988-05-26-mn-4905-story.html (accessed 13 July 2021).

57 Orlando, *Confessions*, 211–21.

58 Vardis Fisher, *Orphans in Gethsemane: A Novel of the Past in the Present* (Denver: A. Swallow, 1960), 927.

59 Agatha Christie, *The Adventure of the Christmas Pudding* (London: Collins, 1960).

60 Fred Kaplan, *Gore Vidal: A Biography* (London: Bloomsbury, 1999), 269–72.

61 Gore Vidal, *Palimpsest: A Memoir* (New York: Penguin, 1996), 167.

62 Cameron Kay [Gore Vidal], *Thieves Fall Out* (London: Titan Books, [1950] 2015), 32, 162, 208–9, 236.

63 Kaplan, *Gore Vidal*, 370.

64 Gore Vidal, *The Judgment of Paris* (New York: E.P. Dutton, 1952), 238–9.

65 Ibid., 245.

66 Lawrence Durrell, *Mountolive* (1958) republished as part of *The Alexandria Quartet* (London: Faber & Faber, 1962); For commentary, see Roger Bowen, *Many Histories Deep: The Personal Landscape Poets in Egypt, 1940–45* (London: Associated University Presses, 1995), 162–85; Anne Ricketson Zahlan, 'The Destruction of the Imperial Self in Lawrence Durrell's *The Alexandria Quartet*', *Perspectives on Contemporary Literature* 12, no.1 (1986): 3–12.

67 Mike Diboll, 'The Secret History of Lawrence Durrell's *Alexandria Quartet*: The Mountolive-Hosnani Affair, Britain and the Wafd', in *Lawrence Durrell and the Greek World*, ed. Anna Lillios (Selsingrove, PA: Susquehanna University Press, 2004), 79–106. See also Donald Kaczvinsky, 'Memlik's House and Mountolive's Uniform: Orientalism, Ornamentalism and *The Alexandria Quartet*', *Contemporary Literature* 48, no.1 (2007): 93–118.

68  Durrell, *Alexandra Quartet*, 598–601.
69  Clive Fisher, 'Barbara Skelton', *The Independent,* 2 February 1996. Available online: https://www.independent.co.uk/news/people/obituary-barbara-skelton-1316869.html (accessed 13 July 2021).
70  Jeremy Lewis, 'Skelton, Barbara Olive (1916–1996)', *Oxford Dictionary of National Biography.* Available online: https://doi.org/10.1093/ref:odnb/583111 (accessed 14 July 2021).
71  Barbara Skelton, *A Young Girl's Touch* (London: Weidenfeld and Nicolson, 1956), 101–4.
72  Ibid., 139–45.
73  Ibid., 118.
74  For example, Stadiem, *Too Rich*, 76–8. For the account of her relationship with Farouk in her autobiography, see Skelton, *Tears before Bedtime*, 64–5.
75  Ibid., 117–18.
76  Skelton, *Young Girl's Touch*, dust wrapper.
77  Ibid., 116, 197, 214–18.
78  D. J. Taylor, 'Barbara Skelton: The Socialite Networker', *The Guardian*, 27 August 2017. Available online: https://www.theguardian.com/books/2016/aug/27/barbara-skelton-socialite-networker-dj-taylor (accessed 13 July 2021).
79  Fisher, 'Barbara Skelton'.
80  For a sympathetic reading of Skelton, see D. J. Taylor, *Lost Girls: Love, War and Literature, 1939–1951* (London: Constable, 2019).
81  'All the King's Men', *Picturegoer*, 16 January 1954, 13.
82  Thomas McNulty, *Errol Flynn: The Life and Career* (Jefferson, NC: McFarland, 2004); Simon Callow, *Orson Welles: One Man Band* (London: Jonathan Cape, 2015). Like Farouk, Flynn spent much of his European years in the nightclubs of Rome.
83  'It's All about a Playboy Monarch', *Daily Mirror,* 6 November 1953, 1.
84  'She'll Be a Girl Who Spurned a King', *Daily Mirror,* 14 November 1953, 16.
85  Donald Zec, 'Farouk by Any Other Name…', *Daily Mirror,* 21 December 1953, 2.
86  Margot Shore, 'The King Who Was Not Farouk', *Picture Post*, 24 April 1954, 24.
87  Donald Zec, 'Kay's a Beeg Girl Now', *Daily Mirror,* 25 October 1954, 2.
88  British Film Institute [hereafter BFI] Script S990 'Abdullah the Great (Release Script)'.
89  *Kinematograph Weekly,* 6 December 1956, 21.
90  *Daily Film Renter,* 3 December 1956, 4.
91  *Kinematograph Weekly,* 6 December 1956, 21.
92  Reviewers indicated that audiences might struggle with the fact that the ruler of an Arab state possesses a 'thick Russian accent', *Variety,* 4 April 1956, 16.
93  Several reviewers were highly impressed by the use of the authentic settings of Farouk's yacht, Egyptian palaces and Monte Carlo: *Film Daily,* 18 June 1956, 6.

94  BFI Script S990, folio 4/2.
95  Jane Dalley, *White Fright: The Sexual Panic at the Heart of America's Racist History* (New York: Basic Books, 2020); Buettner, 'Would You Let Your Daughter'.
96  BFI Script S990, folios 12/1, 4/5.
97  That the Egyptian government might hope to use the film to further discredit Farouk was a thought that had occurred to some more perceptive British observers, Henry Lane, 'What – No Farouk?' *Picturegoer,* 17 April 1954, 8.
98  *Monthly Film Bulletin,* January 1957, 5.

# Conclusion

1  McBride, *Farouk of Egypt*, 222–3; McLeave, *The Last Pharaoh*, 299–301.
2  *Daily Mail*, 18 March 1965, 1.
3  'Seven Women Weep for the Dead Playboy Ex-King Farouk', *Daily Mail,* 19 March 1965, 2; 'Crying… The Butler Who Slept under the Bed', *Daily Mail,* 20 March 1965, 6.
4  'In Mourning…. The Women in the Life of Farouk', *Daily Mirror*, 19 March 1965, 9.
5  *Tribute to Churchill: His Life, His Passing, His State Funeral* (London: Daily Mirror Publishing, 1965).
6  As evidenced in title of, among others, Readers Digest, *Man of the Century: A Churchill Cavalcade* (Boston: Little Brown, 1965). For the creation of the Churchill legend, see John Ramsden, *Man of the Century: Winston Churchill and His Legend since 1945* (London: HarperCollins, 2002).
7  *The Noel Coward Diaries*, ed. Graham Payn and Sheridan Morley (Boston, MA: Little, Brown, 1982), 591.
8  Cannadine, *Ornamentalism*, 73–7.
9  Wm Roger Louis, 'Churchill and Egypt, 1946–1956', in *Churchill*, ed. Wm Roger Louis and Robert Blake (New York: W. W. Norton, 1993), 473–90.
10  David Lough, *No More Champagne: Churchill and His Money* (London: Head of Zeus, 2016).
11  Mostyn, *Egypt's Belle Epoque*, 171–7.
12  For example, Sadit, *A King Betrayed*.
13  Stadiem, *Too Rich*.
14  The series is available (as of July 2021) via the Arab-language streaming service Shahid, https://shahid.mbc.net/en/series/Al-Malek-Farouq-Season-1/season-69229-68673 (accessed 15 July 2021).
15  Hala Sakr, 'Thirty Episode Series on King Farouk', *History News Network*, 26 October 2017. Available online: https://historynewsnetwork.org/article/44113 (accessed 15 July 2021).

16 Alasdair Soussi, 'Farouk: The Last King of Egypt', *The National News* (United Arab Emirates), 27 February 2020. Available online: https://www.thenationalnews.com/arts/farouk-the-last-king-of-egypt-a-monarch-who-was-dapper-yet-divisive-1.985210 (accessed 15 July 2021).
17 'Forum: Giza Things to Do', Available online: https://www.tripadvisor.co.uk/ShowUserReviews-g294202-d17736472-r785258801-KING_FAROUK-Giza (accessed 15 July 2021).
18 Programme for *The Fat Show: Watford Palace Theatre*, 6–29 September 1979.
19 Len Deighton, *City of Gold* (London: Century, 1992).
20 Barry Gifford, 'The Yellow Palace', in *New Mysteries of Paris* (Livingston, MT: Clark City Press, 1991).
21 Warren Adler, *Mother Nile* (New York: Rosetta Books, 2016).
22 Patrick Modiano, *Family Record*, trans. Mark Polizzoti (New Haven: Yale University Press, 2019).
23 John Whitbourn, *Nothing Is True: The First Book of Farouk* (New York: Parvus Press, 2018).
24 Stuart Husband, 'King of Bling: Farouk of Egypt', *The Rake* (April 2018). Available online: https://therake.com/stories/icons/king-of-bling-farouk-of-egypt/ (accessed 15 July 2015).
25 See the discussion at https://www.springsteenlyrics.com/lyrics.php?song=aintgotyou (accessed 15 July 2021).
26 Webster, *Empire and Englishness*, 186–94, 216–17.
27 *Young Winston* (1972), [Film] Dir. Richard Attenborough UK: Columbia Pictures.
28 Steven Fielding, Bill Schwarz and Richard Toye, *The Churchill Myths* (Oxford: Oxford University Press, 2020).
29 The nadir of this unedifying controversy was the ill-judged forum on 'The Racial Consequences of Mr. Churchill' hosted by Churchill College, Cambridge, in February 2021, and its aftermath. Typical of the overheated and ill-informed responses that characterized both sides of the argument were Priyaamvada Gopal, 'Why Can't Britain Handle the Truth about Winston Churchill?' *The Guardian*, 17 May 2021, https://www.theguardian.com/commentisfree/2021/mar/17/why-cant-britain-handle-the-truth-about-winston-churchill (accessed 15 July 2021); Andrew Roberts and Zweditu Gebreyohanes, 'The Racial Consequences of Mr. Churchill: A Review', *Policy Exchange*, 28 February 2021. Available online: https://policyexchange.org.uk/wp-content/uploads/The-Racial-Consequences-of-Mr-Churchill.pdf (accessed 15 July 2021).
30 Richard Toye, *Churchill's Empire: The World That Made Him and the World He Made* (Basingstoke: Macmillan, 2010).
31 Antoinette Burton, *The Trouble with Empire: Challenges to Modern British Imperialism* (Oxford: Oxford University Press, 2015), 5, 7, 3.

32  Beers, 'A Model MP', 234–5.
33  Boorstin, *The Image*, 60–1.
34  David Cannadine, 'Thrones: Churchill and Monarchy in Britain and beyond', in his *In Churchill's Shadow*, 45–84.
35  Bingham and Conboy, 'Monarchy and Celebrity', in *Tabloid Century*, 97–130.
36  Frank Mort, 'The Permissive Society Revisited', *Twentieth Century British History* 22, no.2 (2011): 269–98.
37  Stern, *Farouk Uncensored*.
38  'Palace under Pressure', *The Guardian,* 8 March 2021. Available online: https://www.theguardian.com/uk-news/2021/mar/08/palace-under-pressure-to-respond-to-harry-and-meghan-racism-claims

# Bibliography

## Unpublished sources

British Cartoon Archive, University of Kent:
    Cartoons by Joseph Lee (JL)
    Cartoons by Carl Giles (CG)
    Cartoons by David Low (LSE)
British Film Institute Archive, London:
    Script S990 'Abdullah the Great (Release Script)', n.d.
Mass-Observation Archive, University of Sussex:
    File Report 3026 'The British Sense of Humour', August 1948.
    Topic Collection 16-3-F 'Music Hall Report: Caprice Parisien, Brixton Empire', 22 January 1940.
    Topic Collection 14-I-L 'Famous Persons: King George VI', February 1952.
Middle Eastern Centre, St. Antony's College, Oxford:
    Diaries of Sir Miles Lampson (Lord Killearn)
UK National Archive, Kew:
    Foreign Office
        FO 141, FO 371, FO 421, FO 954
    Prime Minister's Office Records
        PREM 11
    German Foreign Ministry Records, 1867–1945 Captured by the British
        GFM 33

## Newspapers and magazines

*Artfix*
*Billboard*
*Birmingham Daily Post*
*Chicago Defender* (Daily Edition)
*Chicago Defender* (National Edition)
*Daily Express*
*Daily Film Renter*
*Daily Mail*
*Daily Mirror*

*Daily Telegraph*
*Film Daily*
*Financial Times*
*The Guardian*
*Illustrated London News*
*The Independent*
*Jet*
*Kinematograph Weekly*
*Ladies' Home Journal*
*Life*
*Liliput*
*Liverpool Echo*
*Los Angeles Times*
*Miami Herald*
*Monthly Film Bulletin*
*New York Daily News*
*The Observer*
*Picture Post*
*Picturegoer*
*Punch*
*San Bernadino Sun*
*Stage and Television Today*
*Time*
*The Times (London)*
*Variety*
*Vice Squad*
*Yorkshire Post*

## Books and articles

Abelson, Susan. *When Ladies Go A-Thieving: Middle-Class Shoplifters in the Victorian Department Store*. Oxford: Oxford University Press, 1989.

Adler, Warren. *Mother Nile*. New York: Rosetta Books, 2016.

Aldrich, Robert. *The Seduction of the Mediterranean: Writing, Art and Homosexual Fantasy*. London: Routledge, 1993.

Alexandra, Queen of Yugoslavia. *For Love of a King*. New York: Doubleday, 1956.

Amery, Julian. *Sons of the Eagle: A Study in Guerrilla Warfare*. London: Macmillan, 1948.

Amery, Leo. *The Framework of the Future*. London: Oxford University Press, 1944.

Arielli, Nir. *Fascist Italy and the Middle East, 1933–1940*. London: Palgrave Macmillan, 2010.

Auslander, Leora. 'Beyond Words'. *American Historical Review* 110, no.4 (2005): 1015–45.
Bailey, Peter. 'Champagne Charlie and the Music-Hall Swell Song'. In his *Popular Culture and Performance in the Victorian City*, 101–27. Cambridge: Cambridge University Press, 1998.
Bailey, Peter. 'White Collars, Gray Lives? The Lower Middle Class Revisited'. *Journal of British Studies* 38, no.2 (1999): 273–90.
Bailey, Roderick. *The Wildest Province: SOE in the Land of the Eagle*. London: Jonathan Cape, 2008.
Bailkin, Jordanna. *The Afterlife of Empire*. Berkeley, CA: University of California Press, 2012.
Bailkin, Jordanna. *Unsettled: Refugee Camps and the Making of Multicultural Britain*. Oxford: Oxford University Press, 2018.
Ball, Simon. *The Bitter Sea: The Brutal World War Two Fight for the Mediterranean*. London: HarperCollins, 2009.
Baring-Gould, Sabine. *A Book of the Riviera*. London: Methuen, 1909.
Barzini, Luigi. *The Italians*. New York: Atheneum, 1964.
Bayly, Christopher and Tim Harper. *Forgotten Wars: The End of Britain's Asian Empire*. London: Allen Lane, 2004.
Beers, Laura. 'A Model MP? Ellen Wilkinson, Gender, Politics and Celebrity Culture in Interwar Britain'. *Cultural and Social History* 10, no.2 (2013): 231–50.
Behdad, Ali. *Belated Travelers: Orientalism in the Age of Colonial Dissolution*. Durham, NC: Duke University Press, 1994.
Bennett, Tony. 'Hegemony, Ideology, Pleasure, Blackpool'. In *Popular Culture and Social Relations*, edited by Tony Bennett, Colin Mercer and Janet Woollacott, 135–54. Milton Keynes: Open University Press, 1986.
Berger, Diane. *Riviera Style*. London: Scriptum Editions, 1999.
Bertelli, Giovanna. *Dolce Italia: The Beautiful Life of Italy in the Fifties and Sixties*. New York: Rizzoli, 2005.
Bigland, Eileen. *Journey to Egypt*. London: Jarrolds, 1948.
Bin Talal, Hussein. *Uneasy Lies the Head: An Autobiography by King Hussein of Jordan*. London: Heinemann, 1962.
Bingham, Adrian. *Family Newspapers? Sex, Private Life and the British Popular Press, 1918–1978*. Oxford: Oxford University Press, 2009.
Bingham, Adrian. *Gender, Modernity and the Popular Press in Interwar Britain*. Oxford: Oxford University Press, 2004.
Bingham, Adrian and Martin Conboy. *Tabloid Century: The Popular Press in Britain, 1896 to the Present*. Oxford: Peter Lang, 2015.
Birkenhead, Lord. *Walter Monckton*. London: Weidenfeld and Nicolson, 1969.
Blake, Nicholas. *The Widow's Cruise*. New York: Harper and Brothers, 1959.
Bland, Lucy. *Modern Women on Trial: Sexual Transgression in the Age of the Flapper*. Manchester: Manchester University Press, 2017.

Blandford, Linda. *Oil Sheikhs: Inside the Supercharged World of the Petrodollar*. Littlehampton: Star Books, 1976.

Bocca, Geoffrey. *Bikini Beach: The Wicked Riviera, as It Was and Is*. New York: McGraw Hill, 1962.

Bocca, Geoffrey. *Kings without Thrones: European Monarchy in the Twentieth Century*. New York: Dial Press, 1959.

Bocking-Welch, Anna. *British Civil Society at the End of Empire*. Manchester: Manchester University Press, 2019.

Bogdanor, Vernon. *The Monarchy and the Constitution*. Oxford: Oxford University Press, 1995.

Boorstin, Daniel. *The Image, or What Happened to the American Dream*. London: Weidenfeld and Nicolson, 1961.

Botman, Selma. *Egypt from Independence to Revolution, 1919–1952*. Syracuse, NY: Syracuse University Press, 1991.

Bowen, Roger. *Many Histories Deep: The* Personal Landscape *Poets in Egypt, 1940–1945*. London: Associated University Presses, 1995.

Bowker, Gordon. *Through the Dark Labyrinth: A Biography of Lawrence Durrell*. London: St Martin's Press, 1997.

Bradford, Sarah. *George VI*. London: Fontana, 1991.

Braudel, Fernand. *La Mediterranee et Le Monde Mediterraneen a L'Epoque de Philippe II*. Paris: Armand Colin, 1949.

Braudel, Fernand. 'Personal Testimony'. *Journal of Modern History* 44, no.4 (1972): 448–67.

Braudy, Leo. *The Frenzy of Renown: Fame and Its History*. New York: Oxford University Press, 1986.

Breckman, Warren G. 'Disciplining Consumption: The Debate about Luxury in Wilhelmine Germany, 1890–1914'. *Journal of Social History* 24, no.3 (1991): 485–505.

Bret, David. *Gracie Fields: The Authorized Biography*. London: Robson Books, 1995.

*British Culture and the End of Empire*, edited by Stuart Ward. Manchester: Manchester University Press, 2001.

Buchan, John. *The House of the Four Winds*. London: Hodder and Stoughton, 1935.

Buettner, Elizabeth. '"Would You Let Your Daughter Marry a Negro?" Race and Sex in 1950s Britain'. In *Gender, Labour, War and Empire: Essays on Modern Britain*, edited by Philippa Levine and Susan R. Grayzel, 219–37. Houndmills: Palgrave Macmillan, 2009.

Bulwer-Lytton, Edward. *The Last Days of Pompeii*. London: Richard Bentley, 1834.

Burton, Antoinette. *The Postcolonial Careers of Santha Rama Rau*. Durham, NC: Duke University Press, 2006.

Burton, Antoinette. *A Primer for Teaching World History: Ten Design Principles*. Durham, NC: Duke University Press, 2012.

Burton, Antoinette, *The Trouble with Empire: Challenges to Modern British Imperialism*. Oxford: Oxford University Press, 2015.

Burton, Antoinette. 'Who Needs the Nation? Interrogating British History'. *Journal of Historical Sociology* 10, no.3 (1997): 227–48.
Callow, Simon. *Orson Welles: One Man Band*. London: Jonathan Cape, 2015.
Campbell, Neil. 'Landscapes of Americanisation in Britain: Learning from the 1950s'. In *Issues in Americanisation and Culture*, edited by Neil Campbell, Jude Davies and George McKay, 126–43. Edinburgh: Edinburgh University Press, 2004.
Cannadine, David. *In Churchill's Shadow: Confronting the Past in Modern Britain*. Oxford: Oxford University Press, 2003.
Cannadine, David. 'The Context, Performance and Meaning of Ritual: The British Monarchy and the "Invention of Tradition", c.1820–1977'. In *The Invention of Tradition*, edited by Eric Hobsbawm and Terence Ranger, 101–64. Cambridge: Cambridge University Press, 1983.
Cannadine, David. 'Food'. In *The Pleasures of the Past*, 230–6. New York: Norton, 1991.
Cannadine, David. *Ornamentalism: How the British Saw Their Empire*. London: Penguin, 2002.
Cartland, Barbara. *The Scandalous Life of King Carol*. London: Frederick Muller, 1957.
*Celebrity Colonialism: Fame, Power and Representation in Colonial and Postcolonial Cultures*, edited by Robert Clarke. Newcastle upon Tyne: Cambridge Scholars Publishing, 2009.
Chapman, James. *Past and Present: National Identity and the British Historical Film*. London: I.B. Tauris, 2005.
Chibnall, Steve. 'Rome, Open for British Production: The Lost World of "Britalian" Films, 1946–1954'. *Historical Journal of Film, Radio and Television* 33, no.2 (2013): 234–69.
Christie, Agatha. *The Adventure of the Christmas Pudding*. London: Collins, 1960.
Cirkaman, Asli. *From the 'Terror of the World' to the 'Sick Man of Europe': European Images of Ottoman Empire and Society from the Sixteenth Century to the Nineteenth*. New York: Peter Lang, 2005.
Clapson, Mark. *A Bit of a Flutter: Popular Gambling in England, c.1820–1961*. Manchester: Manchester University Press, 1992.
Clark, Anna. *Scandal: The Sexual Politics of the British Constitution*. Princeton, NJ: Princeton University Press, 2004.
Clark, Sydney. *All the Best in Italy*. New York: Dodd, Mead and Company, 1953.
Cleveland. Les. 'Soldiers' Songs: the Folklore of the Powerless'. *New York Folklore* 11, no.1 (1985): 81–3.
Cocteau, Jean. *Past Tense: Diaries, Volume Two*, translated by Richard Howard. New York: Harcourt Brace Jovanovich, 1988.
Cohen, Deborah. *Family Secrets: Shame and Privacy in Modern Britain*. Oxford: Oxford University Press, 2013.
Cohen, Deborah. 'The Geopolitical Is Personal: India, Britain and American Foreign Correspondents in the 1930s and 1940s'. *Twentieth Century British History* 29, no.3 (2018): 388–410.

Cohen, Gerard Daniel. *In War's Wake: Europe's Displaced Persons in the Postwar Order*. New York: Oxford University Press, 2012.
Cohen, Julia Philips. 'Oriental by Design: Ottoman Jews, Imperial Style, and the Performance of Heritage'. *American Historical Review* 119, no.2 (2014): 364–98.
Cohen, William B. 'The Colonized as Child: British and French Colonial Rule'. *African Historical Studies* 3, no.2 (1970): 427–31.
Colla, Elliott. *Conflicted Antiquities: Egyptology, Egyptomania, Egyptian Modernity*. Durham, NC: Duke University Press, 2008.
Collins, Marcus. *Modern Love: An Intimate History of Men and Women in Twentieth-Century Britain*. London: Atlantic, 2003.
Conboy, Martin. *The Press and Popular Culture*. London: SAGE, 2002.
Conekin, Becky. 'Fashioning the Playboy: Messages of Style and Masculinity in the Pages of *Playboy* Magazine, 1953–1963'. *Fashion Theory* 4, no.4 (2000): 447–66.
Cooper, Artemis. *Cairo in the War, 1939–1945*. London: Penguin, 1993.
Cooper, Artemis. *Writing at the Kitchen Table: The Authorized Biography of Elizabeth David*. New York: HarperCollins, 1999.
Cooper, Gordon. *A Fortnight around the Bay of Naples*. London: Percival Marshall, 1955.
Costigliola, Frank. *Roosevelt's Lost Alliances: How Personal Politics Helped Start the Cold War*. Princeton, NJ: Princeton University Press, 2012.
Coward, Noel. *The Lyrics of Noel Coward*. London: Methuen, 2002.
Cunningham, Hugh. *Grace Darling: Victorian Heroine*. London: Continuum, 2007.
Daly, Nicholas Daly. 'Modernism. Operetta and Ruritania: Ivor Novello's *Glamorous Night*'. In *Popular Modernism and Its Legacies*, edited by Scott Ortolano, 43–62. New York: Bloomsbury, 2017.
Dalley, Jane. *White Fright: The Sexual Panic at the Heart of America's Racist History*. New York: Basic Books, 2020.
Darwin, John. 'An Undeclared Empire: The British in the Middle East, 1918–1939'. *Journal of Imperial and Commonwealth History* 27, no.2 (1999): 159–76.
David, Elizabeth. *A Book of Mediterranean Food*. London: John Lehmann, 1950.
Davis, Melton S. *All Rome Trembled*. New York: G.P. Putnam, 1957.
Davison, Roderic H. 'Where Is the Middle East?'. *Foreign Affairs* 38, no.4 (1960): 665–75.
De Grazia, Victoria. *Irresistible Empire: America's Advance through Twentieth-Century Europe*. Cambridge, MA: Harvard University Press, 2005.
Deighton, Len. *City of Gold*. London: Century, 1992.
Delfont, Lord. *Curtain's Up! The Story of the Royal Variety Performance*. London: Robson Books, 1989.
Diboll, Mike. 'The Secret History of Lawrence Durrell's *Alexandria Quartet*: The Mountolive-Hosnani Affair, Britain and the Wafd'. In *Lawrence Durrell and the Greek World*, edited by Anna Lillios, 79–106. Selsingrove, PA: Susquehanna University Press, 2004.

*Displacement, Diaspora and Geographies of Identity*, edited by Shadar Lavie and Ted Swedenburg. Durham, NC: Duke University Press, 1996.

Docker, Lady. *Norah: The Autobiography*. London: W.H. Allen, 1969.

Double, Oliver. *Britain Had Talent: A History of Variety Theatre*. Houndmills: Palgrave Macmillan, 2012.

Douglas, Sholto. *Years of Command*. London: Collins, 1966.

Durrell, Lawrence. *The Alexandria Quartet*. London: Faber & Faber, 1962.

Dutton, David. *Anthony Eden: A Life and Reputation*. London: Arnold, 1997.

East, John M. *Max Miller: The Cheeky Chappie*. London: W.H. Allen, 1977.

East, William Gordon. 'The Mediterranean: Pivot of Peace and War'. *Foreign Affairs* 31, no.4 (1953): 619–33.

El-Barawy, Rashed. *The Military Coup in Egypt: An Analytic Study*. Cairo: Renaissance Bookshop, 1952.

El-Gawhary, Mahmoud. *Ex-Royal Palaces of Egypt*. Cairo: Dar Al-Maaref, 1954.

Elkins, Caroline. *Britain's Gulag: The Brutal End of Empire in Kenya*. London: Jonathan Cape, 2005.

Ellis, Matthew. 'Repackaging the Egyptian Monarchy: Faruq in the Public Spotlight, 1936–1939'. *History Compass* 7, no.1 (2009): 181–213.

Featherstone, Simon. 'The Mill Girl and the Cheeky Chappie: British Popular Comedy and Mass Culture in the Thirties'. *Critical Survey* 15, no.2 (2003): 3–22.

Fielding, Steven, Bill Schwarz and Richard Toye. *The Churchill Myths*. Oxford: Oxford University Press, 2020.

Fischer, Bernd J. *Albania at War, 1939–1945*. West Lafayette, IN: C. Hurst, 1999.

Fisher, Vardis. *Orphans in Gethsemane: A Novel of the Past in the Present*. Denver: A. Swallow, 1960.

Flaiano, Ennio. *The Via Veneto Papers*, translated by. John Satriano. Marlboro, VT: Marlboro Press, 1992.

Fleming, Ian. *Casino Royale*. London: Penguin, [1953] 2004.

Forth, Christopher E. 'Fat, Desire and Disgust in the Colonial Imagination'. *History Workshop Journal* 73 (2012): 211–39.

Francis, Martin. 'The Domestication of the Male? Recent Research on Nineteenth- and Twentieth Century British Masculinity'. *Historical Journal* 45, no.3 (2002): 637–52.

Francis, Martin. 'Set the People Free? Conservatives and the State, 1920–1960'. In *The Conservatives and British Society, 1880–1990*, edited by Martin Francis and Ina Zweiniger-Bargielowska, 58–77. Cardiff: University of Wales Press, 1996.

Francis, Martin. 'Wounded Pride and Petty Jealousies: Private Lives and Public Diplomacy in Second World War Cairo'. In *War: An Emotional History*, edited by Claire Langhamer, Lucy Noakes and Claudia Siebrecht, 98–115. Oxford: Oxford University Press, 2020.

Freeman, Thomas S. 'A Tyrant for All Seasons: Henry VIII on Film'. In *Tudors and Stuarts on Film*, edited by Susan Doran and Thomas S. Freeman, 30–45. London: Palgrave Macmillan, 2009.

*The French Emigres in Europe and the Struggle against Revolution, 1789–1814*, edited by Kirsty Carpenter and Philip Mansel. Houndmills: Palgrave, 1999.

Fritzsche, Peter. 'Specters of History: On Nostalgia, Exile and Modernity'. *American Historical Review* 106, no.5 (2001): 1587–618.

Fryxell, Allegra. 'Tutankhamen. Egyptomania and Temporal Enchantment in Interwar Britain'. *Twentieth Century British History* 28, no.4 (2017): 516–42.

George, Rosemary M. *The Politics of Home: Postcolonial Relocations and Twentieth-Century Fiction*. Berkeley, CA: University of California Press, 1999.

Gifford, Barry. *New Mysteries of Paris*. Livingston, MT: Clark City Press, 1991.

Gilbert, Fred. *The Man That Broke the Bank at Monte Carlo*. London: Francis Day and Hunter, 1891.

Gilroy, Paul. *'There Ain't No Black in the Union Jack': The Cultural Politics of Race and Nation*. London: Routledge, 2002.

Gilroy, Paul. *Postcolonial Melancholia*. New York: Columbia University Press, 2005.

Glubb, John Bagot. *The Story of the Arab Legion*. London: Hodder and Stoughton, 1948.

Gorer, Geoffrey. *Exploring English Character*. New York: Criterion, 1955.

Grafftey-Smith, Laurence. *Bright Levant*. London: John Murray, 1970.

Graves, Robert. *I, Claudius*. London: Arthur Barker, 1934.

Green, Nile. 'Spacetime and the Muslim Journey West: Industrial Communications in the Making of the "Muslim World"'. *American Historical Review* 118, no.2 (2013): 401–29.

Grob-Fitzgibbon, Benjamin. *Imperial Endgame: Britain's Dirty Wars and the End of Empire*. Houndmills: Palgrave Macmillan, 2011.

Gross. Ken. 'The Last Pharaoh and His Ferrari'. *Automobile Quarterly* 27, no.2 (1989): 149–59.

Guldi, Jo and David Armitage. *The History Manifesto*. Cambridge: Cambridge University Press, 2014.

Gundle, Stephen. *Death and the Dolce Vita: The Dark Side of Rome in the 1950s*. Edinburgh: Canongate, 2011.

Gundle, Stephen. *Glamour: A History*. Oxford: Oxford University Press, 2008.

Hahn, Peter. *The United States, Great Britain and Egypt, 1945–1956*. Chapel Hill: UNC Press, 1991.

Hammond, Andrew. 'British Literary Responses to the Suez Crisis'. *Literature & History* 22, no.2 (2013): 53–72.

Hanley, Will. *Identifying with Nationality: Europeans, Ottomans and Egyptians in Alexandria*. New York: Columbia University Press, 2017.

Harper, Sue. *Picturing the Past: The Rise and Fall of the British Costume Film*. London: BFI Publishing, 1994.

Heinlein, Frank. *British Government Policy and Decolonisation, 1945–1963: Scrutinizing the Official Mind*. London: Routledge, 2002.

*Henry 'Chips' Channon: The Diaries, 1938–43*, edited by Simon Heffer. London: Hutchinson, 2021.

Heyer, Georgette. *Regency Buck*. London: William Heinemann, 1935.

Hickman, Tom. *The Call Up: A History of National Service*. London: Headline, 2005.

Higgins, Patrick. *Heterosexual Dictatorship: Male Homosexuality in Postwar Britain*. London: Fourth Estate, 1996.

*Histories of the Aftermath: The Legacies of the Second World War in Europe*, edited by Frank Biess and Robert Moeller. New York: Berghahn, 2010.

Hoare, Philip. *Noel Coward: A Biography*. New York: Simon and Schuster, 1996.

Hobbs, Allyson. *A Chosen Exile: A History of Racial Passing in American Life*. Cambridge, MA: Harvard University Press, 2014.

Hoggart, Richard. *The Uses of Literacy*. Harmondsworth: Penguin, 1957.

Holland, Robert. *Blue-Water Empire: The British in the Mediterranean since 1800*. London: Allen Lane, 2012.

Holland, Robert. *The Warm South: How the Mediterranean Shaped the British Imagination*. New Haven: Yale University Press, 2018.

Hopkins, Harry. *The New Look: A Social History of the Forties and Fifties in Britain*. London: Secker and Warburg, 1963.

Hopwood, Derek. *Sexual Encounters in the Middle East*. Reading: Garnet Publishing, 1999.

Horn, Adrian. *Juke Box Britain: Americanization and Youth Culture, 1945–60*. Manchester: Manchester University Press, 2009.

Hoskins, James. *Biographical Object: How Things Tell the Stories of People's Lives*. New York: Routledge, 1998.

Houlbrook, Matt. *Prince of Tricksters: The Incredible True Story of Netley Lucas, Gentleman Crook*. Chicago: University of Chicago Press, 2016.

Howe, Peter. *Paparazzi*. New York: Artisan Books, 2005.

Howe, Stephen. 'When (if Ever) Did Empire End? "Internal Decolonisation" in British Culture since the 1950s'. In *The British Empire in the 1950s: Retreat or Revival?*, edited by Martin Lynn, 214–37. Houndmills: Palgrave Macmillan, 2006.

Huggins, Mike. *Horseracing and the British, 1919–1939*. Manchester: Manchester University Press, 2003.

Hungerford, Edward. 'Durrell's Mediterranean Paradise'. *Studies in the Literary Imagination* 24, no.1 (1991): 57–69.

Husband, Stuart. 'King of Bling: Farouk of Egypt'. *The Rake*. April 2018. Available online: https://therake.com/stories/icons/king-of-bling-farouk-of-egypt/ (accessed 15 July 2015).

Inglis, Fred. *A Short History of Celebrity*. Princeton, NJ: Princeton University Press, 2010.

Israel, Kali. *Names and Stories: Emilia Dilke and Victorian Culture*. New York: Oxford University Press, 1998.

Jackson, Stanley. *The Aga Khan: Prince, Prophet and Sportsman*. London: Odhams, 1952.

Jackson, Stanley. *Inside Monte Carlo*. New York: Stein and Day, 1975.

Jacob, Wilson Chacko. *Working Out Egypt: Effendi Masculinity and Subject Formation in Colonial Modernity, 1870–1940*. Durham, NC: Duke University Press, 2011.

Jarvis, Anthea. 'There Was a Young Man from Bengal: The Vogue for Fancy Dress, 1830–1950'. *Costume* 16 (1982): 33–46.

Jensen, John. 'Giles, Ronald [Carl] (1916–1995)'. *Oxford Dictionary of National Biography*. 2004. Available online: https://doi.org/10.1093/ref:odnb/60110 (accessed 15 July 2021).

Johnston, John. *The Lord Chamberlain's Blue Pencil*. London: Hodder and Stoughton, 1990.

Joshel, Sandra. *Imperial Projections: Ancient Rome in Modern Popular Culture*. Baltimore: Johns Hopkins University Press, 2001.

Judt, Tony. *Postwar: A History of Europe since 1945*. London: William Heinemann, 2005.

Kaczvinsky, Donald. 'Memlik's House and Mountolive's Uniform: Orientalism, Ornamentalism and *The Alexandria Quartet*'. *Contemporary Literature* 48, no.1 (2007): 93–118.

Kamugisha, Aaron. 'Finally in Africa? Egypt, from Diop to Celenko'. *Race & Class* 45, no.1 (2003): 31–60.

Kaplan, Caren. *Questions of Travel: Postmodern Discourses of Displacement*. Durham, NC: Duke University Press, 1996.

Kaplan, Fred. *Gore Vidal: A Biography*. London: Bloomsbury, 1999.

Karayanni, Stavros. *Dancing, Fear and Desire: Race, Sexuality and Imperial Politics in Middle Eastern Dance*. Waterloo: Wilfrid Laurier University Press, 2004.

Kay, Cameron [Gore Vidal]. *Thieves Fall Out*. London: Titan Books, [1950] 2015.

*Keith Douglas: The Complete Poems*, edited by Desmond Graham. London: Faber & Faber, 2000.

Kelly, David. *The Ruling Few*. London: Hollis & Carter, 1952.

Khan, Yasmin. 'Sex in an Imperial War Zone: Transnational Encounters in Second World War India'. *History Workshop Journal* 73, no.1 (2012): 240–58.

*The Killearn Diaries, 1934–1946*, edited by Trefor Evans. London: Sidgwick & Jackson, 1972.

King, Laura. *Family Men: Fatherhood and Masculinity in Britain, 1914–1960*. Oxford: Oxford University Press, 2015.

Kirk-Greene, Anthony. *Britain's Imperial Administrators, 1858–1966*. Houndmills: Macmillan, 2000.

Klein, Christina. *Cold War Orientalism: Asia in the Middlebrow Imagination, 1945–1961*. Berkeley, CA: University of California Press, 2003.

Kolinsky, Martin. *Britain's War in the Middle East: Strategy and Diplomacy, 1936–1942*. Houndmills: Macmillan, 1999.

Kracauer, Siegfried. 'The Hotel Lobby' (1963), reprinted in *The City Cultures Reader*, edited by Malcolm Miles, Tim Hall and Iain Borden, 2nd edn. 33–9. London: Routledge, 2003.

Kyle, Keith. *Suez*. London: Weidenfeld and Nicolson, 1992.

Kynaston, David. *Family Britain, 1951–1957*. London: Bloomsbury, 2009.
Lamming, George. *The Pleasures of Exile*. Ann Arbor: University of Michigan Press, [1960] 1992.
Lane, Edward William. *Manners and Customs of Modern Egyptians*. London: Charles Knight, 1836.
Langhamer, Claire. 'Adultery in Postwar England'. *History Workshop Journal* 62, no.1 (2006): 86–115.
Langhamer, Claire. *The English in Love: The Intimate Story of an Emotional Revolution*. Oxford: Oxford University Press, 2013.
Lassner, Phyllis. *Colonial Strangers: Women Writing the End of the British Empire*. New Brunswick, NJ: Rutgers University Press, 2004.
Lawrence, Jon. 'Class and Gender in the Making of Urban Toryism, 1880–1914'. *English Historical Review* 108, no. 428 (1993): 629–52.
Leslie, Doris. *The Great Corinthian: A Portrait of the Prince Regent*. London: Eyre and Spottiswoode, 1952.
Levenstein, Harvey. *We'll Always Have Paris: American Tourists in France since 1930*. Chicago: University of Chicago Press, 2004.
Levy, Shawn. *The Last Playboy: The High Life of Porfirio Rubirosa*. New York: Harper, 2005.
Lewis, Jeremy. 'Skelton, Barbara Olive (1916–1996)'. *Oxford Dictionary of National Biography*. Available online: https://doi.org/10.1093/ref:odnb/583111 (accessed 14 July 2021).
Lewis, Joanna. 'Daddy Wouldn't Buy Me a Mau Mau: The British Popular Press and the Demoralization of Empire'. In *Mau Mau and Nationhood: Arms, Authority and Narration*, edited by E. S. Atieno Odhiambo and John Lonsdale, 227–50. Athens, GA: University of Georgia Press, 2003.
Lewis, Norman. *Naples '44*. New York: Pantheon Books, 1978.
Linkof, Ryan. '"The Photographic Attack on His Royal Highness": The Prince of Wales, Wallis Simpson and the Prehistory of the Paparazzi'. *Photography and Culture* 4, no.3 (2011): 277–92.
Lockman, Zachary. *Contending Visions of the Middle East: The History and Politics of Orientalism*. Cambridge: Cambridge University Press, 2009.
Lord, John. *The Maharajahs*. New York: Random House, 1971.
Lott, Emmeline. *Harem Life in Egypt and Constantinople*. London: Richard Bentley, 1867.
Lough, David. *No More Champagne: Churchill and His Money*. London: Head of Zeus, 2016.
Louis, William Roger. *The British Empire in the Middle East*. Oxford: Oxford University Press, 1984.
Louis, William Roger. 'Churchill and Egypt, 1946–1956'. In *Churchill*, edited by Wm Roger Louis and Robert Blake, 473–90. New York: W.W. Norton, 1993.
Lovell, Mary S. *The Riviera Set, 1920–1960: The Golden Years of Glamour and Excess*. London: Abacus, 2017.

Luckett, Moya. 'Travel and Mobility: Femininity and National Identity in Swinging London Films'. In *British Cinema, Past and Present*, edited by Justine Ashby and Andrew Higson, 233–45. London: Routledge, 2000.

Lyth, Peter J. 'From Privilege to Popularity: The Growth of Leisure Air Travel since 1945'. *Journal of Transport History* 15, no.2 (1994): 101–15.

McAlister, Melani. *Epic Encounters: Culture, Media, and US Interests in the Middle East since 1945*. Berkeley: University of California Press, 2005.

McBride, Barrie St Clair. *Farouk of Egypt*. London: A.S. Barnes, 1968.

McCarthy, Helen. 'Petticoat Diplomacy: The Admission of Women to the British Foreign Service, c.1910–1946'. *Twentieth Century British History* 20, no.3 (2009): 85–321.

McIntosh, Elizabeth P. *Sisterhood of Spies: The Women of the OSS*. Annapolis, MD: Naval Institute Press, 1996.

McKibbin, Ross. *Classes and Cultures: England, 1918–1951*. Oxford: Oxford University Press, 1998.

McKibbin, Ross. *Ideologies of Class: Social Relations in Britain, 1880–1950*. Oxford: Oxford University Press, 1990.

McLeave, Hugh. *The Last Pharaoh: Farouk of Egypt, 1920–1965*. New York: McCall Publishing, 1970.

McNulty, Thomas. *Errol Flynn: The Life and Career*. Jefferson, NC: McFarland, 2004.

Mais, S. P. B., and Gillian Mais. *Italian Holiday*. London: Alvin Redman, 1954.

Mak, Lanver. *The British in Egypt: Community, Crime and Crises, 1882–1922*. London: I.B. Tauris, 2017.

Malick, Qayyum A. *His Royal Highness Prince Aga Khan: Guide, Philosopher and Friend of the World of Islam*. Karachi: Ismailia Association, 1954.

Mansel, Philip. *Sultans in Splendour: The Last Years of the Ottoman World*. London: Andre Deutsch, 1988.

Margadant, Jo Burr. *The New Biography: Performing Femininity in Nineteenth-Century France*. Berkeley, CA: University of California Press, 2000.

Marshall, P. David. *Celebrity and Power: Fame in Contemporary Culture*. Minneapolis: University of Minnesota Press, 1997.

Maugham, Robin. *Escape from the Shadows: An Autobiography*. New York: McGraw-Hill, 1973.

Maxwell, Elsa. *The Celebrity Circus*. London: W.H. Allen, 1964.

Maxwell, Elsa. *RSVP*. New York: Little Brown and Co., 1954.

Mayhall, Laura Nym. 'The Prince of Wales versus Clark Gable: Anglophone Celebrity and Citizenship between the Wars'. *Cultural and Social History* 4, no.4 (2007): 529–43.

Mazower, Mark. *Dark Continent: Europe's Twentieth Century*. London: Allen Lane, 1998.

Medhurst, Andy. *A National Joke: Popular Comedy and English Cultural Identities*. London: Routledge, 2007.

Melman, Billie. *Women and the Popular Imagination in the 1920s*. Basingstoke: Palgrave Macmillan, 1988.

Mitchell, Rebecca N. 'The Victorian Fancy Dress Ball, 1870–1900'. *Fashion Theory* 21, no.3 (2017): 291–315.

Mitchell, Timothy. *Colonising Egypt*. Berkeley: University of California Press, 1989.

Modiano, Patrick. *Family Record*, translated by Mark Polizzoti. New Haven: Yale University Press, 2019.

Modiano, Patrick. *Villa Triste*, translated by John Cullen. London: Daunt Books, [1975] 2016.

Mohanram, Radhika. *Imperial White: Race, Diaspora and the British Empire*. Minneapolis: University of Minnesota Press, 2007.

*Moments of Modernity: Reconstructing Britain, 1945–1964*, edited by Becky Conekin, Frank Mort and Chris Waters. London: Rivers Oram, 1999.

Monaco, James. 'Celebration'. In *Celebrity: The Media as Image Makers*, edited by James Monaco, 3–14. New York: Dell, 1978.

*The Monarchy and the British Nation, 1780 to the Present*, edited by Andrzej Olechnowicz. Cambridge: Cambridge University Press, 2007.

Montgomery, Bernard. *From Alamein to the River Sangro*. London: Hutchinson, 1950.

Morgan, Simon. 'Celebrity: Academic "Pseudo-Event" or a Useful Concept for Historians?'. *Cultural and Social History* 8, no.1 (2011): 95–114.

Morgan, Simon. 'From Warehouse Clerk to Corn Law Celebrity: The Making of a National Hero'. In *Rethinking Nineteenth Century Liberalism: Richard Cobden Bicentenary Essays*, edited by Anthony Howe and Simon Morgan, 39–55. London: Routledge, 2006.

Mormorio, Diego. *Tazio Secchiaroli: Greatest of the Paparazzi*, translated by Alexandra Bonfante-Warren. New York: Harry Abrams, 1999.

Morsy, Laila. 'Britain's Wartime Policy in Egypt, 1940–1942'. *Middle Eastern Studies* 25, no.1 (1989): 64–94.

Morsy, Laila. 'Farouk in British Policy'. *Middle Eastern Studies* 20, no.4 (1984): 193–212.

Mostyn, Trevor. *Egypt's Belle Epoque: Cairo and the Age of the Hedonists*. London: Quartet, 1989.

Mort, Frank. *Capital Affairs: London and the Making of the Permissive Society*. New Haven, CT: Yale University Press, 2010.

Mort, Frank. 'Love in a Cold Climate: Letters, Public Opinion and Monarchy in the 1936 Abdication Crisis'. *Twentieth Century British History* 25, no.1 (2014): 30–62.

Mort, Frank. 'The Permissive Society Revisited'. *Twentieth Century British History* 22, no.2 (2011): 269–98.

Muhammed Shah, Sultan, Aga Khan III. *World Enough and Time*. New York: Simon and Schuster, 1954.

Mullen, John. 'Anti-Black Racism in British Popular Music (1880–1920)'. *French Journal of British Studies* 17, no.2 (2012): 61–80.

'Napoleon III at Chislehurst'. *Notes and Queries* Series 22 10, no.242 (1914): 135.

Naquib, Mohammed. *Egypt's Destiny: A Personal Statement*. New York: Doubleday, 1955.
Nasaw, David. 'Historians and Biography'. *American Historical Review* 114, no.3 (2009): 573–8.
Nation Associates. *The Record of Collaboration of King Farouk of Egypt with the Nazis, and Their Ally, the Mufti: Memorandum Submitted to the United Nations*. New York: Nation Associates, 1948.
Nead, Lynda. 'Red Taffeta under Tweed: The Color of Post-War Clothes'. *Fashion Theory* 21, no.4 (2017): 365–89.
Nead, Lynda. *Tiger in the Smoke: Art and Culture in Postwar Britain*. New Haven: Yale University Press, 2017.
Nell, Dawn. 'Helping Yourself: Self-Service Grocery, Retailing and Shoplifting in Britain, c.1950–75'. *Cultural and Social History* 8, no.3 (2011): 371–91.
Nelson, Nina. *Shepheard's Hotel*. London: Barrie and Rockliff, 1960.
*The New Elizabethan Age: Culture, Society and National Identity after World War Two*, edited by Irene Morra and Scott Anthony. London: Bloomsbury, 2016.
Nicolson, Harold. *Diplomacy: A Basic Guide to the Conduct of Contemporary Foreign Affairs*. London: Thornton Butterworth, 1939.
Nixon, Rob. 'Refugees and Homecomings'. In *Travellers Tales: Narratives of Home and Displacement*, edited by George Robertson. London: Routledge, 1994.
*The Noel Coward Diaries*, edited by Graham Payn and Sheridan Morley. Boston, MA: Little, Brown, 1982.
Novello, Ivor. *King's Rhapsody, Written and Directed by Ivor Novello*. London: Palace Theatre, 1949.
Novello, Ivor and Christopher Hassall. *Glamorous Night: A Romantic Play with Music*. London: Samuel French, 1939.
Nuttall, Jeff. *King Twist: A Portrait of Frank Randle*. London: Routledge, 2007.
*Official Campaign History: The Mediterranean and the Middle East* 6 vols., edited by I. S. O. Playfair. London: HMSO, 1954–1987.
O'Brien, Patricia. 'The Kleptomania Diagnosis: Bourgeois Women and Theft in Late Nineteenth Century France'. *Journal of Social History* 17, no.1 (1983): 65–77.
Offer, Avner. *The Challenge of Affluence*. Oxford: Oxford University Press, 2007.
Olechnowicz, Andrzej. 'Britain's "Quasi-Magical" Monarchy in the Mid-Twentieth Century'. In *Classes, Cultures and Politics*, edited by Clare V. Griffiths, James J. Nott and William Whyte, 70–84. Oxford: Oxford University Press, 2011.
Oppenheim, E. Phillips. *Mr. Grex of Monte Carlo*. London: Methuen, [1915] 1925.
Orlando, Guido. *Confessions of a Scoundrel*. Philadelphia: John C. Winston, 1954.
Orwell, George. 'The Art of Donald McGill'. *Horizon* 4, no.21 (September 1941): 379–80.
Osborne, John. *The Entertainer*. London: Faber & Faber, 1957.
Osgerby, Bill. *Playboys in Paradise: Masculinity, Youth and Leisure-Style in Modern America*. Oxford: Berg, 2001.
Otte, Otto, Thomas G. *The Foreign Office Mind: The Making of British Foreign Policy, 1865–1914*. Cambridge: Cambridge University Press, 2011.

Owens, Edward. 'All the World Loves a Lover: Mass Media and the 1934 Royal Wedding of Prince George and Princess Marina'. *English Historical Review* 133, no.562 (2018): 597–633.

Owens, Edward. *The Family Firm: Monarchy, Mass Media and the British Public, 1932–1953*. London: University of London Press, 2019.

Paquet, Sandra. *Caribbean Autobiography: Cultural Identity and Self-Representation*. Madison: University of Wisconsin Press, 2002.

Parsons, Nicola. *Reading Gossip in Early Eighteenth Century England*. Houndmills: Palgrave Macmillan, 2009.

Paul, Kathleen. *Whitewashing Britain: Race and Citizenship in the Postwar Era*. Ithaca, NY: Cornell University Press, 1997.

Pemble, John. *The Mediterranean Passion: Victorians and Edwardians in the South*. Oxford: Oxford University Press, 1987.

Perry, Kennetta Hammond. *London Is the Place for Me: Black Britons, Citizenship and the Politics of Race*. New York: Oxford University Press, 2015.

Peter II of Yugoslavia. *A King's Heritage*. New York: G.P. Putnam, 1954.

Pimlott, Ben. *The Queen: A Biography of Elizabeth II*. London: HarperCollins, 1997.

Pinkus, Karen. *The Montesi Scandal: The Death of Wilma Montesi and the Birth of the Paparazzi in Fellini's Rome*. Chicago: Chicago University Press, 2003.

*Politics and Diplomacy in Egypt: The Diaries of Sir Miles Lampson, 1935–1937*, edited by Malcom Yapp. Oxford: Oxford University Press, 1997.

Pollard, Lisa. 'From Husbands and Housewives to Suckers and Whores: Marital-Political Anxieties in the "House of Egypt", 1919–48'. *Gender and History* 21, no.3 (2009): 647–69.

Porter, Laraine. 'Tarts, Tampons and Tyrants: Women and Representation in British Comedy'. In *Because I Tell a Joke or Two: Comedy, Politics and Social Difference*, edited by Stephen Wragg, 65–93. London: Routledge, 2004.

Powell, Eve M. Troutt. 'Brothers along the Nile: Egyptian Concepts of Race and Ethnicity, 1895–1910'. In *The Nile: Histories, Cultures, Myths*, edited by Haggai Erlich and Israel Gershoni, 171–81. London: Lynne Reiner Publishers, 2000.

Powell, Eve M. Troutt. *A Different Shade of Colonialism: Egypt, Great Britain and the Mastery of the Sudan*. Berkeley, CA: University of California Press, 2003.

Price, Richard. 'One Big Thing: Britain, Its Empire and Their Imperial Culture'. *Journal of British Studies* 45, no.3 (2006): 602–27.

Prochaska, Frank. *Royal Bounty: The Making of a Welfare Monarchy*. New Haven: Yale University Press, 1995.

Purce, Emma. 'Scales of Normality: Displays of Extreme Weight and Weight Loss in Blackpool, 1920–1940'. *Cultural and Social History* 14, no.5 (2017): 669–89.

Quayle, Anthony. *Eight Hours from England*. London: Heinemann, 1945.

Quinn, Edward. *Stars, Stars, Stars: Off the Screen*. Zurich: Scalo, 1997.

Quinn, Robin. *The Man Who Broke the Bank at Monte Carlo*. Stroud: The History Press, 2016.

Ramsden, John. *Man of the Century: Winston Churchill and His Legend since 1945*. London: HarperCollins, 2002.

Ramusack, Barbara. *The Princes of India in the Twilight of Empire*. Columbus, OH: Ohio University Press, 1978.

Rattigan, Terence. *The Sleeping Prince: An Occasional Fairy Tale*. London: Hamish Hamilton, 1954.

Readers Digest. *Man of the Century: A Churchill Cavalcade*. Boston: Little Brown, 1965.

*Re-Envisioning Egypt, 1919–1952*, edited by Arthur Goldschmidt. Cairo: American University in Cairo Press, 2005.

Reid, Donald M. *Contesting Antiquity in Egypt: Archaeologies, Museums and the Struggle for Identities from World War One to Nasser*. Cairo: American University in Cairo Press, 2015.

Renton, James. 'Changing Languages of Empire and the Orient: Britain and the Invention of the Middle East, 1917–1918'. *Historical Journal* 50, no.3 (2007): 645–67.

Rhodes, Joan. *Coming On Strong*. Darlington: Serendipity, 2007.

Riall, Lucy. *Garibaldi: Invention of a Hero*. New Haven: Yale University Press, 2008.

Richards, Jeffrey. *The Age of the Dream Palace: Cinema and Society in Britain, 1930–1939*. London: Routledge, 1984.

Rieger, Bernhard. 'Fast Couples: Technology, Gender and Modernity in Britain and Germany during the Nineteen-Thirties'. *Historical Research* 76, no.193 (2003): 364–88.

Roberts, Andrew and Zweditu Gebreyohanes. 'The Racial Consequences of Mr. Churchill: A Review'. *Policy Exchange*, 28 February 2021. Available online: https://policyexchange.org.uk/wp-content/uploads/The-Racial-Consequences-of-Mr-Churchill.pdf (accessed 15 July 2021).

Roberts, Ben. 'The Complex Holiday Calendar of 1902: Responses to the Coronation of Edward VII and the Growth of Edwardian Event Fatigue'. *Twentieth Century British History* 28, no.4 (2017): 489–515.

Roberts, Mary Louise. *What Soldiers Do: Sex and the American GI in World War Two France*. Chicago: Chicago University Press, 2013.

Robinson, Ronald and John Gallagher. *Africa and the Victorians: The Official Mind of Imperialism*. London: Macmillan, 1961.

Rojek, Chris. *Celebrity*. London: Reaktion Books, 2001.

Ross, Kristin. *Fast Cars, Clean Bodies: Decolonization and the Reordering of French Culture*. Cambridge, MA: MIT Press, 1996.

Rowlatt, Mary. *A Family in Egypt*. London: Robert Hale, 1956.

Rowntree, B. Seebohm and G. R. Lavers. *English Life and Leisure*. London: Longmans, 1951.

Ruger, Jan. *Heligoland: Britain, Germany and the Struggle for the North Sea*. Oxford: Oxford University Press, 2017.

Sabit, Adel. *A King Betrayed: The Ill-Fated Reign of Farouk of Egypt*. London: Quartet Books, 1989.

Sadat, Anwar. *Revolt on the Nile*. London: Allan Wingate, 1957.
Sakr, Hala. 'Thirty Episode Series on King Farouk'. *History News Network*, 26 October 2017. Available online: https://historynewsnetwork.org/article/44113 (accessed 15 July 2021).
Satia, Priya. *Spies in Arabia: The Great War and the Cultural Foundations of Britain's Covert Empire in the Middle East*. New York: Oxford University Press, 2008.
Scheffler, Thomas. 'Fertile Crescent, Orient, Middle East: The Changing Mental Maps of Southwest Asia'. *European Review of History* 10, no.2 (2003): 253–72.
Schofield, Camilla. *Enoch Powell and the Making of Postcolonial Britain*. Cambridge: Cambridge University Press, 2013.
Schwara, Desanka. 'Discovering the Levant: A Heterogeneous Structure as a Homogeneous Historical Region'. *European Review of History* 10, no.2 (2003): 233–51.
Schwarz, Bill. *Memories of Empire Volume 1: The White Man's World*. Oxford: Oxford University Press, 2012.
Schwarz, Bill. 'The Only White Man in There: The Re-Racialisation of England, 1956–1968'. *Race and Class* 38 (1996): 65–78.
Schwarz, Vanessa R. *It's So French! Hollywood, Paris, and the Making of Cosmopolitan Film Culture*. Chicago: University of Chicago Press, 2007.
Schwarzenbach, Alexis. 'Royal Photographs: Emotions for the People'. *Contemporary European History* 13, no.3 (2004): 255–80.
Sessions, Jennifer E. *By Sword and Plow: France and the Conquest of Algeria*. Ithaca: Cornell University Press, 2011.
Sezman, Imre. *Zones of Instability: Literature, Postcolonialism and the Nation*. Baltimore: Johns Hopkins University Press, 2003.
Shay, Anthony and Barbara Sellers-Young. *Belly Dance: Orientalism, Transnationalism and Harem Fantasy*. Costa Mesa, CA: Mazda Publishers, 2005.
Sheffer, Edith. *Burned Bridge: How East and West Germans Made the Iron Curtain*. Oxford: Oxford University Press, 2014.
Shepard, Todd. *The Invention of Decolonization: The Algerian War and the Remaking of France*. Ithaca: Cornell University Press, 2006.
Shlaim, Avi. *Lion of Jordan: The Life of King Hussein in War and Peace*. New York: Alfred A. Knopf, 2008.
Skelton, Barbara. *Tears before Bedtime*. London: Hamish Hamilton, 1987.
Skelton, Barbara. *A Young Girl's Touch*. London: Weidenfeld and Nicolson, 1956.
Slater, Leonard. *Aly: A Biography*. London: W.H. Allen, 1966.
Sluggett, Peter. 'Formal and Informal Empire in the Middle East'. In *The Oxford History of the British Empire, Vol. V: Historiography*, edited by Robin Winks, 416–36. Oxford: Oxford University Press, 1999.
Smiley, David. *Albanian Assignment*. London: Chatto and Windus, 1984.
Smith, Lady Eleanor. *The Man in Grey*. London: Hutchinson, 1941.
Smith, Leslie. *Modern British Farce*. Houndmills: Macmillan, 1989.

Soussi, Alasdair. 'Farouk: The Last King of Egypt'. *The National News* (United Arab Emirates), 27 February 2020. Available online: https://www.thenationalnews.com/arts/farouk-the-last-king-of-egypt-a-monarch-who-was-dapper-yet-divisive-1.985210 (accessed 15 July 2021).

*Sport in Egypt*, edited by J. Wentworth Day. London: Country Life, 1938.

Stadiem, William. *Too Rich: The High Life and Tragic Death of King Farouk*. New York: Carroll and Graf, 1991.

Stark, Freya. *The Arab Island: The Middle East, 1939–1943*. New York: Alfred Knopf, 1945.

Stearns, Peter N. *Fat History: Bodies and Beauty in the Modern West*. New York: NYU Press, 1997.

Steedman, Carolyn. *Landscape for a Good Woman: A Story of Two Women*. London: Virago, 1986.

Stern, Michael. *Farouk Uncensored*. New York: Bantam Books, 1965.

Stockwell, Sarah. *The British End of the End of Empire*. Cambridge: Cambridge University Press, 2018.

Stoler, Ann Laura. 'On Degrees of Imperial Sovereignty'. *Public Culture* 18, no.1 (2006): 125–46.

Stoskopf, Nicolas. 'Deauville: History of an Enterprise'. *Histoire Urbaine* 41, no.3 (2014): 23–44.

Strinati, Dominic. 'The Taste of America: Americanization and Popular Culture in Britain'. In *Come on Down? Popular Media Culture in Postwar Britain*, edited by Dominic Strinati and Stephen Wagg, 46–81. London: Routledge, 1992.

Strang, Lord. *The Foreign Office*. London: Allen & Unwin, 1955.

Strang, Lord. *Home and Abroad*. London: Andre Deutsch, 1956.

Symes, Stewart. *Tour of Duty*. London: Collins, 1946.

Tam, Alon. 'Blackface in Egypt: The Theatre and Film of Ali al-Kassar'. *British Journal of Middle Eastern Studies* 48, no.4 (2021): 733–52.

Taylor, D. J. *Lost Girls: Love, War and Literature, 1939–1951*. London: Constable, 2019.

Thiong'o, Ngugi wa. *Homecoming: Essays on African and Caribbean Literature, Culture and Politics*. New York: Lawrence Hill, 1972.

Thornhill, Michael T. 'Britain and the Collapse of Egypt's Constitutional Order, 1950–52'. *Diplomacy and Statecraft* 13, no.1 (2002): 121–52.

Thornhill, Michael T. 'Farouk [Faruq] (1920–1965)'. *Oxford Dictionary of National Biography*. 2004. Available online: https://doi.org/10.1093/ref:odnb/64939 (accessed 18 June 2021).

Thornhill, Michael T. 'Informal Empire, Independent Egypt and the Accession of King Farouk'. *Journal of Imperial and Commonwealth History* 38, no.2 (2010): 279–302.

Thornhill, Michael T. *Road to Suez: The Battle of the Canal Zone*. Cheltenham: History Press, 2016.

Thorold, Peter. *The British in France: Visitors and Residents since the Revolution*. London: Continuum, 2008.

Tidrick, Kathryn. *Heart Beguiling Araby: The English Romance with Arabia*. London: I.B. Tauris, 1990.

Todd, Selina. *Young Women, Work and Family in England, 1918-1950*. Oxford: Oxford University Press, 2005.

Tralins, S. Robert, and Ruth Barnes (Madam Sherry). *Pleasure Was My Business*. New York: Lyle Stuart, 1961.

*Tribute to Churchill: His Life, His Passing, His State Funeral*. London: Daily Mirror Publishing, 1965.

Tripp, Charles. 'Egypt, 1945-1952: The Uses of Disorder'. In *Demise of the British Empire in the Middle East*, edited by M. J. Cohen and Martin Kolinsky, 112-41. London: Routledge, 1998.

Turner, Graeme. *Understanding Celebrity*. London: Sage Publications, 2004.

Van Der Kiste, and Coryne Hall. *Once a Grand Duchess: Xenia, Sister of Nicholas II*. Stroud: Sutton, 2002.

Vernant, Jacques. *The Refugee in the Postwar World*. London: George Allen sand Unwin, 1953.

Vickers, Hugo. *Cecil Beaton*. London: Weidenfeld and Nicolson, 1985.

Vidal, Gore. *The Judgment of Paris*. New York: E.P. Dutton, 1952.

Vidal, Gore. *Palimpsest: A Memoir*. New York: Penguin, 1996.

Vinen, Richard. *A Generation in Uniform, 1945-1963*. London: Penguin, 2015.

Von Eschen, Penny M. *Race against Empire: Black Americans and Anticolonialism, 1937-1957*. Ithaca, NY: Cornell University Press, 1997.

Walton, John K. *Blackpool*. Edinburgh: Carnegie Publishing, 1998.

Walton, John K. *The British Seaside: Holidays and Resorts in the Twentieth Century*. Manchester: Manchester University Press, 2000.

Waters, Chris. 'Beyond "Americanization": Rethinking Anglo-American Cultural Exchange between the Wars'. *Cultural and Social History* 4, no.4 (2007): 451-9.

Waters, Chris. '"Dark Strangers" in Our Midst: Discourses of Race and Nation in Britain, 1947-1963'. *Journal of British Studies* 36, no.2 (1997): 207-38.

Webster, Wendy. *Englishness and Empire, 1939-1965*. Oxford: Oxford University Press, 2005.

Weintraub, Stanley. *Edward the Caresser: The Playboy Prince Who Became Edward VII*. New York: The Free Press, 2001.

Wheat, Celeste. 'Examining Colonialism and Exile in George Lamming's *In the Castle of My Skin* (1953), *The Emigrants* (1954) and *The Pleasures of Exile* (1960)'. *Journal of Colonialism and Colonial History* 10, no.3 (2009). Available online: https://muse.jhu.edu/article/368533N1 (accessed 15 July 2021).

Whidden, James. *Egypt: British Colony, Imperial Capital*. Manchester: Manchester University Press, 2017.

Whidden, James. *Monarchy and Modernity in Egypt: Politics, Islam and Neo-Colonialism between the Wars*. London: I.B. Tauris, 2013.

Whitbourn, John. *Nothing Is True: The First Book of Farouk*. New York: Parvus Press, 2018.
Whitlock, Tammy. 'Gender, Medicine, and Consumer Culture in Victorian England: Creating the Kleptomaniac'. *Albion* 31, no.3 (1999): 413–37.
Williams, John L. *America's Mistress: Eartha Kitt, Her Life and Times*. London: Quercus, 2014.
Williams, Philip Martin. *Wired to the Moon: A Life of Frank Randle*. Ashton-under-Lyne: History on Your Doorstep, 2006.
Williams, Robert C. 'European Political Emigrations: A Lost Subject'. *Comparative Studies in Society and History* 12, no.2 (1970): 140–8.
Williams, Susan. *Colour Bar: The Triumph of Seretse Khama and His Nation*. London: Allen Lane, 2006.
Wilson, Earl. 'My Secret Life with a Camera'. *Photography* 34 (June 1954): 106–9.
Wilson, Henry Maitland. *Eight Years Overseas, 1939–1947*. London: Hutchinson, 1950.
Winsor, Kathleen. *Forever Amber*. London: Macmillan, 1944.
Withers, Charles W. J. 'Place and the "Spatial Turn" in Geography and in History'. *Journal of the History of Ideas* 70, no.4 (2009): 637–58.
Wolton, Suke. *Lord Hailey, the Colonial Office and the Politics of Race and Empire in the Second World War*. Houndmills: Macmillan, 2000.
Wyke, Maria. *Projecting the Past: Ancient Rome, Cinema and History*. New York: Routledge, 1997.
Young, Wayland. *The Montesi Scandal*. London: Faber & Faber, 1957.
Young, Wayland. *The Profumo Affair: Aspects of Conservatism*. Harmondsworth: Penguin, 1963.
Zahlan, Anne Ricketson. 'The Destruction of the Imperial Self in Lawrence Durrell's *The Alexandria Quartet*'. *Perspectives on Contemporary Literature* 12, no.1 (1986): 3–12.
Zantop, Suzanne. *Colonial Fantasies: Conquest, Family and Nation in Precolonial Germany, 1770–1870*. Durham, NC: Duke University Press, 1997.
Zweiniger-Bargielowska, Ina. 'Royal Death and Living Memorials: The Funerals and Commemoration of George V and George VI, 1936–1952'. *Historical Research* 89, no.243 (2016): 158–75.

## Feature films

*Abdullah the Great* (1955), [Film] Dir. Gregory Ratoff USA: Twentieth Century Fox.
*The Apartment* (1960), [Film] Dir. Billy Wilder USA: Mirisch Company.
*Caesar and Cleopatra* (1945), [Film] Dir. Gabriel Pascal UK/USA: Eagle-Lion.
*Cardboard Cavalier* (1949), [Film] Dir. Walter Forde UK: Two Cities.
*Champagne Charlie* (1944), [Film] Dir. Alberto Cavalcanti UK: Ealing Studios.

*Contempt (Le Mepris)* (1963), [Film] Dir. Jean-Luc Godard France/Italy: Rome-Paris Films.
*Darling* (1965), [Film] Dir. John Schlesinger UK: Joseph Janni Productions.
*The Egyptian* (1954), [Film] Dir. Michael Curtiz USA: Twentieth-Century Fox.
*Forever Amber* (1947), [Film] Dir. Otto Preminger USA: Twentieth-Century Fox.
*The Golden Madonna* (1949), [Film] Dir. Luigi Carpentieri UK/Italy: Pendennis Productions.
*La Dolce Vita* (1960), [Film] Dir. Frederico Fellini Italy: Riama Films.
*Land of the Pharaohs* (1955), [Film] Dir. Howard Hawks USA: Warner Brothers.
*Lawrence of Arabia* (1962), [Film] Dir. David Lean UK: Horizon Pictures.
*Nell Gwynn* (1934), [Film] Dir. Herbert Wilcox UK: Herbert Wilcox Productions.
*The Private Life of Henry VIII* (1933), [Film] Dir. Alexander Korda UK: London Films.
*Say It With Flowers* (1934) [Film] Dir. John Baxter UK: Twickenham Studios.
*The Sheik* (1921), [Film] Dir. George Melford USA: Famous Players-Lasky.
*The Sword and the Rose* (1953), [Film] Dir. Ken Annakin UK/USA: Walt Disney Productions.
*The Ten Commandments* (1956), [Film] Dir. Cecil B. deMille USA: Cecil B. deMille Productions.
*That Dangerous Age* (1949), [Film] Dir. Gregory Ratoff UK: London Film Productions.
*Young Bess* (1953), [Film] Dir. George Sidney USA: Metro-Goldwyn-Mayer.
*Young Winston* (1972), [Film] Dir. Richard Attenborough UK: Columbia Pictures.

## Other visual media

Pathe Newsreels online archive site. https://www.britishpathe.com/search/query/Farouk
R. P. Weston and Bert Lee, 'With Her Head Tucked under Her Arm', performed by Stanley Holloway. Available online: https://www.youtube.com/watch?v=jrxWFuvjsfY (accessed 25 June 2021).

# Index

Abdin (Palace) 15, 101, 128
'Abdin incident' (1942) 19, 37, 111, 119
*Abdullah the Great* 144–7
African-Americans
    Farouk and 132–4
Aga Khan (Sir Sultan Mahomed Shah) 54, 82, 105–7
Albania 15, 30, 31, 96, 141 (*see also* Zog, King)
Alexandra, Queen of Yugoslavia 76, 77
Ali, Mehmet 15, 30, 32, 35, 119
Ali, Prince Mohamed 16–17
Aly Khan (Prince Ali Salman) 33, 107–9
Americanization 46–7, 134–6
Anglo-Egyptian Treaty (1936) 16, 27
Arab League 20, 32
Arabs
    British attitudes towards 32, 104–5

Bacon, Max 43–4
Barnes, Ruth (*see under* Madam Sherry)
belly dancers 35, 145, 147 (*see also* Gamal, Samia)
Blackpool 50, 53
Blake, Nicholas (see *under* Day-Lewis, Cecil)

Cairo
    wartime sexual culture 110–12
Campbell, Sir Ronald 20
Cannes 38, 85, 93, 123
Capri 38, 52, 85–6, 91–3, 94–6
Carol II, King of Romania 67–8, 75
cartoons
    Farouk featured in 49–51, 52, 58, 59
casinos 38, 84–5 (*see also* gambling)
celebrity 25–6, 54–5, 80–1, 85–6
    Farouk and 38–9, 155–6
    monarchy and 64–5, 156–7
Charles II, King of England 68–9
Churchill, Randolph 117
Churchill, Sir Winston
    comparison with Farouk 151, 153–6
    funeral of (1965) 150
Ciemniewski, Joseph 60–1
cigarette cards 59–60
Cocteau, Jean 38
corpulence
    Farouk and 118–22
Coward, Noel 108–9, 150
Crazy Gang (Variety act) 43–4

*Daily Mail* International Cross-Channel Swimming Race 23
Dawson, George 123
Day-Lewis, Cecil (Nicholas Blake) 94
Deauville 81–3, 108, 137–8
Docker, Sir Bernard 123
Douglas, Air Marshal Sholto 30
Douglas, Keith 103
Durrell, Lawrence 34, 89
    *The Alexandria Quartet* 140–1

Eden, Sir Anthony 17, 27, 29, 44
Edward VIII, King (subsequently Duke of Windsor) 19, 65, 66, 70, 74
*Empire News*
    serialization of Farouk's memoirs in 136
exile
    ex-monarchs and 74–9, 104
    postcolonialism and 77–8, 79–80

fancy dress 48–9
Farida (Safinaz Zulficar) Queen of Egypt 18–19, 20, 36, 38, 40, 56–7, 63, 70, 102, 110, 127, 136
Farouk I, King of Egypt
    apocryphal stories 125–7, 136–8
    British popular culture and 43–61
    ex-monarch 74–97
    fictional representations 138–47
    Foreign Office and 24–41

marriages (*see under* Farida, Narriman)
  monarch 61–71
  reputation, posthumous 151–3
  reputation, in United States 127–36
  sexuality 108–16, 120–2
  summary of life 15–22
  wealth 99–103
Fathia, Princess 17, 132
Fields, Gracie 51–2, 94, 96
Fleming, Ian
  *Casino Royale* 82–3
Flynn, Errol 143–4
Ford, Edward 29, 63
Foreign Office (British) 23–4, 26–7, 39–41, 44, 51, 60–1
Frederica, Queen of Greece 39
Free Officers Movement 21–2, 114–16
French Second Empire 31
Fuad, Prince Ahmed (Fuad II) 21, 22
Fuad I, King 15–16, 67, 106, 131, 150

Gamal, Samia 35, 130–1
gambling 22, 54, 100, 137–8 (*see also* casinos)
George, Duke of Kent 62, 70
George IV, King of Britain 68
George VI, King of Britain 24, 43, 63, 64, 70
Giles, Carl 49–50, 52, 58, 59
Gorer, Geoffrey 58
Grafftey-Smith, Laurence 35
Guinle, Irene 29, 117

Hassanein, Ahmed 17, 131, 136
Hayworth, Rita 108, 109
Henry VIII, King of England 69–70
hobbyists
  Farouk's affinity with 58–61
Hofheinz, Roy 131
Hoggart, Richard 47
homosexuality 92
homosociability 55–8
humour 47–9, 51–3 (*see also* cartoons, music hall)
Hussein, King of Jordan 103–4
Husseini, Amin Al- (Mufti of Jerusalem) 32
Hyman, Myers 'Lucky Mickie' 123

indeterminacy, racial (*see under* race)
Ismail, Khedive 15
Italy 16, 29, 30, 31, 76–7 (*see also* Capri, Rome)

Jews
  Farouk and 31–2

Kelly, Sir David 35
Kendall, Kay 144, 146
'King Farouk' (Soldiers' Song) 56–7
kleptomania 116–18
Koubbeh (Palace) 16, 99–100, 113–16, 130

Lamming, George 79
Lampson, Jacqueline 40
Lampson, Sir Miles (Ambassador to Egypt) 16, 17, 19, 27–30, 34, 37, 39–40, 63, 107–8, 110–11, 117, 119, 127, 141, 142
Lee, Joseph 50–1
'Louis Farouk' (furniture) 31
Low, David 49, 52
Lyttelton, Lady Moira 40

McGill, Donald 53
Madam Sherry (Ruth Barnes) 125–6
Maher, Ali 18, 19
masculinity 55–61, 120–1 (*see also* homosociability, sexuality)
Masri, General Aziz el 16–17
Mass-Observation 51, 64
matchbox labels 60
Maxwell, Elsa 109
Mediterranean 10, 88–91 (*see also* tourism, Capri)
modernity
  1930s Egypt 18–19, 27–8
  British understandings of Farouk 36
  gender roles 55
  monarchy 63–65
monarchy
  celebrity culture 64–5, 156–7
  contrasted with Egyptian monarchy 63–6, 156
  explanations for survival 61–2
  and the press 66
Monckton, Sir Walter 19, 110

Monte Carlo 50, 80–1, 83–5, 123
Montesi scandal 88
Morrison, Herbert 24
music hall 45–7, 51–3

Nahas, Mostafa el 18, 19
Narriman, Queen of Egypt 20–1, 35, 39–40, 58, 80, 91, 93–4, 96, 102, 122, 129, 130, 144
Nasser, Gamal 19, 22, 34, 149
national service 46, 55–6
Nazli, Queen of Egypt (Farouk's mother) 17, 63, 131–2
Novello, Ivor 67–8

Oppenheim, E. Phillips 83
orientalism 9, 34–6, 100, 109, 124, 129, 140, 146
Orlando, Guy 137–8
Orwell, George 53

palaces, Egyptian royal 101, 115–16, 129–30 (*see also* Abdin, Koubbeh)
paparazzi 86–8
Parnell, Val 46
Peter II, King of Yugoslavia 75–6
Pharaonic Egypt 32
playboy culture, Farouk and 120–2
pornography 114–15

race 32–4, 109 (*see also* African-Americans)
Rainier, Prince of Monaco 22, 80–1, 84, 85
Randle, Frank 53
Ratoff, Gregory 144–5, 146–7
Reza Pahlavi, Mohammad (Shah of Iran) 67, 111
Rhodes, Joan 52
Rome 40–1, 52, 76, 134 (*see also* Via Veneto)

Ancient 90–1
Farouk's death 22, 97, 149–50
Royal Variety Performance 43–4
Rubirosa, Porfirio 33

Sadat, Anwar 19
Saud, Ibn, King of Saudi Arabia 32, 67, 104–5
seaside resorts 52–3
sexuality 29, 36, 91–2, 110–16, 120–2 (*see also* pornography)
Skelton, Barbara 112, 117, 141–2
   *A Young's Girl Touch* 142–3
stamp collecting 59 (*see also* Ciemniewski, Joseph)
Stevenson, Sir Ralph 27, 39, 40, 44
Sudan 33

tourism 93–6, 130
Tralins, Robert 125–6

United States, press coverage of Farouk in 127–32 (*see also* African-Americans, Americanization)

variety (*see under* music hall)
Via Veneto (Rome) 86–8, 138
Victor Emanuel III, King of Italy 73, 174
Vidal, Gore 139
   *The Judgment of Paris* 140
   *Thieves Fall Out* 139–40

Wafd 18
Welles, Orson 144
Whitehall farces 48
Winsor, Kathleen 69

yachts, royal 32, 73

Zog, King of Albania 74, 75

www.ingramcontent.com/pod-product-compliance
Lightning Source LLC
Chambersburg PA
CBHW062217300426
44115CB00012BA/2112